(Kingsley sent me
this copy in
May 1992, no
inscription)

he cut away
the
← flyleaf

Other Books of Literary and Cultural Criticism by Kingsley Widmer:

The Art of Perversity: D. H. Lawrence's Shorter Fictions (1962)

Henry Miller (1963; rev. ed., 1990)

The Literary Rebel (1965)

The Ways of Nihilism: Melville's Short Novels (1970)

The End of Culture: Essays on Sensibility in Contemporary Society (1975)

Edges of Extremity: Some Problems of Literary Modernism (1980)

Paul Goodman (1980)

Nathanael West (1982)

Counterings: Utopian Dialectics in Contemporary Contexts (1988)

Defiant Desire

Some Dialectical Legacies of D. H. Lawrence

Kingsley Widmer

Southern Illinois University Press
Carbondale and Edwardsville

Library of Congress Cataloging-in-Publication Data

Widmer, Kingsley, 1925–
    Defiant desire : some dialectical legacies of D.H. Lawrence /
Kingsley Widmer.
        p.   cm.
    Includes bibliographical references and index.
    1. Lawrence, D. H. (David Herbert), 1885–1930—Criticism and
interpretation.   2. Nietzsche, Friedrich Wilhelm. 1844–1900—
Influence.   3. Negation (Logic) in literature.   4. Desire in
literature.   5. Dialectic.   I. Title.
    PR6023.A93Z9542   1992
    823'.912—dc20   91-28121
    ISBN 0-8093-1763-X   CIP

"Desire and Denial, Dialectics of Passion in D. H. Lawrence." *D. H. Lawrence Review* 18 (1985–86): 139–150. Reprinted by permission of the publisher.
"Melville and the Myths of Modernism." *A Companion to Melville Studies.*
Edited by John Bryant. Westport, Conn.: Greenwood, 1986. Reprinted by permission of the publisher.
"The Pertinence of Modern Pastoral: The Three Versions of *Lady Chatterley's Lover*." *Studies in the Novel* 5 (Fall 1973): 298–313. Reprinted by permission of the publisher.

Contents

Acknowledgments

From several dozen articles on and around Lawrence, I have selected half a dozen to not only rewrite but to partly reformulate into a fairly continuous argument for this book. Though it deploys mostly different material, I see it as a continuation and extension of the perspective presented in my book on Lawrence a generation ago, *The Art of Perversity: D. H. Lawrence's Shorter Fictions* (Seattle: University of Washington Press, 1962), which was the redoing of a dissertation and a group of essays done in the middle 1950s. But perhaps I have learned a few things in my unceasing dialectic with the subject and some of its ramifications, several of which I explore here.

Obviously there is an ongoing indebtedness to many persons involved over nearly four decades in my arguments with and around Lawrence and the Lawrenceans. Probably there is also an apology due to many as well for my not having learned more fully from their responses and for my not making more charitable acknowledgment. But my weakness at careerist decorums may also be seen to have other, more iconoclastic as well as naive, purposes.

At least I can make brief specific acknowledgment here of the previously published essays, and their energetic editors, that provided the scaffolding for the present book. For the earliest one, James Cox both suggested and raised problems about "The Pertinence of Modern Pastoral: The Three Versions of *Lady Chatterley's Lover*," *Studies in the Novel* 5 (Fall 1973). Difficulties with my gender perceptions in that essay were later discovered for me by Eleanor Rackow Widmer, Vera Mae Fredrickson, and Penny Baldwin Williams, from whom I perhaps perversely failed to fully profit. Thomas Staley bravely asked me to do an 18,000 word critical summary of Lawrence's fiction for his *Dictionary of Literary Biography*, vol. 36,

Acknowledgments

British Novelists, 1890–1929 (Detroit: Gale Research, 1985), even though a house editor had objected to my impious tone in a similar work on Conrad (vol. 34). The late Karl Keller, colleague and fellow critic, warmly suggested, and John Bryant tolerantly edited, an essay partly on Lawrence, "Melville and the Myths of Modernism," for Bryant's *A Companion to Melville Studies* (New York: Greenwood, 1986). G. K. Das asked for, and the late Gāmini Sālgado most tactfully edited, "Desire and Negation: the Dialectics of Passion in D. H. Lawrence," for their long-delayed *The Spirit of D. H. Lawrence*, Centenary Studies (London: Macmillan, 1988). A related piece, "Desire and Denial in D. H. Lawrence," was indulgently allowed as a paper at the D. H. Lawrence: Creativity and Conscience Centennial Conference at Tufts University (June 1985), objected to by Michael Squires and Keith Cushman (along, more informally, with others, such as Charles Rossman, and Mark Spilka, who kindly sent me the manuscript of his forthcoming book on Lawrence), and expertly corrected by Dennis Jackson for publication in the *D. H. Lawrence Review* 18 (Summer/Fall 1985–86). Jeffrey Meyers most responsively asked for, and expertly went over, "Lawrence and the Nietzschean Matrix," for his *D. H. Lawrence and Tradition* (London: Athlone Press, 1985), and "Lawrence's Cultural Impact," for his *Legacy of D. H. Lawrence* (London: Macmillan, 1987), from which I have borrowed, with a twist, my subtitle. Keith Cushman, with an unusually generous tolerance after I had harshly reviewed him, asked for, and Dennis Jackson again most modestly edited, "Lawrence's Bad-Boy American Progeny," for their *Lawrence's Literary Inheritors* (New York: St. Martin's, 1991). An anonymous "reader" for that also made a couple of pertinent objections, and Jeffrey Meyers acutely noted others, to which I am yet attempting to respond. Curtis Clark, of Southern Illinois University Press, caught me up on some bad manners while generously responding to my efforts, and copyeditor Rebecca Schwartz was most patient with an idiosyncratic manuscript. None of them, of course, should be blamed for my waywardness in considerably redoing what they so patiently tried to straighten out. I am too old and set in my ways, after more than ten books of criticism, to try to stop learning and to cease arguing with myself and the world, which is much of what all this effort is about.

I have intentionally kept most of my quotations from Lawrence's writings very brief ("fair use"), and even then from earlier, out-of-copyright, editions (though checked against later editions, as sometimes cited in the notes). I have doubts about synthetic texts, as I have discussed elsewhere.

Acknowledgments

Fortunately, from my irreverent perspective, I have little to positively acknowledge from any institution, its officials, monies, or ambience, other than use of several libraries. But, I might grant, they allowed me some negative freedom, which is appropriate here. Further acknowledgments and introductory remarks appear at pertinent places in the text and notes, where I think they really belong.

Kingsley Widmer
Cardiff by the Sea, California

1

Defiant Desire:
Introduction, Examples, Adumbrations

Some Dialectical Perspectives

A supposedly noted reviewer of one of the preliminary essays for this small book (now rewritten and expanded), comparatively summarized that it was "the best researched, the most provocative, and the most foolish." Given this scholar's conventional pedantic and parochial perspective, I take it as a compliment. But it may also serve as fair warning to the reader. For those continuing beyond such summary, I might note part of the purpose to my learnedly provoking foolishness. The writings of D. H. Lawrence have become a long-established subject—in my mind as well, since I have been critically thinking about him for nearly forty years.[1] Possibly I could cultivate a cautious summary treatment of what I thought I had learned in more than a generation of reading and rereading Lawrence and things about and around him. Or I could attempt some rather specialized plantings. But to confine myself to either of those would be temperamentally uncongenial, and would likely produce small or watery intellectual potatoes, and so I have subordinated both to a more contentious digging. There would seem to be little intellectual utility (though I suppose there could be some worldly advantages) in being either pedantically or swollenly bland. I choose yet again, at the cost no doubt of peculiarity and tendentiousness, in continuing a rather edgy view of the subject, though I try to back it up with some borrowed broad knowledge and some curious cultivation here and there. While I attempt to range a bit, my view is still rooted in immediate responses, including the pervasive sense in rereading Lawrence of a compound of assent and resistance, of combined admiration and irritation, properly resulting in both confirming and countering reactions. I do not

Defiant Desire

really understand how one can take a simple and unilateral view of Lawrence, whether seen as a group of literary artifacts, as a sensibility, as an influence, or as a legacy, which are my concerns here.

Hence some special appropriateness of the dialectical, at the simplest level the pro and con, argument and counterargument, in discussing Lawrence. No doubt such dialectics, which I grant I have also practiced elsewhere, are partly a matter of defiant temperament and radical bias. To perceive much of experience as endless counterings is, one inconveniently discovers, far from universally acceptable. Not just the critic but Lawrence, it seems almost too obvious to note, had such proclivities, irritably and exultingly reaching after what he called "opposition" and "polarities." He was a man often driven by large rages as well as a tender responsiveness, and these tend to reverse, as with his "tenderness" becoming an angry doctrine in his last novel. But for him the oppositional was even more fundamental: as a repeated trope in his early philosophical ramblings has it, "the great systole-diastole of the universe."[2] As the conflicted man wrote in another even more abstracting rumination: "We are two opposites which exist by virtue of our interopposition."[3] Or, in a more Blakean declaration: "It is the fight of opposites which is holy."[4]

His major, recurrent, indeed most insistent, term here for what drives the opposition is *desire*. Desire comes out more central and positive in Lawrence's writings than, for example, *love*, many of whose modes he often wisely treated with scorn as perversions of passional response. Desire, that heightened state of being-in-the-world, that trope for the high-sexual (and sexual "high") intensity of response that he above all insisted upon— even when arguing for "insouciance"[5]—is brigaded with an endless series of defiances, an opposition unto nihilism, a pervasive stance of negation. Thus my framework, both as keying characteristic and as response, is the defiant dialectics of desire and negation.

Of course, I am going to use again, after more than a generation of mulling them over, the terms broadly and variously, though with some recognitions of when they do not apply or work very well. Desire/negation is a conceptual pattern, not intended as a total summary, to suggest a way of carrying out the critical job. And no doubt in the minds of the more moderate, the less dialectical who do not find heightened desiring and nihilistic denying appropriate problematic, I am going to sometimes appear a bit insistent, deviant. Such an emphasis seems to be an issue with the Lawrenceanists. A recent survey of scholarly criticism of Lawrence notes

2

a division into those who consider him and his views "normative" and those fewer who do not, who instead consider him extreme and peculiar.[6] Obviously I belong with the latter, though with the dialectical twist that I consider the peculiar and extreme to often be the truer, however fearfully denied and disguised. A radical view of human meaning, and lack of meaning, is part of the issue. The Lawrence I emphasize is in many ways rooted in a drastic revisionism, an "inhumanism," of much of what is usually taken as the defensible values. Too many, I think, foolishly attempt to "mainstream" Lawrence and his works and effects. Especially inappropriate in regarding Lawrence is the now widely prevalent sentimentalism. As he characteristically and shrewdly noted, "Sentimentality . . . covers viciousness as inevitably as greenness covers a bog."[7]

This, as a recent pleasantly intentioned reader warned me, leads to "ideological criticism" (unbeknownst to him, I have long acknowledged such a label)[8]—ideological both in recognizing one of my own (no academic scientism here) and in treating the other's ideology as an appropriate central concern, including with the literary artifacts. Granted, the ideological, in its now common sense of a loaded engagement with a scheme of ideas and values which serve as a justifying philosophy, carries a good bit of denigrative flagging. Currently, the emphasis unhappily suggests the reductively doctrinaire, most often some form of the neo-Marxist, that usually rather calcified academic power-posturing with which as a libertarian I have but little sympathy.[9] Call the ideologizing, then, "life philosophizing," in the particular directions here of "Lawrenceanism."

In aesthetic matters, an ideological emphasis also may suggest a willful ignoring of the formal qualities and the stylistic and other "artistic" characteristics of the work, as if the arguments and attitudes were not germane to the artistry. Since I have rather relentlessly attempted to counter that division, on Lawrence among others, in earlier writings in which I insisted that the formal qualities (and often their peculiarities or violations) revealed the real ideology, here I am not going to come down so heavily on it but simply assume it. In other words, I am not going to much demonstrate what used to be called "close readings" of the selected texts (really rather remedial work, whether done in symbolistic, psychological, archetypal, or semiotic manner), though I like to think that I have done an adequate bit of several of them before moving on to a rather different focus. And that focus, if one objects to the term ideological, is on the reaches and context of social-cultural ideas. Perhaps what I am practicing should just be called "intellec-

3

tual commentary," except that besides being an impolite comment on my colleagues, it suggests a dispassionate and neutered stance which I have partly learned from Lawrence to abhor. So: the engagement here is a passionate intellectual response to Lawrence's ideology, properly qualified by the way it comes out, by what context seems most germane, and by the dialectical cast.

As focus for the five longish chapters of a small book, I have taken a handful of related problems—proper context for the problematic figure—which often necessarily go beyond particular texts. A nicely old-fashioned one for the next chapter is an "influence" issue, Lawrence's response to and central use of Nietzsche, which has often been done unsatisfactorily, I argue, and which I speculatively suggest issues in a distinctive tradition of "dark prophecy." Another is influence in the other direction, now sometimes called "inheritance." Here, in a chapter of rather thick context, I discuss the use of Lawrence by some later writers, especially of rather rebellious American disposition, such as Henry Miller, Norman Mailer, and some Melvilleans, with a concern for how literary-intellectual inheritance not only oftentimes recreates its subject but doubles back on itself. An earlier chapter takes up issues both in and around one of Lawrence's most disputed (but of course) works, *Lady Chatterley's Lover*, and its radical cast. And the final chapter extends some of Lawrence's role as influential culture hero, which he took on with some of his crucial works, and follows it into such obvious social-cultural issues as censor-object for his blasphemy, as totem figure for feminist-masculinist debate, and as prophet for certain erotic views. Perhaps it will be granted me that these are areas where literature and ideology are especially hard to separate, even if I haven't altogether persuasively made the case in the immediately following abbreviated exposition of examples of some of Lawrence's defiant dialectics.

Hence some dialectics of ideological criticism, some cultural commentary, and not a little radical social-cultural perspective as the matrix for exploring Lawrenceanism. Proper to the dialectical, I critically run in several directions, refusing the critical monotheism of sticking with biography, history, language tropes, or one-way doctrines. One peculiarity—no doubt an old-fashioned prejudice—is that I am still concerned, going back to my earlier essays that I wrote in the mid-1950s (contra F. R. Leavis, Mark Spilka, and other then-reigning Anglo-American normative moralizers), with how best to read Lawrence, how to respond to the experience of the specific works. I do, however, attempt to go beyond the interpretation

Introduction, Examples, Adumbrations

of specific writings to the larger entity—the combination of author/artifact/ context/response—that can plausibly be called "Lawrenceanism." Along my thematic ways, I have provided commentary on the eleven novels— and in several forays—because they serve as the most usual focus of argument, though I still hold that his short fictions, which I only briefly draw upon (not to repeat old arguments) and some of his "miscellaneous" writings are his best. I also discuss a number of his representative essays. And I repeatedly try to draw on a sense of what Lawrence is arguing with and, especially, against. While I have a group of related problems that I am taking up, which engage a number of larger issues of culture and society, and what negative attitude to take towards them, I am still bothered by inadequate, uncandid, and narrowly special pleading with the literary arti- facts. Criticism, of course, must be critical—the failure to constantly at- tempt evaluations is the corruption of our vocation. So indicators of specific literary criticism do mark the larger arguments. But essential to the Law- rencean is not to confine one's responses just to artistic specifics but go on to the fundamental perspective that this has been for quite some time a considerably wrong human world, and we must passionately respond against it, negate it as it is, if we are to be with genuine human desire. The writings have the purposes of defiant desire in the world.

This does not, to my no doubt naive puzzlement, seem to be the insistent thrust of much of the writing on Lawrence. Since for a long generation I have read the larger part of what has been written on and around Lawrence (indeed, have reviewed dozens of books on him), no doubt I am much indebted to the Lawrence criticism and scholarship, however often by negation. On some selected matters, I have attempted some thoroughness in citing it; on others I have confined myself to a few, usually recent, examples. My annotations have come out (due to repeated request) re- strained, undoubtedly because I lack the competence of so many of my colleagues in slyly and smugly dismissive manners. To cite yet more thoroughly, given the immense volume of writing on Lawrence, would have taken out of all proportion what intends to be but a small book. Still, I was lamenting the same weariness with the mania for trivial overproduc- tion (one of the base imperatives of our culture and institutions) in a book written on Lawrence more than three decades ago. The prolix confusion demands attempts at demystification of a number of matters if Lawrencean- ism is to have its due. If in doing so my foolishness is much, perhaps the provocation also still seems evident.

Dialectics Developing

Enough of half-suggesting the critical strategy which, as with much literary theorizing, may be mostly distraction from the real issues, such as what attitudes to discover towards life and antilife—a Lawrencean point. One of those Lawrencean discoveries is, in effect, that the whole humanist enterprise is in deep trouble. Lawrence sought a countering in a deep inhumanism, a more primal concern. His insistent trope of "desire" links with a heightened eroticism, various kinds of peculiar responsiveness, "discriminating sympathetic consciousness," the bringing into awareness of repressed "dark knowledge," and the commitment to "intense vivid life."

On the negative side of the dialectic, we insistently see not only attacks on conventional repressions—the social and moral origins against which Lawrence came to define himself, and without which he is considerably incomprehensible—but also rejections of most "fixities" and "willed" claims to meaning, i.e., the order of the world as usually given. Most basically, Lawrencean "desire" is an encompassing counterclaim.

For example, Lawrence, unlike many narrative and poetic writers in Anglo-American traditions, frequently generalized and moralized his tropes, in and out of his fictions. Take, for what I believe to be a fairly representative instance, one of his statements, a rather moderate one, on the nature of desire from a late essay:

> All that matters is that men and women shall do what they *really* want to do. Though here, as everywhere, we must remember that man has a double set of desires, the shallow and the profound, the personal, superficial, temporary desires, and the inner, impersonal, great desires that are fulfilled in long periods of time. The desires of the moment are easy to recognize, but the others, the deeper ones, are difficult.[10]

Now that may not appear as drastic a dependence on absolutized subjectivity as when written a couple of generations ago, what with more recent placebo rhetoric about "self-actualization," and the like—a partial change of attitude which Lawrence probably helped engender (as I will discuss later). But in its several appropriate contexts, Lawrence's demands for following desire should be understood as a radical disavowal of many usual claims to human meaning and conduct. The extremity might be further emphasized by a key earlier avowal (only partly qualified by the late statement just quoted): "I shall accept all my desires, and repudiate none."[11] All through Lawrence, the peculiarity of desire is central. And it is partly extreme because Lawrence didn't just criticize what is, he hated it, and there is little understanding desire without such negation.

Desire, we may reflect in a way which perhaps parallels Lawrence's thinking, was rarely the positive subject of traditional moralists, who usually assumed that it was all too present and that its constraint or repudiation provided the important issues, the needed conduct. We confront here a crucial reversal, and one not to be simply equated with its partly romantic sources in notions that human desires are not problematic because generally benign, which is not usually Lawrence's logic. As the quote indicates, and as so many of Lawrence's fictions dramatize, finding the deep desire is part of the difficulty. No doubt an important source here is frail and frequently ill Lawrence's own problematic identification with life itself. As some of the biographers sensibly emphasize, he was repeatedly aware of being near death (as a child, as a beginning writer following the death of his mother, as a figure in extremity in Mexico in the mid-1920s, and of course, in the years of illness leading up to his death at age forty-four). We may also see this in the obsessive death-longing as the takeover subject of so many sweeping fables (oddly ignored by many commentators), from the pre–Great War "The Prussian Officer" through *Women in Love*, "The Man Who Loved Islands," and "The Woman Who Rode Away," to the final *The Man Who Died*. But let us not reduce the issues to the biographical (though acknowledging its role), which tends to both undercut the specific writings and neutralize the broader pertinence.

No doubt Lawrence's revulsion at the social and moral climate in which he grew up further encouraged his insistent assaults on what he took to be views centered on the repudiation of desire. Looking through his polemics—and many of his fictions and poems as well as essays are polemical—the repudiators seem to be legion: Christians, of course, but other traditional "idealists" also,[12] and the bourgeois, the rational-industrial, "the mechanical," the scientist (and scientific), the patriotic (and most of his or her fellows), the sentimental, the powerful, the parental, the feminine, the willful, and almost endless others. Lawrence expresses, of course, what can often be partly understood as appropriate negations of the avowed views of many in the last quarter of the last century and the first quarter of this one. But let us also not reduce the issues to the social-cultural history

7

(though attempting to identify some of it), which tends to depersonalize the specifics and antiquate the broader responses.

Lawrence's emphatic reversal of traditional moralist concerns may also be viewed as not isolated but distinctively "modernist," as part of a larger revolt of Western sensibility (I will in several ways return to this) not only to deny past orderings but to affirm root subjectivity against an accelerating order of destructive objectification—modernization in the other sense, with mass overpopulation, overmechanization, overurbanization, endless war, ultimate ecocide, and similar denaturing of the human and the world. In sum, Lawrence desperately wants us, and himself, to *feel* differently, and clearly emphasizes (except in moments of despair) that a change in feelings can change the world. In his quoted casuistry of distinguishing not between good and bad desires but between the shallow and the deep desires, the merely superficial "personal" (in the sense of manipulatively egotistic) and the "primordial" (in the sense of larger-than-consciously fundamental), desiring is itself ultimate being. Desire is not an external ideal but the absolute of subjectivity: "A desire proceeds from within, from the unknown, spontaneous soul or self."[13] But typically, Lawrence often pushes beyond that to make transcendental claims: "We can only know that from the unknown profound desires enter in upon us, and that the fulfilling of these desires is the fulfilling of creation."[14]

I would think that Lawrence could still be seen here by the unsympathetic (as in the famous T. S. Eliot attack on him in *The Sacred Wood*) as an extreme example of the tradition of "inner light" Protestant individualism, which is of course part of his historical and biographical sources. Lawrence's apotheosizing of desire may require a sense of what is being twisted and reversed, such as puritanical spirituality, as well as denied. One condition he repeatedly negates is what was, and often still is, thought of as moral will—the will against worldly desire so paradoxically demanded in his aspiring petty bourgeois Protestant background. As he crucially summarized in reflecting on his most ambitious literary work: "Desire, in any shape or form, is primal, whereas the will is secondary, derived."[15] The form of the statement here suggests some sophistication in moral philosophizing (probably contra Nietzsche, as discussed later). The more general pertinence of Lawrence's repeated castigations of *will* is not only as dialectical counter to desire, though it is certainly that, but as the force behind the modern takeover of society by "sheer instrumentality" (see *Women in Love*). Will is also the dominant motive force of the narrowed rationality and the mechanistic order which imposes the bad modernizing values. Similarly, Lawrence's obsessive denunciations of the *"wilful woman"* are not just examples of his peculiar woman-identifying misogyny, though certainly that (to be discussed later), but also further negation of "will" as the enemy of desire, often in the forms of antisensual women. Passional, not willful, responses must be brought into fuller "consciousness"—Lawrence's most persistent theme and purpose.

Much of Lawrence's fiction may be brought into focus as counterargument to what he took as exemplifications of corrupting moral will. A major one: the archetypal Christian-bourgeois ambience of English vicarage and rectory, savaged in the early tale, "Daughters of the Vicar," obliquely continued through many other fictions, and replayed even more harshly in his penultimate novella *The Virgin and the Gipsy*."[16] Both tales are harshly negating works (both—the last one was never revised for publication— could have artistically used some pruning of tendentious rhetoric and images, but they are works of his nuclear anger). Both are about the emphatic discovery of young female desire (in Louise and Yvette) against representative conditions of its denial, the tabooed transformation. Says the Lawrence persona in religious summary in the latter, "Desire is the most wonderful thing in life." By it, the fairly ordinary young women end up not only becoming different beings but negating their families and societies. It would not be wrong, though it certainly would be incomplete, to use that Christian-daughter-converted-to-passional-desire pattern as a basic paradigm of what Lawrence is about. Granted, it is complicated in the elaborations with Ursula (*The Rainbow*), Alvina (*The Lost Girl*), Constance (*Lady Chatterley's Lover*), and others (whom I will consider shortly), but not all that much changed. Yet what do we find with the interpreters? Earnest fabulist readers pontificate about Lawrence's cerebral versus sensual patterns (as I have), and others chatter about "love story" niceties (or their absence), instead of emphasizing the amoral discovery of desire as a negation of Christianized middle-classdom. The willed repressions of social class, the moral icons of religiose duty and matriarchy (foully "obese" and "fungoid"), and the viciously hypocritical virtues of family and decency and order, as traditionally recognized, are treated with a vituperation quite beyond mere artistic purposes of fable and realism. The countering is in the heightened prose-poetry—so insistent in such stories—that exalts passional desire as the overcoming arête. That is essential Lawrenceanism.

In these tales, and elsewhere, Lawrence certainly did not say that finding and following one's real desire was easy. Indeed, most of the fictions show it as considerably anguished, often in puritan senses. Acting by deep desire is rather more demanding than acting by moral principle. No doubt this presupposes a highly repressive, moral-willed, ambience. Lawrence also does not suggest that the developing passions will be predominantly "nice," nor the consequences necessarily so. As in many of his best-known "love" stories, from the passionately battling couple in the very early "White Stocking," through the middle-period Paul Morel (*Sons and Lovers*) and the Brangwens *(The Rainbow)* and the paradigmatic "Horse-Dealer's Daughter," and on to the final fictions with the misanthropic reluctance for passion, the struggle for desire is often of heroic proportions, frequently the greatest agon in the otherwise ordinary lives of commonplace people. We may find here the domestication of the proportions of tragic passion in everyday life, as against reasonable ordering (and as against the social condescension that dominated English fiction), which one notes not only in the exacerbated language but in such declarations as, "Let it be a great passion and then death, rather than a fake or false purpose."[17] The tradition is of desperate countering, but in ordinary life.

As antimoralist, Lawrence uses "desire" (as in many of his statements that I am quoting) where others would use some ultimate "good." In such countering, he seems to have taken over some of the moral casuistry of distinguishing between "goods" by attempting discriminations between "shallow" and "deep" desires. The metaphoric differences are not always self-evident, but his dramatizations do emphasize desire as not just need or longing but as the transforming power of the body and of consciousness, which he attempts to make one. It is, of course, usually sexual, but the sex not only varies in its shapes but enlarges into a total responsiveness and metaphysics. Certainly in most of his uses, *desire* constitutes a near-total claim to meaning. As he typically insisted, "desire itself [is] beyond criticism and moral judgment." Desire is the *Ding-an-sich*.

Because Lawrence views passionate desire as the basis of most value— or *disvalue* when desire is falsified or corrupted—it frequently appears in sacramental language and scene. Given his countering cast, it is often blasphemously so. That was true from his literary start to his literary end, from the awkward very early story of a rebellious church-vandalizing and sexually consummating serf, "A Fragment of Stained Glass" (ca. 1907), to his final fiction a bit more than two decades later, *The Man Who Died*, with its sexually resurrected and anti-Christian Christ in flight as eternal vagabond-demon. Sacrilege is an important part of the desire-and-negation pattern, from beginning to end. That continuity (as also noted with the sexual rebellion of the clergymen's daughters) seems to need some emphasis. For there still are those narrow (and essentially genteel) commentators who incline to deeply separate early and late Lawrence, such as the supposedly realistic and moderate early fictionist within mainline British traditions, and the deracinated and exacerbated post–Great War prophet. While there are some changes, with the petty bourgeois schoolteacher and aspiring writer having become a wandering bohemian and prolific artistic polemicist, the continuing pattern seems more important. The disguised moralisms of secondary literary history or biographical qualifications would undercut it, as so often in putting the emphasis on manners and the like in place of the living human purposiveness. While we should grant some variations and contradictions (and I will note some) in Lawrenceanism, my emphasis is that the desire/negation dialectics for the two-plus decades of Lawrence's literary activity are distinguishingly largely of a piece, and crucial.

Granted, in his imitative and not very talented first two novels, when he was trying to make his way in the commercial-literary establishment, this dialectic does not have a major role. The stilted and slight *White Peacock*, narrated by an insufficently characterized middle-class youth, Cyril Beardsal, loosely centers on the decline of his farmer friend, George Saxon, who marries down (a pub girl), and within a few years becomes a depressive and defeated drunk. Some of the peculiar forms of desire do, digressively, come up, as with homoeroticism: "I admired the noble white fruitfulness of his form," Cyril says effeminately of George during an obsessively remembered nude swim. He recalls how they rubbed each other dry: "The sweetness and touch of our naked bodies one against the other was superb." In "indecipheral yearning," Cyril always remembers that the young male "love was perfect for a moment, more perfect than any love I have known since, for man or woman."[18] The failure to follow through in deciphering such desire, and relating it to the rest of the action, was to plague Lawrencean eroticism, the burden of *repressed* homosexuality, of ambivalent desire.

Also striking, and inconsistent with the prevailing tone of the novel, is the brief tale of Annable, a local gamekeeper. This outsider is an educated ex-parson, once married to a noble lady and since become a misogynist and apocalyptic prophet. He provides the novel's entitling metaphor by describing a showy white peacock in a graveyard "perched on an angel . . .

11

as if it were a pedestal for vanity. That's the soul of woman—or it's the devil." The peacock, ponderously fabulistic, dirties the angel—"A woman to the end, I tell you, all vanity and screech and defilement." We also learn from young Cyril that the embittered gamekeeper "was a man of one idea—that all civilization was the painted fungus of rottenness." His countering, in one of the earliest declarations of what was to be Lawrence's famous doctrine: "Be a good animal, true to your animal instinct." The misognyny and apocalyptic pronouncements, of course, are a first run for the gamekeeper-lover of Lawrence's last novel, and central to the always Lawrencean dialectic.

But this early snapshot of the Lawrence prophet is cast aside by Annable's death in the middle of the narrative. The rest of *The White Peacock* consists mostly of sentimental adolescent posturing, florid descriptions of nature, and stilted cultural allusions from post-1890s fashions. The novel also reflects Lawrence's mother's lower-middle-class snobberies, including hatred of drinking men and social upgrading of the characters. In his early twenties, Lawrence was still trapped by the need to present his mother's puritanical-genteel values. Not surprisingly, then, women dominate all the relationships in the novel, with the males clearly defeated.

Lawrence's second novel, *The Trespasser*, is a rewriting, probably with dubious popular-fiction motives, of the journal of an uninsightful, antimale schoolteacher friend, Helen Corke, and is labored, alternating the trite and the inflated—"their thoughts slept like butterflies on the flowers of delight."[19] His adaption covers a few days in the life of a near-middle-aged music teacher, nicknamed Siegmund, whose adulterous affair with the semifrigid, younger Helena concludes with his guiltily hanging himself. More than half of the narrative describes five days of a tormented love tryst on the Isle of Wight, with drawn-out, claustraphobic scenes of erotic rituals, heavy with Wagnerian overtones of doomed love. These emphasize the resentful fluctuations in feelings between the lovers, mostly induced by the antisexual, willful, and sentimentally righteous woman. Though inadequately backgrounded and explored, these scenes do carry an essential Lawrence theme: the frigidly erotic woman "rejected" male sensuality, leaving the man feeling like a "balked animal." But the man, too, appears quite inadequate—narcissistic, priggish, and full of resentful self-pity. The scenes with Siegmund's embittered wife and rejecting children also lack dramatic depth. The heavy irony that the wife is not much affected by her husband's death, and takes a lover herself, seems stock. Lawrence's insights do not rise above the maudlin writing. Obviously desire is perplexed, and Lawrence is still questing, mostly negatively, for transcendence.

Several of these points can be reinforced by briefly considering the far better and most "realistic," as well as erotically transforming, of the early novels, *Sons and Lovers*.[20] It is an intensely detailed, emotionally rich, presentation of puritanical-provincial common life. Contra our fashionable quasi-Marxist critics, it is, as presented, rather more aspiring petty bourgeois sensibility than working-class. However Lawrence sometimes romanticized or rejected the proletarian, mostly he and his works were essentially "marginal" in the social sense. Not incidentally, that was to be parcel as well as part of his later role as cultural hero.

We should also properly emphasize the heightened sexual insistence. Cultural history has perhaps exaggerated the Oedipal side of this (granted it is there, and the partly Freudian-cast Frieda may have contributed more than personally to it) as against the restrictive Protestant ethos of the aspiring and anxious petit bourgeois. Protagonist Paul must reject Miriam because she personifies not only the mother, in a rather more mystical version, but much of that Protestant ethos: the antisensual (the graphic revealing scenes with the swing and with the pecking chickens, as well as the too-late "sacrifice" sexuality); the nagging, "fussy," moralistic work quality and the spiritual earnestness for "higher things"; the antispontaneous Christian "martyr" disposition and the puritan willful "proud humility," and so on. While Lawrence did not much comment (as in his letters) on all that (unlike the mother-son problem), it is that ethos which is most thoroughly struggled with and negated—including its social-economic aspirations and character structure—as well as reversed into a more direct sense of deep desire.

While the negation of the antisensual woman was not new in Lawrence's novels (the issue is certainly in his first two), there is now the crucial countering, including the inverted religious metaphors, the sexual "baptism of fire in passion," the erotic culmination of the "dark, impersonal fire of desire." In rather more commonsensical description, Paul's sex in the night field with Clara is "the something big and intense that changes you when you really come together with somebody." The transformation by desire is more than analogous to a religious-conversion experience—it is itself the religious state of being.

A sense of conversion experience was, of course, part of Lawrence's inheritance from his Protestant Christian background (specifically Congregational but probably also Methodist-influenced—the prevailing chapel going in his society—and related). A revealing passage appears in an essay responding to the Great War, several years later than *Sons and Lovers*. Lawrence is discussing a man with the courage to embrace death. It is the great "courage of negation"—a recurrent Lawrencean rhetoric—but it lacks the other courage to embrace "the unknown that should make him new and vivid, to yield himself, deliberately, in faith. Does any story of martyrdom affect us like the story of the conversion of Paul? . . . We dare to gloat on the crucifixion, but we dare not face the mortal fact of the conversion from the accepted world, to the new world which was not yet conceived, that took place in the soul of St. Paul on the road to Damascus."[21] It is transformation to the "new way of creation," to an excitement which surpasseth reasonable understanding, though in Lawrence's usual application it is with St. Paul now reverse-converted to un-Christian Saul. The sense of irony of Lawrence praising one of the creators of the viciously antisexual Pauline ethic which burdened Christianity for millennia may be more ours than Lawrence's. (Figures named Paul, as in *Sons and Lovers* and "The Rocking-Horse Winner," however, were to have libidinal conversion experiences.) Lawrence made the heightened sexual engagement, from at least Midlands Paul (Morel) to his final post-Crucifixion Christ, the real conversion experience.

Now traditional moralists, including some contemporary commentators on Lawrence, might reasonably ask, What follows from this inverted conversion, this erotic transformation? In dramatic and dialectical fact, the consequences are not essentially familial and social ordering, not even a long-enduring relationship (in a peculiarly ambivalent and rather obscene covertly homoerotic action, Paul in *Sons and Lovers* gives Clara back to her estranged husband Baxter, placating the miner–Morel-like crude maleness). For consequences, we are driven back to the coital scene (previously commented on) with its heightened yet harsh sense of immanent life. The significance includes, as almost always in Lawrence, a vibrant external awareness, of the "cry of the pewit" and the night sky "wheel of the stars." The *otherness* of nature and the self has been realized. No less, and not much more. As Lawrence summarized for his postcoital Paul and Clara, "having known the immensity of passion," and its "impersonal" force and revelation, they also know "their own nothingness." (The state of nothingness also concludes the novel—the "Derelict" chapter—more represented by than caused by the dead mother, with Paul's self-negation never adequately "explained.") Thus desire both is and leads to further

14

negations, with the heightened moment of being its own justification in richly unwilled and morally unadulterated responsiveness. To summarize— not all of *Sons and Lovers*, but just one of its most essential, revealing, and continuing dialectics, which I take as more important than the somewhat uncertain development of character and psychology—the negation of the puritan petit bourgeois ethos represented by mother and Miriam is polarized in the revelation of erotic desire, which itself is a negation but heightened as a conversion to that intensity which is one of the primal truths for the human world.

That was and for the most part remained the nuclear Lawrenceanism. Of course Lawrence did other things, in various turns of the realistic and fabulistic, the lyrical, the documentary, and the polemical, in his characteristically heightened responses to various realities. But the crux, I am arguing, was a distinctive sensibility which can be rooted in the evident dialectic partly illustrated by these examples. Certainly in other writings, the tropes of the dialectic of passional ontology vary, a bit, from desire/ nothingness: wonder/oblivion, heat/negation, flame/darkness, and similar metaphors for the state of being amongst the quick and against the dead. And certainly he tried out various claims for consequences of the transforming awareness, though above all emphasizing the transcendent experience with the "unknown," the break with given consciousness and feeling, as the nonobject object of desire. But usually he arrived back at a radically limited view of what can be considered enduring moral and social commitments, and those that he had were considerably utopian. Indeed, the high positive of what Lawrence repeatedly calls "the furious flame of passion" results in far more getting burned than affirmed, the discovery of deep desire brigading most often with the amoral and antisocial, adultery and other violation, flight and other refusal—the dying to the old self and way of life—sometimes including new powers of the destructive, which Lawrence so often equates with the creative. Otherwise put, which the majority of commentators seem to miss, the vitalistic is deeply conjoined with the nihilistic.

What a character says of Lawrence's persona Birkin could well be said of the author: He was distinctive for "his way of seeing some particular things vividly and feverishly, and his acting on this special sight."[22] Whether it be a flower or a phallus, a tremor of touch or a demand for apocalypse, he sought a total, salvational, intensity. Obviously, the reader of the biographies must be deeply convinced, Lawrence was often hard to take as a person, and that applies to his writings as well. Not the kind of man you would want to meet in a dark argument. His exacerbated heightening of individual desire, which is what he was largely aiming at in a modern world he saw as otherwise pretty empty of authentic human values, moves inseparably with the negation of those conditions which lessen such responsiveness. Hence desire depends upon negation, and negation becomes desire.

Adumbrating Some of the Other Novels

Canon is always a literary problem, with an author as well as with a curriculum, a period, a program, or other purpose which it helps determine as well as reflect. Continuing with my purpose, I want to partly reselect Lawrence works as well as the emphasis, or rather, as part of the emphasis. Some of the problems with the critical perspective on Lawrence have, of course, been the conventional focus on the early and middle-period novels, especially *Sons and Lovers*, *The Rainbow*, and *Women in Love*. A generation ago, there was not a long essay, much less a book, on the short fiction, though some of the tales would have to be granted, just on grounds of craft or insight (thus even by the formalist or the psychological reader), as some of Lawrence's best as well as most ranging writing. There was also little about the poetry—now partly corrected, with a change in fashionable poetics to the more open and various. Or for simpler example, one of Lawrence's most effective pieces of writing, his novella-length introduction to the *Memoirs* of Maurice Magnus, and its purpose of recognizing "the bitterness" and peculiarity and using it to "cleanse the blood," only slowly gets some of the attention it obviously merits.[23] The meaning and the significance of Lawrenceanism thus shift in terms of the works and their evaluation. It may even become more persuasive to argue that Lawrence was not primarily a novelist—that role in considerable part determined by the literary marketplace in his time and his intention early on to make a literary living so as to be considerably free of his society and its other institutions (for several generations a major motive for a writing "career"). From most discriminating critical perspectives—however formalist, psychological, stylistic, ideological, or whatever—a literal majority of Lawrence's novels must appropriately be seen as poor to bad. True, he passionately defended the novel (an example will be discussed in a later chapter). But he was of a peculiar sensibility who used the not altogether congenial novel form (though also stories, poems, travel sketches, personal essays, apocalyptic pronouncements, etc., at all periods of his writing), and it may be a fallacy of misplaced concreteness to almost totally concentrate on Lawrence-as-novelist (there goes the majority of critical studies!). Granted, one can put considerable emphasis on the novels (as I will continue to do here—I have discussed most of the stories and novellas elsewhere) because that is where the arguments about Lawrencenism have largely been. (I admit to assuming learned criticism to be considerably the community of argument.)

The reconsideration of the canon may suggest other changes, such as the greater importance to be given to one of his best-shaped, and more lucid, novels, *Lady Chatterley's Lover*, as well as to the nonfictional writings. It may also modify the perspective on what had been treated as canonical. Case in point, *The Rainbow*, which I will briefly and selectively recapitulate as if somewhat of a naive reader, in order not to obscure the essential points.[24] It has been discussed more positively than this suggestive but terribly awkward saga deserves, especially as a story of sexual fulfillment, when it really is more about the obscure negation of fulfillment, an uncertainty which no doubt partly encouraged the repetitious, overblown, carbonized prose. The story is also often ragged and unrealized; the themes are frequently shifting and murky. An obvious frequent failure of fictional craft, *The Rainbow* nonetheless intrigues because of its ambitiousness in pursuing three generations of the provincial Brangwens as they uncomprehendingly undergo major changes in English social values as well as passional relationships, and its positing the dominant power of sexual desire— beyond procreation, lust, and affection. Implicitly, Lawrence acknowledged the novel's weakness by considerable shifts in the style and focus and numerous rewritings into a quite different manner, and even more vehement negations, in what had been the continuation that becomes *Women in Love*. It is not necessary to impose inappropriate models— say, those of James or Nabokov—to realize the problematic nature of Lawrence's novel writing since his own drastic shifts in form and manner insist upon it.

In *The Rainbow*, Lawrencean desire struggles for larger reach, as with first-generation Tom Brangwen's "desire to find in a woman the embodiment of all his inarticulate, powerful religious impulses," however dramatically inchoate it remains. In a language heavy with images of heat, flame, darkness, and other metaphoric churning for the sacralization of erotic torment and wonder, the figure attempts to break through sexual repression.

Defiant Desire

His improbable late marriage to Lydia, a mid-thirties Polish exile widow with a daughter (Anna)—foreignness, as in so much of Lawrence's fiction as well as his life, exotically transmutes Oedipal incest fears and conflict-fully heightens the relation—makes him both erotically excited and frustrated into rages and drinking. In Lawrence's insistent (and sometimes unconsciously self-parodying) sanctification of the erotic, the woman represents for the man the transcendent "unknown," part of heightening desire to "eternal knowledge." Tom sees his marriage as "his Gethsemane and his Triumphal Entry in one" (the obscenity of the puns may not be intentional), his sex with his wife as "blazing darkness" (among other oxymorons), and his heightened desire as his "transformation, glorification, admission" (p. 91) into a religious state.[25] Elsewhere, Lawrence repeatedly calls this the state of "wonder," which is the "holiness" experience (in Rudolf Otto's sense) in erotic-desire conversion, or, later, the romantic and phenomeno-logical metapsychology of relating to the natural universe.

There are a few effective scenes in this first third of the fiction: Tom comforting stepdaughter Anna in the barn while her mother is giving birth (*Rainbow*, pp. 72ff); his drunken speech at Anna's wedding where the sacramental eroticism takes a seriocomic turn ("a married couple makes one Angel" [p. 134]); and some brief touches in the rhetoric-clotted prose in often more vaguely realized scenes. Lawrence is obviously forcing desire beyond his old-fashioned and provincially restricted material. But Tom simply drops out of the narrative ten years before his artistically and metaphysically fortuitous death in a flood (to be later answered by the rainbow), and we then surprisingly hear that his had been part of "the old brutal story of desire and offerings and deep, deep-hidden rage of unsatisfied men against women" (p. 250), which had hardly been dramatically developed, though it was to become a most insistent Lawrence theme. Whether a tale of desire achieved or frustrated remains confusingly ambiguous.

Such perplexity as well as burning of desire passes on to Anna, who has to fight against her stepfather Tom to achieve sex and marriage with cousin Will. Covert incest and its negation heightening is also a frequent part of Lawrencean desire, though I am not aware that he ever explicitly defends the desirability of incest (no Diogenes in this). Part of Anna's self-discovery occurs during the famous surrogate sexual scene in which she and Will shock corn sheaves in the moonlight, itself a poignant-comic muddling of desire (*Rainbow*, pp. 116ff). This second generation's more self-conscious battle of male/female wills plays out in metaphors of heat, birds, unfolding plants, and arching cathedrals (further foreshadowing the rainbow promise but poetically confusing the sexual drama). The marriage bed again becomes "the core of living eternity," but desire, of course, turns into conflict in which "there could only be acquiescence and submission," temporarily salved by the "tremulous wonder of consummation." Anna overcomes, negates, Will when she relinquishes "the adventure to the unknown," i.e., her individuality in desire, for obscenely compulsive breeding (nine pregnancies) and the "violent trance of motherhood" (p. 193). She also forces Will into a resigned "darkness in which he could not unfold," so that his aspirations as a religious artist are reduced to a hobby of making church repairs while he earns a living doing mechanical design work (and later teaching crafts in the schools). He principally serves the female will and family, which is the defeat of individual male desire, of fully intense being. In summary, Anna and Will were never "quite defined as individuals." Again, desire has been acted out but never quite fulfilled, and has become a kind of ontological negation of itself.

The third generation engages even more perplexing and self-conscious struggle to relate desire to "a sense of the infinite." The adolescent eldest, Ursula, center of a rather different novel, also takes up quasi-incestuously with a cousin (tabooed heightening), Anton, whom she does not really like, except for the physical satisfaction he provides ("her sexual life flamed into a kind of disease" [*Rainbow*, p. 322]). We see little of the male figure that Lawrence condemningly gives as conventional, a "conservative materialist" and statist, who goes off to the Boer War as an engineering officer. With all too typical highfalutin rhetoric: Anton's "soul lay in the tomb. His life lay in the established order of things" (p. 326). (In most of his long fictions, Lawrence seems unable to stop himself from generalizing, and sometimes misgeneralizing, his issues.)

Nearly half of the novel turns around third-generation Ursula, much of it in a considerably different, and often more novelistically successful, realistic mode. Partly that may be because Lawrence is closer to his own experiences, as in the gritty scenes to show the teacher's repressed rage at the trivializing, regimented labors of doing a "collective inhuman thing"— compulsory schooling (*Rainbow*, pp. 367ff.). Ursula, a feminist "New Woman" of the time,[26] partly escapes from teaching by taking her amorphous romantic yearnings to a university, where as a student she soon becomes disillusioned with that "apprentice shop" for "making money," that "commercial shrine" and "slovenly laboratory for the factory" (p. 435).

She eventually flunks her exams, and Lawrence sometimes flunks as a novelist in not giving much particularized sense of her student experiences amidst his churning rhetoric of subjective states.

But the history of desire gets more attention. While teaching, Ursula engages in a lesbian relationship with another teacher, taking up "the perverted life of the elder woman" (*Rainbow*, pp. 343ff). (Lawrence uses such terms as *perverted* to describe any sexual situation of which he does not approve, and lesbianism, for reasons discussed later, chapters 3 and 5, was usually one of them.) To Ursula's combined disgust and relief, her lover ends up marrying Ursula's uncle Tom. Though also inadequately described and dramatized, this coal-mining industrialist comes across as perverted in a larger sense, dehumanizing lives in his "putrescent" eagerness to serve "Moloch" (p. 349), the industrial machine, as well as himself, which from then on was to become an insistent Lawrencean focus of strident negation. (Socially dubious people almost always have bad sex in the Lawrencean world, though Anton seems to be a partly incoherent exception.) The negatives—lesbianism, the industrial Moloch, the frustrated woman seeking inappropriate sexual fulfillment, etc.—are, of course, to be more effectively replayed in *Lady Chatterley's Lover*.

While Ursula's development is not altogether clear, she has become a Lawrencean sophisticate, as with making Nietzschean denouncements (see my chapter 2) amidst her rather bovarysme yearnings. She also is the adventurous early twentieth-century female, living with war-returned Anton. The sex seems to be orgasmically good—she "entered the dark fields of immortality" (*Rainbow*, p. 451)—but not good enough to bridge the split between transcendent desire and "the social self." So she becomes a predatory "harpy" (of Lawrence's legion of such), insatiable and out to destroy maleness (p. 479); "will broken," Anton flees to a conventional marriage and a job as a colonialist in India. In the conclusion, the pregnant Ursula, after a semifantasy scene in a field with threatening horses (apparently metaphors for the masculinity which she wantingly fears—the later more sophisticated heroine of *St. Mawr* will choose the horse in a kind of transcendental bestiality), becomes ill and miscarries. Although now the modern, experienced and alienated, woman, she still seeks a man "from the Infinite," but represents an anguished dangling between the lost organic world of her forebears and an unacceptable present dissolution. "She grasped and groped to find the creation of the living God, instead of the old, hard barren form of bygone living" (p. 479). But there is little indication that any such possibility is available to her, only the ersatz Old Testament rainbow promise of a transcendent dimension after three generations of the partial failure of desire. The devolving generations have fractured male/female continuities, and the rhetorically hypothesized organic forms, and so the concluding rainbow promises little but perverse passional yearnings in Lawrence's desperate effort, with fervent incoherences in writing and dramatization, to separate good sexual desire from a badly negative history and society. With three generations of passional fulfillment, which is yet its negation, Lawrence's dialectic has foundered in some confusion, though, the critical history indicates, with a powerful suggestiveness for a number of readers to interestingly rewrite the novel. (I grant that this is but a summary "reading"—I will come back to some of the issues in later chapters—though would the pedantic elaboration of character, psychological, symbolist, archetypal, semiotic, or similar readings really change the issues?)

In the better-crafted *Women in Love*, we still follow Ursula (and get a few details about Anna and Will, and even obscure references to Anton [pp. 145, 466]), but Lawrence has reconceived the incompatibility of male/female, the negations of the given society, and the fiction as more disputatious novel of ideas (his dominant mode in the rest of his long fictions).[27] The rainbow-promise turns into a rather socially barren self-exile. Rootless bohemia—defined as the community of those who live in "rejection and negation" (p. 52)—of course, had become the only class and country of most of the characters as well as of Lawrence and his wife. Lawrence's rage at the Great War gave his writing an increased sophistication and hardness. The England at issue is no longer provincial and familial but industrial and marginal, and distinctively modern (unlike his four preceding novels). Even the old industrial ethic, as embodied by the contradictory Christianized paternalism of mine owner Thomas Crich, is being replaced by the highly rationalized functionalism of his wilful son Gerald—the confusingly charitable patriarch taken over by the ruthlessly instrumental "industrial magnate." Will Brangwen's Ruskinian religious art in *The Rainbow* is replaced by his daughter Gudrun's modernist-abstractionist minisculpture (and by the antihumanist artist Loerke, by primitive art objects, and the like, which Lawrence fascinatedly attacks in what is a more general negation of art). And the fiction is taken over by overt dialectics. Hence *Women in Love* is less a novel, in many of the traditional senses, than intensely metaphoric arguments partly dramatized about the

21

"passionate struggle into conscious being" (as Lawrence wrote in the fore-word) of marginal characters shaped by "the bitterness of the war." Partly trapped in its earlier conception, it ostensibly follows two years of the sisters' love affairs before the war. But the war-engendered modernist apocalyptic vision is at the heart of it.

Much, indeed, is sheer negation, including the novelistic focus on Rupert Birkin, the too-synthetic Lawrence persona who displaces the sisters and makes the often powerful but abstract arguments about tortured subjectivity. The archly awkward conception of the figure as a thirtyish, misanthropic school inspector with a substantial outside income (and a car in that early time) lacks solid personal background and social reality behind the upper-bohemian (marginality with money and social status) way of life. Lawrence was usually socially and masculinely boosting up his personas. Some of the attacks (as on upper-class witch Hermione) are a personal and class "consummation of hatred." But Lawrence's Great War rage also becomes more largely misanthropic (granted, that stance was important at least from Annable in *The White Peacock* on). Thus "humanity is a dead letter" (*Women in Love*, p. 52); "mankind is a dead tree" (p. 118); "man is a mistake; he must go" (p. 469). As even Lawrence notes of his artificial "upped-class" surrogate, "his dislike of mankind . . . amounted almost to a illness" (p. 53). The negations are often acutely focused: against the new functionalist rationalism (as Max Weber was to put it about the same time) of the industrial ordering—"pure organic disintegration and pure mechanical organization" (partly represented by Gerald, who consequently must die); against what Lawrence sees as the closely related dehumanizing modernist art (especially represented by industrial decorator Loerke, who consequently must be a sexual sadistic pervert); against the vestigial upper class (the colliery-ruling Crichs and the decadent upperclass at Breadalby); even against the unrebellious sensation-seeking lesser classes (the colliers' Saturday night, and the few touches with more ordinary folk); and the nastily futile bohemians (Minette and the others, "the half-men"). All must be viewed as "disintegrative" in this social nihilism. The parallel paeans to death are extreme: "How grand and perfect death was, how good to look forward to" (p. 183; not only here, of course, but in the essay "The Reality of Peace," the story "England, My England," the later war-reflecting novel *Kangaroo*). This goes beyond dramatic and dialectical coherence—the sustained argument for viewing the universe as essentially "inhuman" (pp. 257, 470, etc.)—to pure revulsive negation for almost its own sake. The only allowed alternative is heightened individual consciousness and permanent flight.

More dialectical, and sometimes charming, is Lawrence's partial negation of women, since they change desire into controlling "will." This aims not only at the destructive and submissive-dominant man-manipulators (Hermione, Minette, and Gudrun) but more generally, including the positive-lover figure of Ursula, to whom Birkin announces that "woman was always so horrible and clutching, she had such a lust for possession, a greed of self-importance in love. She wanted to have, to own, to control, to be dominant." Inverting his maternal fixation, Lawrence also attacks the "Great Mother of everything," as when Birkin furiously stones the reflections of the female moon and curses Cybele and "the accursed Syria Dea!" (in the chapter "Moony," *Women in Love*, pp. 236ff). No doubt the attacks on the feminine should be linked to the confused desire for heightened male relationships. Partly homoerotic, as in the cancelled "Prologue" of overwrought prose about Birkin's "affinity for men" because of "the hot, flushing aroused attraction" for alien males who "held the passion and the mystery to him,"[28] the longing for "eternal union with a man too" (p. 472) is the concluding thematic statement of desire. The male-on-male passion has been irregularly raised in the novel, as in the attempted "conjunction between two men" of Birkin with Gerald and the *Blutbrüderschaft* ritualization of it, as in the self-consciously forced scene of naked wrestling (improbable and inconsistent in the social ordering) in the "Gladitorial" chapter. No wonder the supposedly happily married man's wife concludes that it is a "perversity" (p. 473) in a statement so personal as to be an anticlimatic dying fall to the ambitious fiction. (Again, I am doing a fairly straight-on reading, rather than "one-upping" other readings by textual overelaborations.)

Lawrencean "desire," it should be honestly noted, takes some extreme forms. Birkin, for example, emphatically tells Gerald that "a man who is murderable is a man who in a profound hidden lust desires to be murdered" (*Women in Love*, p. 27). What happens is what one really desires. This I see as a psychologically suggestive but finally absurd reach of turning desire into an absolute, which denies all chance and other reality. The fiction's final action apparently intends that a variant of Birkin's statement applies to Gerald, whose final weakness of desire in his willful struggle with Gudrun becomes suicidal. (The "murderee" desire less adequately reflects Gerald than it does the self-destructive antiheroines in "None of That" and

"The Woman Who Rode Away.") Even here Lawrence claims a larger reach of desire since industrialist Gerald is the "messenger" of the "universal dissolution into whiteness and snow," the modernist apocalypse without any rainbow promise. The destructive perversity of Gudrun, which encourages Gerald in his suicidal end, seems to be the feared female will engaged in the "mystic frictional activities of diabolic reducing down, disintegrating the vital organic body of life" in her insistence on dominating Gerald. Both figures negatively serve Lawrence's dialectical polarity of desire, and so it is not simply antiwoman.

Lawrence's erotic arguments develop out of, rather than in spite of, the destructive ordering and the nihilistic bent. Thus Birkin-Lawrence engages Ursula-Frieda in a "fine passion of opposition," in scenes generally recognized as some of the most delightful in the novel. Explicitly not a love ethic in any usual sense (like that which goes with despised Christianity), the "strange conjunction" that Birkin demands is "not meeting and mingling . . . but an equilibrium, a pure balance of two single beings; as the stars balance each other" (*Women in Love*, p. 139). No doubt Birkin's individualist stance here partly reflects a fear of merger with woman as well as a contrary desire. Lawrence, of course, is making his own conflicted desires into cosmic doctrine. Understandably, he deploys it in one of his vehement rejections of usual sentimental courtship—elsewhere he scornfully call it "adoration love" (as in the novella *The Ladybird*)—in a metaphysical extension of the common male revulsion against the constraints of courtship. He demands that the passion be "stark and impersonal," as against the sentimental and merging (p. 179)—primordial as against the calculated. Such love, "such fine passion of opposition," it should be acknowledged, precariously orbits with hostility. It is, of course, not confined to *Women in Love* (or a period of the biography) since it runs through all periods of Lawrence's fiction, from the very early "White Stocking" on through the late tales. As Lawrence even more harshly put the issue in an essay of the period of this novel: "Love without a fight is nothing but degeneracy."[29] Such oppositional eroticism is certainly demanding, youthfully heroic (I would now note) as well as extremely ambivalent, and can hardly be taken as very consistently normative.

While Lawrence's Birkin claims equality in the relationship, clearly one star is to be more powerful than the other. Ursula, reasonably enough, repeatedly characterizes her lover's highfalutin demands as male "bullying." The male claim to go "beyond love" to a "pure duality of polarization" (*Women in Love*, p. 193) seems to be a countermetaphysics to a feared merging and submission, as well as a desperate gambit of gender incompatibilities. Lawrence complicates it with woman—here Ursula— reinterpreting the conflicting polarity (as in the hostile "moony" scene) as really a demand for love. The rhetoric presents it as more general truth about women. It is certainly a demand for submission by both. He wants "the surrender of her spirit," something even beyond the "phallic," for which she must forgo her "assertive *will*" (p. 242). According to Birkin-Lawrence, she one-ups him by twisting even that demand to her purposes; she "believed that love was *everything*. Man must render himself up to her. He must be quaffed to the dregs by her. Let him be *her man* utterly, and she in return would be his humble slave . . ." (p. 258). A Hegelian "happy slave" who masters the master? In these contrary and twisting erotic ideologies, where one extremity counters the other, mating becomes a kind of permanent warfare, demanding, exhausting, and tenuous (which, I must suppose, is why most accept other erotic conventions).

Whatever the proportions of a terrible fear of female domination, of contrary homosexual longing and rejection, and of heroic individualism, it seeks to make love into something other. "I don't want love," says Lawrence's spokesman, "I want to be gone out of myself, and you to be lost to your self" (again, the "moony" scene). Such passion seeks the obliteration of mere social roles, and of guilts and self-consciousness, in the yearning to achieve an unanxious "dark involuntary being." The arguments from passional desire really serve a holistic ontology, not mere affectionate relationships, or just sexual gratification (though they may heighten it). One does not have to have Lawrence's sexual peculiarities and problems to recognize some profundity in the search for "dark" being.

This is but another version of Lawrence's polemical demands for the notorious "blood knowledge," and in various other places for "instinct," "intuitive life," "animal nature," and other "dark" (unconscious) states which sometimes slide over into the "demonic." Yet, we might well note, Lawrence's vitalistic doctrines are often treated with a critical intelligence which makes him something other than a mere fundamentalist of his erotic desperation. His Birkin, for just one example, shrewdly attacks Hermione (his mistress before Ursula, and the author's angry personal caricature, say the biographers, of an upper-class domineering lady), who is given some of his doctrinal gestures, such as an insistence on the "spontaneous" over the "self-conscious." Says Birkin-Lawrence of this claim to vitalistic values, "It is the worst and the last form of intellectualism, this love . . . for passion and the animal instincts." (chapter 3, "Class-room"; or, as Lawrence repeated the point in the essay "On Human Destiny": Modern man's "very spontaneity is just an idea . . . fathered in the mind, gestated in self-consciousness.") Lawrence here perceives and provides the line of what was to be the major attack on himself. I also see the complex strategies of such intellectual anti-intellectualism, which insists on the "marriage between mind and emotion" (same essay), as part of the post-Enlightenment "crisis" ideology of modernism.

Curiously, Birkin grants of his transcendental desire that "his spirituality was concomitant of a process of depravity." We might see the demand for female submission as depraved—the fear is of course pervasive in the novel: Diana Crich dragging her lover to his death in Willey Water; old Mrs. Crich attacking her husband; Hermione smashing Birkin's head with a paperweight; Gudrun pushing Gerald to choking hatred and suicide; and on and on. But the depravity also has a more literal sexual dimension. In Ursula's affectionate surrender in the Sherwood Forest night scene, Birkin's domineering eroticism apparently takes the form of anal sexuality—"the darkest poles of the body" found "at the back and base of the loins" (*Women in Love*, p. 306). How this relates to the "star-equilibrium" of trumpeted Lawrencean relationship must remain a bit obscure in its reversal, not least because it also seems to be the "perversity" of Gudrun and Gerald's hostile sexuality (p. 403). Not much further specification of the buggery is suggested, though the insistence is a little less obscurely repeated in *Lady Chatterley's Lover* (see the discussion below), and seems to be part of the point of the even vaguer, voluptuously "shameful" sexual practices of Will and Anna in *The Rainbow*.[30] We should link it not only with female submission in passivity, but with homosexual longings and with the "dark passion" violations of genteel adoration love.

Still, the suggestive courtship, presented in intense and even sometimes witty scenes, remains powerful, partly because of the oppositional in its endless provocative dialectic, as does the larger adaption of desire in which the man desperately quests for "his resurrection" by way of "ultimate marriage." "Sick" Birkin is reborn in the Sherwood Forest dark dalliance, though mostly in nullifidian ways, which immediately follow. In *Woman in Love* eroticism is granted to be a "religious mania," not a family institution. It is no longer confused with the domestic ordering of *The Rainbow*. In *Women in Love*, the erection of desire, whether by "shameful" sex, female submission, heroic conflict, or whatever, can only result in asocial marriage with even the most positive couple in isolated flight. Neither sister achieves traditional marriage and a community. The old world is dead in the most intimate as well as larger senses. The relationship of Ursula and Birkin depends on their being, as he announces, "disinherited"—declassed, deracinated, defamilied—though the protagonist, like the author, retains wistful utopian longings for male bonding and even a new community—"I always imagine our being really happy with some few people" (p. 471). Utopianism was the other side of Lawrence's nihilism (which I will return to). But the longings in *Women in Love*, as Lawrence's overreaching metaphors and dialectics suggest, can have only quite limited positive issue. The perplexities of desire have not really been resolved, nor those of any large purpose. As Birkin says near the end, "Whatever the mystery which has brought forth man and the universe, it is a non-human mystery . . . man is not the criterion" (p. 469).

So human efforts, erotic rebirth, and other heightening of desire, provide only a momentary counter against the nothingness. This awareness may be taken as the deep modernist disenchantment. That is part of the importance of *Women in Love*, Lawrence's most thoroughly wrought long fiction (though as balanced narrative it does not match *Sons and Lovers* and *Lady Chatterley's Lover*, and for quality of craft and insight it does not equal the best of the short fictions). Its force, I suggest, comes from Lawrence's intense quest for passional possibility which is combined with perplexed dialectics and vivid metaphoric scenes, such as the fatal water party at the Crichs', Gerald's willfully fighting his horse against the railroad machine, Hermione's smashing Birkin, the stoning of the feminine moon's reflection, the rabbit scoring Gudrun's arm, Gerald's death in the snow—all scenes of extremity and destructiveness. The revelation of subterranean negative motives heightens the scenes—indeed, may be taken as their purpose and achievement. But it is a more general Dostoyevskian principle with Lawrence, who usually looks for the conflict and extremity. As Birkin pronounces, even the "most normal people have the most subterranean selves" (*Women in Love*, p. 200). The dialectics work similarly: Birkin's arguments with Gerald carry homoeroticism as well as anti-industrialism; the lovers' quarrels engage hostile gender metapsychology as well as courtship; the erotic doctrines concern cultural nihilism as well as sexuality; even the descriptions of art (including implicitly his own) becomes an attack on the falsity of all art, including his own. The fulfillment of desire becomes a kind of inverse something else. Such intensification provides much of Lawrence's distinctive quality, and fascinating literary importance.

As a coda to this brief survey of some of the dialectics of the best-known middle-period novels, consideration of *The Lost Girl* might be appropriate.[31] Less ambitious than *The Rainbow* and *Women in Love*, it is also carelessly written (especially in the switches in tone), but is more interesting than the trite critics neglect of it would suggest. Probably taking off from Arnold Bennett's *Anna of the Five Towns* (1902)—therefore more novelistically traditional than any other long fiction between *Sons and Lovers* and *Lady Chatterley*, and perhaps thus to be handled with some disdain by the increasingly convention-contemptuous Lawrence—it provides a study of shabby lower-middle-class provincial life, though the novel's often railing tone suggests the author's would-be mocking distance from his parochial past.

The Lost Girl is about a somewhat perverse feminism in its "liberation" of a Midlands spinster, Alvina Houghton, a failed shopkeeper's only child who frees herself to become a nurse, then a vaudeville piano player, then the wife of an Italian peasant. The rigid moral-social system of the small colliery town produces the "Dead Sea fruit" of bitter old maids—the near-thirtyish virgin Alvina and the poignantly earnest viragos, Miss Frost and Miss Pinnegar—women unable "to submit" to desire (p. 34) and "yield, yield, yield"—who take care of her after her mother develops heart disease "as a result of nervous repressions" (p. 10). Other sad fruits of the old order include Alvina's father, a quasi-comic, always failing entrepreneur who finally becomes proprietor of a sleazy working-class vaudeville and cinema house. That entertainment center and the Congregational chapel Alvina attends encompass most of provincial culture, in all the oppressive narrowness Lawrence was forever fleeing.

Lawrence only thinly presents much of the material, including virgin Alvina's would-be male predators and two fiancés: a rigid, social-climbing colonial schoolteacher and a pompous older doctor little boys with a domineering, manly veneer. No wonder that she prefers to have as friend odd little Mr. May (based on Maurice Magnus?), the theater partner and a cryptotransvestite (as we see in his costuming and manner). Alvina seeks "not mere marriage" but deeper desire for a "profound and dangerous inter-relationship" (*Lost Girl*, p. 71). Much of the quest, of course, is by negation—here escape from the puritanical small-town "mechanical" and "mediocre" (as in the concurrent American literature of Sherwood Anderson, who soon recognized some appropriate affinity with Lawrence). Alvina is *declassee* (p. 132) by playing piano for the vaudeville acts (as usual in Lawrence, the pursuit of desire must violate class and defy social status), and even more so by her attraction to Cicio, an image of alien, dark sensuality, and a crude wandering Italian performer (he plays a vaudeville Indian in some very silly scenes—Lawrence has been reading Cooper novels). She marries him for his "dark flicker of ascendancy," usual metaphor of Lawrence's demon-lovers (as with Romero in "The Princess," et al.). While merging with him, without "will," he made "her his slave" (pp. 223, 256–57, etc.). Lawrence paradoxically insists that this also provides a kind of completion of the woman, a "perfected" self. She becomes "bewitched" in a "sleep-like submission to his being," even feeling at times like "a sacred prostitute" (p. 315). The "atavistic" and "desperate passion that was in him sent her completely unconscious" of egotism and social role (pp. 313, 318). Yet, we should note, though completely yielding in the "acquiescent passion" of the primordial female, the loss of self remains incomplete. Is this failure or victory of female masochism? But Lawrence's point is a richer sense of self. Alvina's orgasmic sexual submission—"a paroxysm of unbearable sensation" (p. 194)—paradoxically becomes her individual completion. (Whether, to refer to an issue discussed later, her sexual paroxysm is clitoral or just a broader psychological submission does not seem clearly indicated in the text.) Lawrence also may be seen as holding, as so often, to the famous Tiresias prophecy that women have the greater sexual gratification. Having gotten that in exchange for giving up nursing and midwifery (and possibly a comfortable marriage to a middle-aged doctor) for the life of a primitive farm family in the Abruzzi, Alvina has certainly gone to the social extreme to satisfy desire. And Lawrence, as in so many of his fictions and poems, presents some of the extreme in his travel descriptions of an alien "spirit of place," which carries on, as so often, his desire/negation dialectics. Treated without sentimentality, these are places which "resist us" and "have the power to overthrow our psychic being" (p. 343). As with much of his other foreign-scene descriptions (the prewar and postwar Italian travel pieces, the sketches and fictions using Mexico and the American Southwest), the Abruzzi focuses some powerful writing. The place is not pretty: Lawrence evokes savage pagan gods, a "malevolent" spirit, dirt, crudeness, "venomous" inhabitants, and other repulsions (especially pp. 354ff). There is, as so often, a negative exaltation which becomes a passional affirmation.

Defiant Desire

The very harshness and extremity can liberate Alvina (and Lawrence) from the tight, gray English scene, bringing an expansive awareness of a humanly indifferent universe and a nihilistic vitality. Though the heroine fatalistically subordinates herself to the harsh scene and her demon-lover (with whom she can hardly even converse—traditional Mediterranean male, he talks mostly to other men in public places), we are to see her as transformed. But problematically. The poor, pregnant, aging English "girl," left on the harsh peasant farm when her husband is conscripted for World War I—though they yearningly plan to flee to America—remains "lost" in the simple sense as well as the orgasmic. A once pathetic "old maid," the ironically liberated heroine is unlikely to repeat her mother, who withdrew into invalidism, or the devastated, cold, vinegarish spinsters, in the repression and emotional mediocrity of puritanical, lower-middle-class provincial life. Lawrence was probably right again that it takes drastic assaults on the psyche to transform Protestant petty bourgeois sensibility, though he was so convinced that he was rather sloppy and jeering in this handling of a sometimes moving fiction of the rebellion and sexual conversion experience which was his as well as his heroine's. For Alvina has followed desire into problematic realms of passional being, however wedded to the negative, and thus into fuller experience and meaning. And that is much of what is at issue in Lawrence's terribly insistent demands for "more vivid life!"

Just short of relentlessness in this annotation of the dialectics of desire in the fictions, let me add as postscript brief consideration of yet another middle-period "novel," *Mr. Noon*.[32] The crudity of the incomplete fragments posthumously glued together may provide a bit of deconstructing reminder. (They were first published together in 1984; the previously published part 1, a rather superficial would-be comic-satiric account of provincial lower-middle-class adolescent seduction—"spooning"—need not concern us here.) Much of the emphasis is again as usual: "Oh wonderful desire: violent, genuine desire!" (p. 136) However, rather archly, the self-conscious narrator contemptuously mocks his readers—"oh gentle but rather cowardly and imbecile reader" p. (292), etc.—and also, consciously or not, mocks himself: "I insist on apostrophizing desire" (p. 137), though curiously in somewhat surreal ways since, as with from a failing love, "his poetry, like pus, flowed from the wound" (p. 141).

Gilbert Noon, a provincial schoolteacher, like his author, skips out abroad when he finally connects with a post-"spooning" sexual woman whom he pursues to Germany, Johanna (obviously autobiographical— Frieda). It is, again, transcendent eroticism, for she "took her sex as a religion" (*Mr. Noon*, p. 139). Lawrence repeats, though in rather crass abbreviation, many of the desire/negation motifs of *Women in Love*. It is also the "love of two splendid opposites." And "wonderful opposition!" with "mating always half a fight" (p. 186). In conversion by "the sacred magnetism of desire" (p. 211), it again includes negation of the conventional repression that made "sex, and the sacred, awful communion . . . degraded into a thing of shame. . . ." For love "is no spiritual union. It is the living blood soul in each palpitating from the shock of a new metamorphosis," a "second birth" (p. 226). For this conversion is required the negation of the old life, and that they flee "the horror of that middle-class milieu" (p. 199).

But in both literary context (the account is underdeveloped and inconsistent in tone) and in larger eroticism, much, indeed, is problematic. Pathetic Gilbert Noon, for example, admires soldiers and repeatedly longs for male connections; he desperately wanted to "really mix and mingle with men" (*Mr. Noon*, p. 227). Poor effeminate and envious Paul Morel-ish Lawrence! Though being reborn in heterosexual passion, he also repeatedly longs for a "womanless life" (p. 209). An odd light is cast on the romantic passion by the frustrated male longing for men. So apparently does Johanna who, in a few days of high romance also manages to have casual sex with at least two other men. Noon's responses seem short-circuited and confused jealousy. He appears to have other sexual problems as well, not least evident in his boast that "it isn't every man who can love a women three times in a quarter of an hour" (p. 141). Nor is it every man who wants to, leaving a woman dissatisfied and pursuing other men. (Isn't this a rather sad adumbration of Lawrence's legion of dissatisfied women, and of his attacks on their clitoral aggressiveness? [discussed later]) While it is no doubt unfair to make a literary-ideological evaluation of Lawrence in terms of draft fragments, the Noon revelations do tend, given the same desire and negation motifs, to confirm the problematic nature of Lawrencean desire more complexly evident in his other writings. Hardly normative, Lawrencean desire provides crucial and profound issues, but there is little sense in ignoring its difficulties and self-negations.

Defiant Desire

Some Further Consequences

In the first passage I quoted from Lawrence on desire, he said that the "deep desires" may be "fulfilled in long periods of time." Are here implied all sorts of social affirmations, especially in his fictional use of marriage-tale forms—however ambiguous and antique-appearing now? Does that not suggest an enduring order resulting from his defiantly religious eroticism, and one which goes beyond his harsh negations? Yes, I will argue, but not really. Simply too earnest commentators have for long been twisting Lawrence's *Ding-an-sich* of desire/negation and its vivid being into not only tritely overcoming all denials but as the base of inappropriate conventional pieties.

Certainly Lawrence dallied with clusters of affirmations around marriage in his tales, novels, poems, and discursive statements—and many could be quoted, early and late—however pyrrhonized in the dramatization and undercutting motives and descriptions. As just noted of *The Lost Girl*, sexually converted Alvina marries her primitivistic alien, "atavistic," dark lover, goes to live on a farm in the Abruzzi, and becomes pregnant, though the conclusion is left with Lawrence's usual drastic openness, uncertainty. Constance Chatterley appears to be on the way to a similar family-and-farm permanency (in Scotland) in Lawrence's last novel, though also with considerable uncertainty. So, too, with quite a range of Lawrence stories, such as his novella, *The Captain's Doll* (so often cited as marital positiveness, especially since the absurdly hyperbolic praise of F. R. Leavis),[33] which adds to family farming (in Africa this time) the quaintly ancient marriage rhetoric of a wife as traditionally "obedient" and a "patient Griselda." In context, if that is not to be taken as comic rhetoric, it must be seen as a bad joke, especially given the independent-minded anti-doll Hannele (though it seems to have partly worked for a while on Frieda). Even more undercutting appears, for example, in the coda to *The Fox* about the marriage to the dissatisfied ex-lesbian, after totemic pursuit and murder, so that it can hardly be read as moral and social affirmation. But perhaps I need not further rehearse here the drastic ambiguities of Lawrence's marriage-family-farming tropes in his life, utopian dreams, and fictions (though I may not have sufficiently emphasized them in past commentary). The marriages are at best perplexed and the nexus of social purpose is less farming than flight (to Canada, Africa, Scotland, Italy, New Mexico, etc.), as Lawrence himself was always in flight from modern society and pretenses at traditional values and permanency. The crucial tales (examples already cited), and the crucial episodes in the longer fictions, tend to be antimarriage, antifamily, anticommunity. Not surprisingly, even those tales with marriage-family-farming resolutions are almost always given a skeptical uncertainty, if not irony. Such ostensible resolution may now sound a poignant dying fall. Otherwise put, Lawrence's fictions may have been undercuttingly entrapped in a convention for a dying mode of sexual resolution—organic family life. Lawrence, of course, is hardly to be blamed for his dialectics of desire and negation not really resolving male/female polarities and his radical rebellion not finding permanent moral and social forms. In his time, as in ours, they may not be generally resolvable.

But a good many commentators on Lawrence may be to blame for imposing on him simple love-ethic and social-ethic affirmations. The "dying" to reach regenerative desire includes the death of much of the social-moral forms and obligations, even when not resulting in apocalyptic demands for change. It is not incidental that Lawrence's most successfully achieved artistry in his fictions often turns around negations (as in the destructive scenes in the novels previously cited, or in such of his best fables as "The Rocking-Horse Winner"—defeat by superficial bourgeois desires—or "The Man Who Loved Islands"—defeat by idealist antidesires). The realization of the deep desires, often including the disturbing, ugly, or destructive, and the drastic denial of those conditions which would negate or distort desiring, seem so crucial with Lawrence that the onus, not only of misreading but of moral falsification, must lie on those who do not give them full place in the peculiar and radical perspective of Lawrenceanism.

A bit tendentiously, let me add to the issue some brief consideration of a few speculative-polemical essays, mostly from *Reflections on the Death of a Porcupine*. These, I take it from the critical literature, are not much responded to even by Lawrence specialists, though it was the sort of thing he insistently went at again and again as the social-political dimensions of desire/negation. The ignoring is partly understandable, for the pieces are diatribes, full of sarcasms, put-downs, crass bigotries, and views quite unacceptable to most of those who would affirmatively moralize Lawrence. For example, ". . . Love Was Once a Little Boy"[34] (one of his longest essays of the mid-1920s), attacks usual bland conceptions of love (hence the sarcastic title), Wordsworthan nature sentimentality ("eternal absurdity," silly "anthropomorphism"), St. Francis (ditto), the phony individuality appealed to by advertising ("sawdust manikin"), fashionable promiscuity

Defiant Desire

("Don Juanery, sex-in-the-head, no real desire") and most insistently, the equality of women. I partly refer to the piece in this context because it uses Lawrence's key term *desire* literally dozens of times. "In its essence, love is no more than the stream of clear and unmuddied, subtle desire which flows from person to person, creature to creature, thing to thing." In humans, it is, of course, a polarity—"balanced against the opposite desire, to maintain the integrity of the individual self." Sentimentality loses the conflicting individuality; modern love is especially false in egoizing desire, thus corrupting it into kinds of "prostitution." Lawrence's usage certainly varies, from the metaphysical ("Desire itself is a pure thing, like sunshine, or fire, or rain. It is desire that makes the whole world living. . . .") to the crass (it is the essence of women to be "desirable"). Though desire is one of the poles of the life force, "the living stream of sexual desire itself does not often, in any man, find its object, its confluent, the stream of desire in a woman into which it can flow." (The obscenity again seems unconscious.) He pushes the separate rivers-of-desire metaphor hard, "because the individualities of men and woman are incommensurable. . . ." Man and woman are no more to be equalized than "I can equilibrate myself with my black cow Susan," whom he goes on about at some length to show her errant but finally submissive, though deeply different, cowishly feminine, ways. The real center of the essay is an attack on heterosexual equality as the enemy of desire. There is no real living balance "that equates the cock and the hen." "It is a pity of pities women have learned to think like men." For "making the sexes alike" destroys not only oppositional desire but "the original individuality of the blood. . . ." But it is hard to find much individuality, much less heroically oppositional female "star-equilibrium," associated with the cow and hen analogies. (Lawrence has been married too long and unhappily.)

That is much of Lawrence's love ethic. As for the larger social ethic, that is also vehemently antiegalitarian, as we see in the contiguous essay, "Reflections on the Death of a Porcupine."[35] The dogma is simple: "There is no such thing as equality." It is indeed too simple, in the way he got from guiltily killing a nuisance porcupine to social Darwinian reflections on the struggle for existence generally as "conquest," the struggle of higher and lower as "the inexorable law of life." Granted, he attempts some qualifications on the difference between individual "being" and the struggle necessarily engaged in by the group and "species." He has also reversed the prevailing form of social Darwinism, via the works of Herbert Spencer, and related sources, that he probably read in teacher's college, and he repeatedly alludes to in *Sons and Lovers*, "Study of Thomas Hardy," and in a number of these later essays, by *not* taking it as economic struggle.[36] Lawrence's very language (as in passages earlier cited) is Spencer's, such as giving the evolutionary process a semireligious cast coming from the "unknowable," adding a dubious social-moral purpose to biological processes, and insisting on ruthless competition (including classical-liberal "free-enterprize" in Spencer but not in anticommerce Lawrence), with a brutal lack of mitigation for suffering and injustice. Lawrence concludes his essay by vehemently attacking "money and money standards," which will lead the "moneyless" to "set our house on fire, and burn us to death." We apparently deserve it for our obsession with money standards, which makes us lose all "vitality," and which most of the essays are out to negate. Competition in life-vitality has replaced economic competition in Lawrence's righteous version of social Darwinism.

But, a countercritic might reply, this is a wayward polemical essay, not art. That argument does not apply well to Lawrence, for essentially the same social Darwinism and metaphors provide, for example, the poetic vision of the last pages of the novella *St. Mawr* (a "battle" to "win" over "the lower stages of creation"), and somewhat less overtly are evident in, among others, *The Rainbow* and *Women in Love*, and restated in *The Plumed Serpent* (discussed later). The repeated social-moralized evolutionism may also partly contradict Lawrence's insistent anti-anthropomorphism of nature perceptions. To see snake and fish and mountainous place as having their own and quite inhuman "spirits" may not accord with hierarchical chains of being, culminating in the superior human. Yet Lawrence's biologism must be taken as central to most of his writings and views (and necessarily frames my later discussions).

In the related "Aristocracy,"[37] Lawrence continues the argument by loose analogies. The "daisy is more alive" than the torpid fern, the bee than the flower, until we get to man in particular, "the highest, most developed, most conscious, most *alive* of the animals: master of them all." The dubious switch from aliveness to domination provides the social ethic, with the forced "infinite" difference applying within a species as well. Thus the more alive men must dominate the Christian meek and poor of both sexes, for, by a dubious pun, "the poor in life are the most impure, the most easily degenerate." This nastily follows social Darwinism, then and now (as in current right-wing "libertarian-capitalist" ideology). "Aristocracy of birth is bunk" but there is *"natural* aristocracy," exemplified by Caesar and Cicero, by Dostoyevsky ("more vividly alive than Plato" though a negative aliveness), by all those (here, exceptionally in Lawrence, of many races) who have a connection with the sun as metaphor of cosmic vitality. Riding his metaphor in a fundamentalist way, he concludes that all those who have the magical connection with the sun, apparently not only intensified responsiveness but a new vision of the cosmos, are "lords of the earth" and "the aristocracy of the world," "a confraternity of the living sun," who will rule all and negate the now world-controlling finance-industrialism.

"Blessed Are the Powerful"[38] (the shortest of this group of essays) rejects what Lawrence takes to be the Nietzschean notions of will and power, and the contemporary political manifestations of it (Mussolini, Primo de Rivera, Woodrow Wilson, Lenin, and, of course, money-power) for what he takes to be passionate religious and ethical power, the "Holy Spirit" which Jesus got rather wrong in his negating desire for equality. As by implication, Lawrence previously had, too. In a later aesthetic-utopian essay he writes: "In the flush of youth, I believed in Socialism, because I thought it would be thrilling and delightful. Now I no longer believe very deeply in Socialism, because I am afraid it might be dull, duller even than what we've got now." To reject—as a libertarian might well do—what prevails seems the most continuous purpose of Lawrence's porcupinish reflections. The carryover socialism (which, with Nietzsche, he usually condemningly connects with Christianity), leads to his elitism being practically anticonservative, always attacking money-power, always vaguely pointing to a directed economy, and still socialistically demanding "basic provision" for all, to eliminate the "money problem." The rebellion inclines to anarchism, the exasperation to authoritarianism, the history and economics to socialism, the metaphysics to extreme individualism. Hardly a stable mix. But it may serve Lawrence's most basic purpose—provocation.

It is, in "Blessed Are the Powerful," those who can teach us intense living who provide "the real *exercise* of power." "Living consists in doing what you really, vitally want to do . . . [which] is terribly difficult." (This is simply another version of the first quote I started with above on desire, though apparently written about five years earlier.) So, inverting the gospel message, "Blessed are the powerful, for theirs is the kingdom of earth." But not blessed is the serpent of the absolute in "Him with His Tail in His

Mouth"[39] (perhaps the least exacerbated and exasperating of this group of essays), which helps him, Nietzsche style, reject Christianity and Platonism, yet again, for a somewhat pluralistic-pantheistic view of the universe since there is "no eternal goal," no ultimate value but experiential desire. Because he feels "the life-urge weakening"—not least that there are "too many people" (strangely, magically, that is not a social or ecological problem, as it obviously is, but one of too much consciousness and self-consciousness, thus blocking the primal). History, then, has become a downward path ("Hadn't somebody better write Mr. Wells' History backwards, to prove how we've degenerated since the cave-men?" Lawrence was to do a bit of reverse-Wells later in *Lady Chatterley's Lover*). Only the "pure spark" of desire, of vital relationship, can possibly redeem us. And it takes the exceptional, a vital elite, to do that.

Nor are these views an aberrant phase of Lawrence's thought. In an essay written half a dozen years earlier, "Democracy,"[40] he was raging against equality: "Men are not equal . . . and never will be. . . ." Equality is just idealizing an anti-individualist abstraction, "The Law of the Average," and imposing it on the individual for material, functional, purposes. Scornfully taking off from Whitman's glorification of the *mass*, democratic "One Identity"—as so often, Lawrence attacks the figures he is attracted to and uses (as with Dostoyevsky, Nietzsche, Blake, and others)—he holds that more than a minimal material view of equality is the enemy, by way of deadening abstractions such as nation, state, internationalism, and the like, which defeat "the full spontaneous being" of the desiring self. Such questions as whether some should have more material or comfort than others, or some should have power beyond that of their desiring vital being, are not at all considered. He is simply dismissing in his flailing manner all social-political issues—and prevailing authorities, mere "servants" (a libertarian disenchantment)—for his metaphysics of exceptional desiring individuals. While Lawrence may be properly disgusted at the politics of his time, and at the dubious majoritarianism justifying it, it is hardly a considered view. Without much subtlety or probing, Lawrence demands unmaterialistic individualism, and that would be real "democracy." But in none of these essays is there much sense of drastic social injustice—indeed, Lawrence seems totally obtuse on that historically most crucial push for democracy.

Obviously in such summary treatment of this group of central essays, I am ignoring both some of the suggestive metaphors and some of the nastiness, but the cast should be clear: the negation of the high ideals of Western civilization (Christian, Platonic, Enlightenment, finance-industrial, liberal-democratic) for a prophetic demand for the religious experience of intense desire, heightened relationship with person and place, exceptional vitality. Lawrence is out to negate much of the civilization, no less, since he sees even the best in Western civilization as the denial of true desire. And he was to persist in that, with the later essays simply more exacerbated and colloquially defiant. Again, there is little sense of Lawrence without recognizing his constant, indeed, obsessive, negation of what he saw as dominant, such as capitalist "democracy," which, of course, has often been contemptibly inadequate for the more intense individual truths.

No doubt some of this radical spirit can be explained away as the angers of an exasperated, repeatedly ill, irascible, frail, tormented, alienated, failing, angry man. Some of it perhaps comes from the very taking on of a prophetic role in a dubiously appropriate form—the colloquial personal essay uncomfortably heightened to the denouncing voice from the New Mexico wilderness. Surely some of it is ugly, especially, I would say, in its authoritarian attack on equality, both of women he could not dominate and of the modern society he was constantly fleeing. Much of it also seems incoherent. While the main impetus in more than a decade of such pronouncements seems to be the negation of all that would negate the vital individualism of desire, the passional evolutionism and the exaltation of hierarchy and authoritarianism would obviously defeat that. The crass positing of "aristocracy" undercuts his even more insistent attacks on social class. The rejection of social-economic equality produces the very money-power that he repeatedly curses. His negations dominate in his revulsions to the war-state, bourgeois democracy, and the reformist dogmas as well as doctrines for maintaining the commercial-industrial mechanisms that he viewed as overwhelmingly destructive. Much of the Lawrence social-political perspective has reasonably been summarized as an extremely "emphatic and bizarre individualism."[41]

And surely there is more to be said (and I will), in qualification and understanding, of these negations and desires. But it also seems evident that in demanding and broadly projecting the exceptional experiences of desire and transformation of being, Lawrence yet often furthered the enemies of the exceptionally alive, negating the Lawrencean. However, it may often be salutary for the Lawrencean of the way not to go in deductions, as it were, from the go-for-broke eroticism. Desire too entirely becomes negation.

Much of the critic's job, I am also suggesting, is to try to recognize what is significantly there, and then to attempt to relate it to a possibly better truth, including its own better truth. Nothing less really engages the experience of the writing in the world.

2

Dark Prophecy of Negative Desire: Lawrence's Nietzschean Matrix

Lawrence's Education in Nietzsche

$\mathbb{M}$uch, I am suggesting, of D. H. Lawrence can only be understood within contexts of most perplexing and exasperating directions of sensibility, such as nihilistic and counternihilistic prophecy *in extremis*. There are shapings, post-Enlightenment negations, for understanding the insistence on redemptive desire. Yet, in a parochialism often almost as evident in American literary study as in British, the continuities with Lawrence frequently come out as some sort of "olde" English "great tradition."[1] His significant forerunners, therefore, are the major nineteenth-century British novelists, from George Eliot to Thomas Hardy.[2] A somewhat less narrowly nativist-moralist view of the inheritance allows for the Brontës and the English romantics, especially in his responsiveness to nature scenes (though much of that, as in the Abruzzi scene in *The Lost Girl* or the New Mexico descriptions in *St. Mawr*, or the birds and beast poems, is of a quite unromantic and untranquil harshness, a biocentric rather than humanistic view of nature). A rather more suspicious perspective gives some sources in more eccentric writer-prophets, whether denunciatory Carlyle or, rather obscurely, the Midlands homosexual apologist Edward Carpenter.[3] A less intellectual provincialism tends to submerge Lawrence in his lower-class Midlands background—"the coal-miner's son"— whether somewhat patronizingly, as with his early supporters, or somewhat sentimentally, as with his later biographers and quasi-Marxist commentators.[4] The obvious partial truth of these emphases helps to confirm their inadequate perspectives, which quite fail to respond to the peculiarity of the sensibility evident in some of his most distinctive writings.

Lawrence's Nietzschean Matrix

Lawrence's fictions and poetry, slowly evolving out of conventional origins, obviously did partly relate to those of his British predecessors. He certainly also had some deep continuities with the romantics, especially Blake and Whitman, though he was usually rather dismissive of them.[5] (Often when Lawrence is dismissive, as with Dostoyevsky or, as we shall see, with Nietzsche, his dependent antagonism is part of his self-definition, as would be expected from a rebellious and dialectical temperament— contrary to the perspective of many discussions of "influences.") Surely, too, Lawrence was marked by his provincial origins and his class resentments in a snobbish-status society, and especially (though this has been less emphasized) marred by his mother's petty bourgeois repressions and aspirations, and that beyond his early, and then rejected, role as a rather priggish schoolteacher. But too much emphasis on these ploddingly limited sources and lineaments must miss much of Lawrence's peculiarity. And thus one insufficiently recognizes this exacerbated man's rebellions against his origins and, more generally, against English, and the larger Western, society and culture. Parochially oriented criticism encourages misestimations of Lawrence's cultural role (which is part of my special concern in this book). Lawrence, I am holding, will be better understood and responded to when seen as a *révolte*, an outsider prophet, considerably belonging to a different and darker matrix of sensibility.

There are, plausibly enough, several of these matrices, including some religious heterodoxies and, typical modernist syncretism of the times, odd mixtures of classical and primitivist mythologies. Here I want to mostly pursue just one lineage of an intellectual cast, without claiming any completeness. Now it is often granted that some other-than-English intellectual "influences" reached Lawrence in his later twenties (his intellectual and artistic maturation was relatively slow), including from 1912 on, his German-reared wife's enthusiasms for Nietzsche and Freud.[6] But clear evidence, repeatedly noted long ago, indicates that the influence of Nietzsche on Lawrence was pre–Frieda von Richthofen Weekley. Some of the early commentaries, though out of academic fashion, still seem quite pertinent.[7] Lawrence's crucial editor-mentor, Ford Madox Ford, described Lawrence amidst his Eastwood friends about 1910: "All the while the young people were talking about Nietzsche and Wagner and Leopardi and Flaubert and Karl Marx and Darwin."[8] Ford's accounts, it is frequently noted, tended to the hyperbolic, and so the details here may not be literal, though there seems little reason to suspect the general direction of his report about the intellectual breadth and energy of those Lawrencean provincials. Ford also had a considerable knowledge of German thought (and he half-rightly noted the social Darwinism I discussed in the preceding chapter). But note, too, in context the tone of surprise in Ford's reaction. As with many successful and fashionable literati, he did not expect such intellectual vitality in the outlands and out-classes (though one could well have, given the effects of the few-decades-earlier Education Acts, access to libraries and inexpensive books for seekers out of a puritan background, and early twentieth-century social and cultural ferment). The rather smug insularity, now as well as then, of established intellectual circles (even with a relatively open and sympathetic figure such as Ford) should be part of the corrective issue when we discuss cultural "traditions."

Otherwise put, a significant part of Lawrence's intellectual development took place "amid the neo-Nietzschean clatter," as Pound says in *Mauberley,* of the years when "the last metaphysician" was having considerable literary effect (though not on professional philosophy) in Britain, including on G. B. Shaw, W. B. Yeats, T. E. Lawrence, Wyndham Lewis, J. C. Powys, and others. More than a generation ago, comparativists pointed to the passage in the memoirs of Jessie Chambers, Lawrence's adolescent girl-friend, about his early school teaching days: "It was in the library at Croydon that Lawrence found Nietzsche. He never mentioned him directly to me, nor suggested that I should read him, but I began to hear about the 'Will to Power,' and perceived that he had come upon something new and engrossing."[9] While the account is missing something (Chambers, if Lawrence had not mentioned Nietzsche, must have had other evidence than the rhetorical tag—seeing the books? comments from others, such as Helen Corke?), her point has literary confirmation. In a stilted and mawkish early autobiographical story about his first love (Jessie, the Miriam of *Sons and Lovers,* here called Muriel), "A Modern Lover" (completed by 1911), Lawrence has his "superior" and priggish young protagonist summarize his intellectual education as having *started* with Brontë and Eliot, then moving through Russian and French writers, with Nietzsche as a concluding high point.[10] Given the strong autobiographical cast of such Lawrence fictions, there is no reason to doubt the personal pertinence of the characterization.

Some Nietzschean elements may also be recognized a bit later in Law-rence's bad second novel, *The Trespasser* (published 1912), his adaption of schoolteacher friend Helen Corke's diary, and his personal attack on women who sexually defeat men. The fiction carries not only references to

Lawrence's Nietzschean Matrix

Nietzsche (and Heine, Turgenev, Wagner, nihilism, etc.) but related motifs of battle of wills, art as intensity, and the inadequacy of middle-class emotions, and also in the late German romantic protagonist, nicknamed Siegmund, an adulterous music teacher who commits suicide.[11]

In a bit more mature book review (1913), Lawrence explicitly praised Nietzsche for "demolishing" the "Christian religion as it stood."[12] Mental warfare with Christianity was a fundamental nexus for Nietzsche and Lawrence, both piously Protestant-raised literary prophets. So was sexual rebellion. In his "Study of Thomas Hardy" (written in 1914 but not published in his lifetime), Lawrence wrote of one major style of lover, of what we now call the *macho* male, in his "passion": "The female administers to him. He feels full of blood, he walks the earth like a Lord. And it is to this state that Nietzsche aspires in *Wille zur Macht*." However aslant that erection of his source, and however similar to his own views and dramatizations in his later demon-lovers (especially in the shorter fictions, but also in the leading males in *The Plumed Serpent*), Lawrence attacks this Nietzscheanism as really a *fear* of the female which results in compensatory roué compulsiveness. Thus, concludes Lawrence, "the *Wille zur Macht* is a spurious feeling."[13] Here, as elsewhere over the years, as in "Blessed Are the Powerful" ([1925] previously discussed), his attacks on the Will to Power (an essentially ambiguous notion, for what has to be willed lacks deeper power in Lawrence's usual view) are based on seeing it as an expression of ego, rather than deeper, spontaneous vitalities. This was almost always Lawrence's antipuritanical concern, and therefore he claimed the Nietzschean to be detestably manipulative, tyrannical, and bullying. (That Nietzsche often meant something more primordial by "will" than self-conscious aggrandizement will come out later.) Midway between these obvious responses to Nietzsche is another countering in which Lawrence defends the "*dark* volition of man," a deep desire which stands against will:

> Not that miserable mental obstinacy which goes by the name of *will* nowadays. Not a will-to-love or a will-to-any-thing else. All these wills to this, that, and the other are only so many obstinate mechanical directions. . . . You may choose the idea of power, and fix your mechanical little will on that, as the Germans did. . . .[14]

Pretty obviously, he had Nietzsche (and perhaps Schopenhauer) in mind, and in a kind of desperate counterassertion he goes on to propound an

antithetical "primal will," physiologically based in a "great volitional centre" to be found at "the base of the spine" (and which is curiously suggestive
of intellectualizing the sodomistic emphasis covertly appearing in some of
his fictions).

If we look at a bit earlier fiction, we might note a somewhat more
positive use of Nietzschean terms and perspectives in Lawrence showing
the self-destructive inadequacy of Egbert in "England, My England"
(1915).[15] He was taken as representative of the traditional liberal-English
culture for which Lawrence had an outsider's scorn because the indulged
man explicitly lacked "will" and primordial life-affirming power. In other
fictions of the Great War period and reaction to it, Lawrencean Nietzscheanisms also appear. In *The Rainbow* (written 1912–15), the last third of the
ragged generational saga centers on Ursula, Lawrence's version (beyond
the slighter Clara in *Sons and Lovers*) of the modern female, the trumpeted
"New Woman" of the time, struggling for defiant self-definition. Perhaps
a bit improbably for a provincial adolescent girl and then elementary schoolteacher, she becomes the vehicle for some Nietzschean declarations. While
still a child, Lawrence gives her an emphatic rejection of humble Christian
morality. "And she didn't want to do what the gospels said. She didn't
want to be poor." "Nor could one turn the other cheek." When her sister
slaps her, Ursula tries cheek turning, gets slapped again, and "went meekly
away." But she soon revolts in anger and shame and beats her sister,
"feeling unChristian but clean." In a summation which would be quite in
place in *The Genealogy of Morals*, "There was something unclean and
degrading about this humble side of Christianity" (*Rainbow*, p. 283). Like
a good adolescent Nietzschean, Ursula then has fantasies of being an
aristocratic lady. However, I am not suggesting that all of her defiance of
conventional Christianity (as in her later blasphemous insistence on sexual
foreplay in a cathedral) need be related to the anti-Christian philosopher
with whom Lawrence had for some time been fascinated. Lawrence, of
course, had good personal reasons from his own repressive background and
society as well as other intellectual influences for rejecting the usual religious prohibitions and impositions.

But certainly the unexpected, and hardly prepared for, political statements that Ursula is given near the end of the novel are also of Nietzschean
cast. In the process of choosing and then rejecting marriage with her lover,
the conventional, colonial army officer, Anton Skrebensky, she announces:
"I shall be glad to leave England. Everything is so meagre and paltry, it is so

unspiritual—I hate democracy." Defending herself against Anton's hostile response, she goes on: "Only the greedy and ugly people come to the top in democracy . . . because they're the only people who will push themselves there. Only degenerate races are democratic" (*Rainbow*, pp. 460–61).[16] So, it is generally agreed, held Nietzsche, and certainly the dominance of the greedy and mediocre in the power structures of Western nations properly angered both writers. Ursula hates "equality on a money basis. It is the equality of dirt." Instead, she wants an "aristocracy" of the spiritually superior—or, implicitly, in her psychological castration of Anton, some more obscurely fulfilling potency, some transcending *Übermensch*. Incidentally, this certainly contradicts the several commentators who hold that Lawrence's antidemocratic views (for he can plausibly be linked with Ursula, as with no other character in the novel) are post-*Rainbow*. (I am drumming again on Lawrencean continuity.)

However, such fantasy longings do not at all get fulfilled in *The Rainbow*, and remain ambiguous in the partial continuation in *Women in Love* (1920, but mostly written 1915–17), though the partly reconceived Ursula does marry a supposedly superior man and flees degenerate northern climes for the meridional (as Lawrence and Nietzsche repeatedly did, both allegorically and literally). Her earlier doctrines have been displaced to her new lover, an obvious Lawrence persona (though vaguely, and compensatorily, upper-class in education, private income, and social-erotic life), Rupert Birkin. Typically, some of Lawrence's Nietzscheanism is put in reverse ways here, as in the canceled opening section of the novel, later published as "Prologue to *Women in Love*," where the homoeroticism of the book's protagonist was made more explicit. Here we find Birkin "holding forth against Nietzsche."[17] The crux of his attack, central dialectic for much of Lawrence, rests on the polarity between "desire" and "will" (as I have previously discussed): "A man cannot create desire in himself, nor cease at will from desiring. Desire, in any shape or form, is primal, whereas the will is secondary, derived. The will can destroy, but it cannot create."[18] The counter-Nietzschean dialectic is set as his affirmative variation on Nietzscheanism.

In the rest of the novel, Lawrence partly creates a straw Nietzscheanism. For example, Ursula describes Gerald Crich spurring his horse until it bled at a railroad crossing as "a lust for bullying—a real *Wille zur Macht*—so base, so petty" (*Women in Love*, p. 170). Birkin ostensibly accepts her commonsensical anti-Nietzschean point: "I agree that the *Wille zur Macht* is a base and petty thing," yet he goes on to argue for a willful male domination quite like it, though slightly redefined in French to slip ambiguously around Nordic bullying—"a *volonte de pouvoir*, if you like, a will to ability." By such verbal sleight of hand, Lawrence confirms an essential Nietzscheanism, as he was repeatedly to do.

"Will" is an obsessive subject in *Women in Love*, as in many of Lawrence's fictions, and one which may require a sense that Lawrence is both drawing negatively upon the puritan emphasis on moral will and reversing the philosophy of Will to Power. In an application little evident in the earlier Nietzsche, who quite lacked an angry sense of the developing technocracy (and therefore lacks some of Lawrence's later pertinence), Gerald Crich in "The Industrial Magnate" chapter seems to be a Nietzschean villain, for "what he wanted was the pure fulfillment of his own will" (*Women in Love*, p. 255). In Lawrence's condemnation of the industrial system, Crich moves toward this by substituting impersonal management and dehumanized relationships (what post-Nietzschean Max Weber described as "modern rationalization") for the old paternalistic order in the family mines. Something like this is often noted, but not Lawrence's equally vehement rejection of the old order in a Nietzschean attack on the Christian ethic of the previous generation's paternalism (as with the elder Crich). For what that encouraged was "the whining, parasitic foul human beings who came crawling after charity, and feeding on the living body of the public like lice" (pp. 245–46). Lawrence, then, hates the Will to Power of the new industrial order, which he has oppositionally yoked to Nietzscheanism. However, Lawrence also hates the Christian charity antithesis which Nietzsche, too, so thoroughly excoriated, and which prejudice was part of widespread social-evolutionary dogmas. Both prophets strikingly lack most proclivities towards social justice and reform—one of the uglier characteristics of both—which was the more usual alertly discontented intellectual response. But the double condemnation, of both traditional Christianized and modern rationalized power, was to lead Lawrence to repeated attempts at a utopian vision which certainly was engaged to revulsive social radicalism.

In the concluding pattern of *Women in Love*, Gerald Crich's will to live breaks—a somewhat obscure fictional argument, I think, suggesting that his will has been destroyed by a false passion and woman (Gudrun), by the destructive willfulness of modern art which parallels modern denaturing industrialism (Gudrun's choice of Loerke, who in his ruthlessness may be read as a caricature *Übermensch*), and by the price of exalting will itself, which is a lack of organic vitality, of the deepest desire. Yet Lawrence seems to be finally less attacking than redefining the will to mastery. When Birkin demands that Ursula give up *her* "assertive *will*" and surrender to him (*Women in Love*, pp. 286ff., but one example of several), she rightly enough sees this as a demand of bullying male will, though she submits out of need and love, and discipleship. Lawrence has hardly succeeded in transforming the Will to Power into a clearly different "superiority," vitality, "fuller being," or "dark power," however much he attacks will as cerebral, manipulative, and destructive. He might rather be seen as doing variations within the Nietzschean matrix. He longed for something similar as an answer to modern destructiveness and nihilistic loss of meaning, a new god-term and force. As with Nietzsche, Lawrence attacked "equality" as the reigning religion (*Women in Love*, p. 217, as also in the essays previously discussed) and a source of passional mediocrity, and therefore to be overcome. It is a postscientific prophetic purpose, one centrally dependent on the nihilistic recognition that the "universe is non-human" (p. 257). Thus it requires a "dark" power, a Nietzschean "revaluation of all values." That becomes, in the majority of Lawrence's fictions, a destructive process. Or as Nietzsche had put it: "Whoever wants to be creative in good and evil, he must first be an annihilator and destroy values."[19]

As we can note of yet another version of Lawrence's argument from another novel of the same period—and centering on yet another slavish submission of a woman to vital male will in an inhuman universe—*The Lost Girl*: "The puerile world went on crying out for a new Jesus. . . . When what was wanted was a Dark Master from the underworld" (p. 57).[20] Obviously Dionysianism—and from where else than Nietzsche?

But before pursuing some of that "dark" heroism, let me recall the polarity. For Lawrence, "will" and vital "desire" appear counterpoised; the icy will of annihilation that killed Gerald Crich must somehow be countered by a will-annihilating force, which turns out to be a dark, passionate, primordial version of the will to life. "Will" for Lawrence was a frequent and mostly negative term, and was especially dominant in describing his witch figures of "willful" women (obviously based in part in the domineering maternal, but also in social reality), and to characterize the cerebral overriding the fuller passional. (For an extreme example, there is the suicidal rich bitch Ethel using "will" against her own sexuality in "None of That" [1924],[21] as well as the related character, the destructive Hermione braining the obdurately passional Birkin in *Women in Love*.) Lawrence frequently used "will," from at least Gerald Crich on, to characterize modern industrial civilization, which he saw as inherently producing the Great War and other destructiveness instead of more organic community and persons. Lawrence sometimes seems to attempt to separate "will" from power, as in his distinction in a late essay (1925): "We have a confused idea that *will* and power are somehow identical. We think that we can have a will to power."[22] But since he finds authentic power in the passional, as in unwilled sexual desire, spontaneous responsiveness, and intense individual being, he condemns Will to Power again as just tyrannical "bullying." He was clearly again attacking Nietzsche, who may have sometimes used Will to Power in this way (the term is certainly often ambiguous, in its permutations from encompassing life-will in Schopenhauer) but Nietzsche also sometimes used it in ways parallel to Lawrence's perspective, as when he clearly equates "Will-to-Power" with "Will-to-Life" in *Beyond Good and Evil* (as in aphorism 259). It can also plausibly be argued that both saw ultimate "power" as richer individual "being."[23] And, indeed, this seems to me to be the most important sense of it.

Even more generally, I suspect that both Nietzsche and Lawrence were similarly looking for an affirmative dialectic based in sweeping negation in which the "oppositional" stance against their times and culture was itself crucial. What the Nietzschean commentators refer to as his dominant sense of "antithesis," and what the Lawrencean commentators rightly emphasize as his dominant sense of "polarity," is a nub here. From at least *Beyond Good and Evil* on, Nietzsche was insisting on the "revaluation of all values," and at least from the period of his reading Nietzsche on, Lawrence is practicing the revaluation. That, of course, seems to have generally been the appeal of Nietzscheanism in the time.

Much of the pattern of Lawrence's overt relation to Nietzsche might be summarized thus: Discovery and influence in a crucial period of his intellectual development and his emotional watershed (mother dying, breaking with provincial origins, larger literary reach, social anger), then reinforcement a couple of years later by his upper-bohemian German lover's fragmentary ideological enthusiasm, developing into an obsessive dialectic both as domestic counterassertion and as a variant propounding of his own somewhat similar philosophy. Lawrence's Nietzscheanism seems to have been sometimes imitative, sometimes confirming, sometimes oppositional, but long persisting. In essential ways, Lawrence had thus become an English

Nietzsche. I put it this way not just because of the obvious strong influence of his predecessor but because of the anti–traditional English role he had emphatically taken on as prophet of nihilism and passionate being.

Historical Notation

Now, in spite of the dominant "normative" English-y cast of Lawrence studies, which I started with, there has long been a smaller stream of commentators who emphasized Lawrence's Nietzscheanism.[24] A still useful liberal polemic briefly pointing up the relationship nearly two generations ago was Eric Bentley's *A Century of Hero-Worship, A Study of the Idea of Heroism in Carlyle and Nietzsche, with Notes on Wagner, Spengler, Stefan George and D. H. Lawrence.* Another comparativist, H. Steinhauer, lightly but acutely sketched out a sense of some of the linkages. I too briefly summarized in footnotes, a generation ago, a bit of comparison of the two (and covertly employed it more extensively). Shortly later in a book on Lawrence, Eugene Goodheart in scattered comments drew loosely large ideological parallels with Nietzsche. Ronald Gray sweepingly suggested similarities, centering on *Women in Love.* Some historians of Nietzscheanism (Thatcher), rather weakly just commented in passing on Lawrence's relation to Nietzsche, or simply summarized the case for influence (Bridgewater). Emile Delavenay, in an intellectual biography of Lawrence's early years, disapprovingly catalogued, without much analysis, some of the similarities with Nietzsche. John B. Humma in an article reasonably emphasized the continuities of thought. Eleanor Green pointed up political similarities of Lawrence and Nietzsche, especially with the "leadership novels" (which I modify below). John Burt Foster, Jr., in *Heirs to Dionysus,* suggested probable relations between *Twilight in Italy* and *Twilight of the Idols,* though was merely ingenious with *Women in Love* and vague with the other novels. Jennifer Michaels-Tonks (in a study I had previously missed) made a point similar to my emphasis on Lawrence's twisting Nietzsche (only applied mostly to *Aaron's Rod*): Lawrence chose to "misinterpret Nietzsche" in order to "distance himself" from what he was aware of being very close to. Of another fiction, she notes that "this life-urge that Lawrence describes would be called the will-to-power by Nietzsche." She also claims that Ramon in *The Plumed Serpent* "embodies Lawrence's most positive conception of the overman" (I suggest some alternatives). A recent, and the most lengthy study, Colin Milton's *Law-*

rence and Nietzsche, which, apparently in ignorance and a not uncommon British scholarly parochialism, does not mention most of the earlier studies, talks about characters, metaphors, and similar "nature" to show that Lawrence was making "the Nietzschean point." The literalized but too broad similar ideas are given as anti-Christianity, emphasis on the sexual body and motives, "perspectivism" (Nietzsche's sophisticated philosophical counter to reigning epistemological views, which could not have been of much interest or comprehension to Lawrence), and the like, leading to the unexceptional conclusion that Nietzsche "did indeed profoundly affect Lawrence's whole vision and with it the character of the fictional world he created." Some very recent studies, such as that of May, counter to fact claim that "Lawrence was scarcely influenced by Nietzsche, but independently arrived at his own similar views on, especially, will to power." (This missing the dialectical relationship is compounded by poorly discriminating, and sometimes erroneous, summaries of the novels in loose parallelism to some Nietzchean notions.) Another recent argument (H. M. Robinson) contrastingly notes that Lawrence's efforts "constitute a thorough imaginative and analytic investigation of the plausibility of Nietzsche's philosophy." But, from a liberal-Christian perspective, he failed not only in the brutalism of many of his 1920s explorations but also in the final inadequacy of his attempts at "the immersion of intelligence in physicality," though it was an heroic effort to carry out the Nietzschean modernist-materialist project.

While this nearly half-century sampling of views on Lawrence as English Nietzsche is not complete, it may be sufficient to point up the parochial narrowness of a majority of discussions on influences and affinities on Lawrence.[25] Granted, my countering of the fashionable parochialism may itself turn into a new parochialism in a never done critical redefinition. But I suggest that more generally the critical-lineage misemphasis has been part of a kind of unwarranted domestication and academic intellectual neutralization of Lawrencean peculiarity and extremity.

The Prophets of Dionysus

Nietzsche had characteristically written: "There is more reason in your body than in your best wisdom."[26] Lawrence, of course, notoriously agreed. Nietzsche had also insisted on locating passional reason in the ancient pagan traditions connected with Dionysus. Lawrence, though lacking Nietzsche's impetus from classical philology, repeatedly and elaborately put the late-adopted Dionysianism into fictional practice. Both were affirming paganism in the mental warfare with Christianity (a conflict, I think, much underrated for several millennia in our cultural history), and using the Dionysian for purposes of passional liberation.

Lawrence had for some years been insisting that we cannot have "the profound and *primary* sacredness of the passion of the living blood," the true "sensuality," "until we re-instate the great old gods of the passionate communion" such as "Dionysus." Some of this appears quite emphatically in a relatively late story retroactively placed in the post–Great War German scene, "The Border Line" (1924).[27] On the biographical level of motivation, the story apparently savages (as do several others) Lawrence's longtime friend, the critic Middleton Murry, here named Philip, for his erotic involvement with Frieda Lawrence, here named Katherine. In the fictional version, Katherine has married Philip after the death in the war of her first husband, here named Alan, a British army officer (an indeed weirdly inappropriate and presumptuous fantasy role of Lawrence's, as also in the protagonist of *The Captain's Doll* and others, including Major Eastwood in *The Virgin and the Gipsy* and ex-officer Mellors in the final version of *Lady Chatterley's Lover*).[28] Alan-Lawrence is an amoralist Nietzschean *Übermensch*—a "born lord" who "had an weird innate conviction that he was beyond ordinary judgment," a "real man" with a special sense of "fate." Alan had gone to war with a cool superiority since "only the strength of a man, accepting the destiny of destruction, could see the human flow through the chaos and beyond to a new outlet. But the chaos first, and the long rage of destruction." Typical Lawrencean rhetoric of negation. Passional lover as well as neo-Nietzschean nihilist, he had the very *macho* eroticism I earlier quoted Lawrence as condemning in Nietzsche; he showed "an implacable pride and strength" and "expected a woman to bow down to him." Yet he also explicitly had a "contempt of Nietzsche," apparently in part because his wife "adored" the similar thinker. The wife, after a vision of anti-Christian apocalypse, has a sexual consummation in the woods of Germany with the demon-ghost of her dead husband, and, again, in the marital hotel bed as her craven intellectual present husband fearfully dies. This rather forced ghost tale of sexual revenge clearly affirms the Nietzscheanism it ostensibly denies.

More generally, Lawrence partly follows Nietzsche (and also earlier romantic lineages) in exalting the ecstatic and erotic pagan deity, variously

Dionysus (as, for example, with Count Dionys—also a military officer—in the long, sticky mythopoetic tale *The Ladybird*) and Pan (repeatedly, as in *St. Mawr*, *The Plumed Serpent* and the end of *Lady Chatterley*). In a much earlier rumination, toward the end of his philosophizing excursus in "The Crown": "If I look at the eternity behind, back to the source, then there is for me one eternity, one only. And this is the pagan eternity, the eternity of Pan. This is the eternity some of us are veering around to, in private life, during the past few years." I take it that the "private life" means the passional, the sexual conversion experience, in Lawrence's usual extension of the autobiographcal to the metaphysical. He goes on to dialectically emphasize a synthesis of the "Pagan, aristocratic, lordly" which subsumes "the Christian, humble, spiritual, democratic," to bring us to the revelation that "there is no eternity, there is no infinite, there is no God, there is no immortality."[29] In the somewhat confused and confusing abstract tropes here, he wants a new "absolute" which is yet not absolute, in the sense of fixed and final. Ultimate values are lived relationships and qualities which might be summarized as neo-pagan. But Lawrence's neo-paganism is often more fundamentalist, primitivist, than the more rationalist Nietzsche.

In Christian iconography, such pagan deities as Dionysius and Pan merged with other figures to become devils, later reactively being reheroized as demon-lovers, as with demon-ghost-lover Alan in "The Border Line." Now the fit with Nietzschean tropes, of course, is only partial; Lawrence has no admirable "blonde beast" (probably itself a combination of the tawny lion [Arthur Danto's suggestion] and the Nordic hero). But many of Lawrence's pagan echoes—usually around alien, dark aristocratic figures, with Satanist imagery—seem to have similar resonances and functions.

And they seem to have similar doctrines, as I might briefly adumbrate from Lawrence's notorious "leadership novels." *Aaron's Rod* (first published in 1922, though partly written in 1917) never directly cites Nietzsche (that I can recall), but it may be seen as providing an overlay for similar views.[30] Written with sloppy haste, it is a half-hearted, ideological-picaresque novel about an ex–coal miner become flute-playing bohemian wanderer, questing and despairing, in London and then in postwar Italy after deserting his family. His homoerotic companion and intellectual guru, Rawdon Lilly, an obvious Lawrence persona, is a weakly realized figure who egomaniacally asserts "a certain belief in himself as a saviour" because he is a superior man of true "knowledge" whose "soul was against the whole world" as it was (*Aaron's Rod*, pp. 78, 301). His sermonizing includes raging condemnations of modern mass society, some racist ranting, and near-mystical demands for a revived "sacred" individualism to replace the dead absolute now "there's no God outside." The work has some ideological interest, evident in a number of semiliterary fascinations with it (see, for example, the discussion in chapter 4).

But it has drastic novelistic inadequacies. With insufficient dramatization, we learn that "love was a battle in which each person strove for the mastery of the other's soul." No doubt this reflects Lawrence's domestic difficulties with the sexually and ideologically errant Frieda, just as Zarathustra's pronouncements on women in the later sections of that work may reflect Nietzsche's rejection by Lou Salome. But ideologically both writers were also repeatedly insisting on love as a power battle (though without the ironic wit of the Laclos-Stendahl-Murdoch-etc., tradition of that view). Lily-Lawrence claims to resolve erotic power here with the demand that "woman must now submit," though in a way that goes beyond "slavery" to a "deep unfathomable free submission" (*Aaron's Rod*, pp. 135, 235, 311).[31]

But it is not altogether unfathomable since the subordination of eros to power serves a larger subordination of "love" which includes social compassion. Throughout *Aaron's Rod*, Lawrence not only inverts in reevaluation but attacks, Nietzsche-style, the traditional base of goodness in Western culture. As Aaron says, "To hell with good-will. It was more hateful than ill-will" (p. 27). Or, as a more elaborate Lilly-Lawrence lecture has it:

> The ideal of love, the ideal that it is better to give than to receive, the ideal of liberty, the ideal of the brotherhood of man, the ideal of the sanctity of human life, the ideal of what we call goodness, charity, benevolence . . . all the whole bee-hive of ideals—has got the modern bee-disease, and gone putrid, stinking. (*Aaron's Rod*, p. 293)

As with Nietzsche's attack, in the *Genealogy of Morals* (and elsewhere), on Christian-engendered morality, Lawrence also sees it as having "its logical sequence in Socialism and equality." It is a continuation of the Nietzschean attack on democracy by Ursula in *The Rainbow*. While Lawrence does not bother to explain its genesis in the herd's Christian-engendered weakness and resentment of superiority, he assumes it for modern mass-man. And in later angry declarations, trumpets it, as (with one previously cited in part): "When Jesus came, the inferiors, who are by no means the meek they *should be*, set out to inherit the earth." For "the poor in life are the most impure, the most easily degenerate."[32]

We might well see Lawrence's Nietzschean view, as a thoughtful minor Jewish character in *Aaron's Rod* notes, as "nihilism." That seems to be both diagnosis and demand, as in Nietzsche (as I read him, following Danto and others). The power resolution seems similar. Lilly-Lawrence, like a Grand Inquisitor, puts it harshly: In consequence of the nihilism, the modern masses should and "will elect for themselves a proper and healthy and energetic slavery." "I mean a real committal of the life-issue of inferior beings to the responsibility of a superior being" (*Aaron's Rod*, p. 294).[33] However, the arrogant megalomania of this is often undercut, as within a page where Lawrence's spokesman anarchistically asserts the absolute of holy individualism and denounces the "*bullying*" of the individual as a most hateful vice, though it would seem necessary for the submissions.

Aaron's Rod concludes with more of Lawrence's Nietzschean attack on "herd morality": "Religion and love—and all that. It's a disease now." The inevitable "recoil" from the love-disease becomes violent and horrific, apparently including the symbolically castrating bombing earlier in the narrative—the social love ethic itself the source of modern terrorism. So goes Lawrence's paradoxical argument (for we usually link violence to power rather more than to love), man must leave off the "love-whooshing" and "passionately" embrace the deep, dark "power motive" (*Aaron's Rod*, pp. 303, 307, 310). (For Nietzsche, one commentator summarizes, "Nihilism is the problem to which the will to power is the answer."[34]) So men (as well as the more obvious needing women) must "submit to some greater soul than theirs," submerge themselves in the "heroic soul," voluntarily, magically, in order to reestablish values against the nihilism of "love," and thus achieve wholeness and purpose. For Lawrence and for Nietzsche, a kind of organic being was almost always the issue, but this way of manipulative power hardly corresponds with it.

From a libertarian perspective, I hold that this is no "transvaluation" of values but, rather, a remystification of the disease of love control in the form of the disease of hero control, which is really the same displaced eroticism. Probably Lawrence's Nietzschean-style hero worship and Will to Power can partly be related to personal problems, such as he gave to his Aaron: deracination and alienation, sexual failure and ambivalence, and illness and despair. And personal resentments (that so often undervalued motive of social morality). More broadly, of course, Lawrence's extreme ideology reflects in an ugly way the Great War "disillusion as never before" (Pound), and other horrors of hopelessness in Western mass society against which it makes countering assertions. Power is the desperate dosage for loss of meaning.

Postwar flight from England, then from Europe, was to provide Lawrence and his protagonists little relief, as his further Nietzschean-style ideologizing was to show.[35] So with *Kangaroo* (written hastily in a few weeks in 1922).[36] It also suffers from shapelessness and ranting, along with some not especially knowledgeable Australian travel writing, some usual intense descriptive passages, and some digressive memories of the earlier war period.[37] The latter include Lawrence's account of his extreme revulsion even to being examined for military conscription (when living isolated in Cornwall), from which he was excused for poor health—pathetic prelude to his repeated postwar fantasies of projection into military officers. (In partial contrast, Nietzsche volunteered, though he was a Swiss citizen, for Prussian military submission in 1870, serving until he was invalided out, and seemed smugly proud of his military submissiveness in later years.) The Australian novel also has fragmentary bits of the Lawrences' marital struggle of wills, and some of Lawrence's skittishness about social class— was he a "gentleman" or still of his ostensible "working-class" origins?— an issue he was not to make serious efforts to resolve until the declassed Mellors of the third version of *Lady Chatterley's Lover*.[38] And *Kangaroo* is riddled with a half-repressed homosexuality as Lawrence both yearns for and rejects "mate-ness" and mergence with male heroes. Lawrence's persona, in one of his own revealing self-definitions, is a "shifty she-man." The novel chatters too much about Lawrence's egotism and ambivalent sexuality and other illnesses, as well as resentfully bigoted ranting, to be a very good fiction in its own right.

In *Kangaroo*, the synthetic political issue for the touring English essayist and Lawrence persona, Somers, concerns ostensible socialists and a fascistic nationalist group, "the diggers," led by a rich homosexual Jewish lawyer nicknamed Kangaroo. He dies as a result of political terrorism, and Lawrence-Somers' ambivalent rejection. While much of the politics comes out as ill-informed and ill-conceived bluster, it does display Lawrence's demands for a passional-religious "new bond between men" to transvalue the loss of human communion and community. This might be viewed as an uncertain enlargement of the mystic blood brotherhood of Birkin-Gerald in *Women in Love*. But Lawrence's spokesman skittishly turns away from the homoerotic politics (made easier by the fascination-repulsion of anti-Semitism?). Similarly, he longs for apocalyptic change in the empty modern world but then disdainfully notes, "I'm afraid . . . that, like Nietzsche, I no longer believe in great events." (Just what of Nietzsche he has in mind, beyond a general disillusionment with contemporary possibilities, I cannot determine.) Yet in spite of the disillusionment, Lawrence is full of spiteful demands for some sort of authoritarianism, though he finds both its socialist and fascist forms false because based, yet again, on the mediocrity and deathly ethic of the "will-to-love" (*Kangaroo*, pp. 180, 233). Exceptional-man individualism and fearful exclusiveness seems to be at the gut of such declarations.

Fused with this is the attack on "mob" morality, in which Lawrence outdoes Nietzsche on the resentments of "herd morality," defined by Lawrence as that "collection of all the weak souls . . . that lusts to glut itself with blind destructive power." But it is truly a "dark god" speaking through Somers-Lawrence, as with the description of the English people: "They are *canaille*, carrion-eating, filthy mouthed *canaille*, like deadmen-devouring jackals. I wish to god I could kill them. I wish I had the power to blight them . . . slay them in thousands and thousands" (*Kangaroo*, pp. 323, 277). And on and on. Hatred here does not produce the art it sometimes does in Lawrence, perhaps because it is too generalized a misanthropy. In utter rage against the "compulsions" of the Great War and the like, Somers-Lawrence incoherently insists on even greater compulsions. Since those compulsions of the war, and of industrial-bourgeois societies more generally, were costumed in benevolence, we have again, as in *Aaron's Rod*, the central Nietzschean rejection of the destructiveness of idealism: "For the idea, or Ideal of Love, Self-Sacrifice, Humanity united in love, in brotherhood, in peace—all this is dead" (*Kangaroo*, p. 291). The attack on ideal brotherhood is also a persistent subject of the essays from the early Great War period on. This includes, of course, the Christianity out of which it historically developed and, in the rather ragged deployment in *Kangaroo*, the socialism and fascism seen as still depending on the same mass-love idealism. The argument, I suggest, is implicitly powerful, for many of the massive crimes of Western civilization have come in the shapes of benevolent idealism, such as those Lawrence was especially sensitive to—the destruction of the natural order for mass progress and comfort, the exploitative industrial-commercial ugliness for mass expansion, the pathological great wars for massed power. But it can hardly be said that this fiction develops the issues with much specificity, subtlety or other persuasiveness.

In his rage to demystify destructive Western civilization, Lawrence is ready to remystify "the great life-urge which we call God" (*Kangaroo*, p. 324). By an old logic of mystagogy, that cosmic vitalism is displaced unto supposedly superior men. But the fiction's examples, such as the left and right demagogues (and the resentful protagonist), rather undercut the argument, as do the rhetorical references to Caesar and Napoleon (also hero-worshiped by Nietzsche, even more insistently, plus the even grosser Caesar Borgia, though his humanistic culture heroes—not Lawrence's— such as Sophocles and Michelangelo and Beethoven, are rather more enduring, and endearing). In the texture of *Kangaroo* (as often in Nietzsche's more poetic writings), the exaltation of the gross power figure all too patently suggests sources in the psychological and social compensations of the weak outcast, the author. Somers-Lawrence rhetorically insists on the "aristocratic principle, the *innate* difference between people" (as he was also to do in the essay "Aristocracy," previously discussed, among others) perhaps partly because of social Darwinism, and partly because little tangible difference is evident (*Kangaroo*, p. 305).[39] Isn't this but another form of what Nietzsche acutely perceived as the *ressentiment* of the weak?[40] Fortunately, I would suggest, Lawrence partly undercuts his symptomatic bombast not only by its overstatement but by pyrrhonistic dramatization— his redeeming skepticism, so evident in the endings of most of his novels.

In a related side of his overweaning and desperate individualism—"the self is absolute"—Lawrence restates, perhaps more appropriately this time, the positive meaning of the Nietzschean Will to Power: "It is a will-to-live in the further sense, a will-to-change, a will-to-evolve, a will towards the further creation of the self" (*Kangaroo*, pp. 309, 324).[41] Nietzsche sometimes makes a similar point explicit, as in equating "Will-to-Power" to "Will-to-Life" in *Beyond Good and Evil*. Furthermore, by some creative "polarity" of agonistic conflict between the spiritual aristocrats who assert Will to Power and the reluctant "mass," a new stage in civilizing "evolution" will be reached, and hence a new "*being*." This is the most positive, and perhaps most persuasive, version of the social Darwinized Will to Power. But the ontology remains an abstract speculation, in personal identification as well as narrative fact, since Somers simply flees Australia (as did Lawrence), the vitalist figure rejecting all social movements for "one's own isolate being," which Nietzsche's heroes also tended to do. That inevitably returns one to defiant individualist nihilism, that is, the explicit denial of the adequacy of "any meaning," any social-moral order, which should really be the center of what we mean by the Nietzschean matrix (*Kangaroo*, pp. 361, 366).[42] The flight from Western idealistic nihilism simply comes full circle in the despairing but defiant outcast last individual.

Lawrence tried again and again to bring the individual into a communion and community, to resolve the defeating isolation by translating the Will to Power into social-political mythology. And perhaps to transcend the Nietzscheanism he had so strongly absorbed. But while it may be seen as heroic effort, it certainly resulted in fictional and ideological failure. His next, and in many ways most repulsive, novel, *The Plumed Serpent* (completed 1925), a work written in physical and moral illness, and domestic failure (his wife had left him), the argument is synthetically mythologized. The entitling image probably draws not just on the Quetzacoatl of Aztec mythology but on Nietzsche's recurrent image of snake and bird in *Thus Spoke Zarathustra*. In both sources, the commanding trope suggests a fusion of polarities of earth and sky, higher and lower impetuses. But it might be emphasized that Lawrence's religious awareness of the need for community gave a different direction than Nietzsche's near-solipsistic metapsychology.[43]

The transvaluatory fusions in *The Plumed Serpent* mostly come out as high bombast for low impetuses. The desperate individualist is this time a fortyish Anglo-Irish widow, Kate Leslie, in alien Mexico and its revolutionary turmoil, yearning, in Lawrence's somewhat patronizing perspective, to join a regenerative movement—again the centrality of the conversion experience. One crux is a confused rebirth: "Ye must be born again. Out of the fight with the octopus of life, the dragon of degenerate or incomplete existence, one must win this soft bloom of being." Kate Leslie hungers "to be merged in desire beyond desire, to be gone in the body beyond the individualism," and become a "morning star" female goddess in submission to the dark sun of generic man (*Plumed Serpent*, pp. 55, 128).[44] More literally, she self-hatingly subordinates herself to two fanatical thugs, dark Dionysian beyond-good-and-evil ideologists, "Natural Aristocrats," exemplars of the "Pan male" and "demon-lover," authoritarian landed gentry Ramon and his devotee General Cipriano, homoerotic lovers (p. 367) and

Lawrence's Nietzschean Matrix

European-educated men of resentment. They are out to destroy Christianity (chapter 18, "Auto da Fe") and revive Aztec cultism with themselves as incarnations of the gods. They are murderers who peddle a synthetic Aztec Methodism and its authoritarian politico-religiosity.[45] This largely consists of a ritualism developed at intolerable length in a rather bad prose-poetry, the main traditions here probably being neither anthropological nor philosophical but Lawrence's early Protestantism and other subliterary languages and longings. The ambivalent antiheroine submerges intelligence, sensibility, sexual gratification (the now notorious "Aphrodite of the foam" attack on "clitoral" orgasm [pp. 422–23]) and despairing selfhood.[46] She literally kisses Cipriano's heels (p. 328), rejects her own common sense (such as that she is victim of "high-flown bunk" [370]), takes the passively submissive role, and surrenders her European individuality.

While there are intermittent bits of Lawrence's perceptiveness and descriptive power (usually at the start of chapters before the hysterical ritualization overcomes all), the novel is mostly ugly, perhaps most importantly because it is caught up in the "fathomless lust of resentment, a demonish hatred of life itself," which it only pretends to transform into a new communion (*Plumed Serpent*, p. 132).[47] The descriptions of Mexico, and Mexicans, are not only often patronizing (as also in the travel sketches of *Mornings in Mexico*), and burdened with heavy vehemence—"garbage," "filth," "hate," "resentment," "disgust," "evil,"—but repeatedly racist, including insistent "blood" metaphors, which are not to be separated from the author. After all, says the social Darwinist dark prophet: "The dark races belong to a bygone cycle of humanity. They are left behind in a gulf out of which they have never been able to climb. And on to the particular white man's levels they never will be able to climb" (p. 145). Sometimes they make good servants, though, except when stirred by agitators into "resentment" and "insolence." But not much can be done with people who have "a strange perversity which makes even the squalid, repulsive things seem part of *life* to them" (p. 21). Lawrence's ugly contempt overwhelms all.

The writing is bad in various ways: inconsistency (on p. 253, Cipriano suddenly has a full trimmed beard; Kate variously identifies herself as Leslie and Forrester; Mexican politics are muddled; the social-political history is jerry-rigged into a couple of paragraphs, p.420); mixed and overextended religious metaphors, muddying Aztec, Christian, and other cults; and a pervasive redundancy and nastiness. In small qualification, I guess, one could note that Lawrence's nastiness is only intermittent, perhaps not full-scale sexual sadism. It seems forced, imposing upon himself as well as the reader, and Lawrence was to considerably counter it in following works and views.

Even considered as a Nietzschean "thought experiment" or a Lawrencean "shedding" of sickness, *The Plumed Serpent* defeats the intelligence and sensitivity engaged in the anguished revaluation of values which, after all, provides the justification of such efforts. Iconoclasm, the matrix's real strength, reverses into icon masturbation and pseudomyths for, of course, mythic orderings are not the products of individual artists and thinkers, and therefore seem mostly the result of megalomaniac resentment. Instead of religious experience, we have religious myth (the defeat of intelligence); instead of blasphemy, attempted new orthodoxy. In the context of much of Lawrence's other writings, it is also self-violation. That, indeed, is the darkness of prophecy. It is not, to take up charges that have been mismade, unambiguous primitivism, since the social Darwinist author insists that humans cannot "return to the older previous levels of evolution" (p. 137), which reinforces the racism. Bigoted, surely, but not Nazism. While the characters snarlingly reject socialism and capitalism, both forms of machine worship, they do so in terms of an arts and crafts emphasis (loving descriptions there, as of the handmade fabrics) and "the old communal system" (p. 360). Lawrence's usual antitechnocratic utopianism, however inadequately deployed. It is also not simple female subservience: not only does Kate have endless reservations, and an attentuated part-time submission to Cipriano rather than any fuller marriage, but we are repeatedly reminded of male-female incompatability—"the gulf can never close up" (p. 251). There is little desire to overcome the disparity, perhaps mostly because the *Serpent* antidesire and responsiveness aim for power and domination.

Of course, *The Plumed Serpent* may, in spite of, or perhaps because of, various redundant insistencies, not have much coherence in its ideology. While overman spokesman Ramon centrally claims to be "nauseated with humanity and the human will" (p. 69)—Lawrence's recurrent reversed Nietzscheanism—he also repeatedly exalts Will to Power, to change, to mastery (pp. 66, 385, etc.), in a suprapolitical mass-conversion movement. Surely it willfully violates Lawrence's own dialectics of desire, gone overboard in fears and hatreds. As with Nietzsche, Lawrence's powerful countering, negative perceptions of religious and social-political pathology have gone over into pseudopositive prescriptions of more pathology.

Lawrence's Nietzschean Matrix

As the darkness of madness approached, Nietzsche ecstatically identified himself as both sides of his dialectic of icons, as both rapturous idealist and heroic overcomer, as both "the Crucified One" and "Dionysus" (*Ecce Homo*). As the darkness of his fatal illness approached, Lawrence, in his last novella, *The Man Who Died*, combined basically similar tropes and commitments into a blasphemously fornicating Christ who rejects his messianic social-moral role for a life-affirming myth of endless rebellion.[48] The Dionysian demon of passion and fertility no longer pretends to be a leader, only the eternally recurring outcast deity of defiance. Granted, the Nietzscheanism had been more modestly continued in Lawrence's previous work and last novel, both in its negations of the idealist heritage (the "mental-lifer" attitude, as the antipassional is there described—"and Socrates started it," as Nietzsche, too, had insisted in *The Birth of Tragedy*) and in the harsh negations of modern mass society, seen as coming to an apocalyptic end. But in his later love story, Lawrence had some positives of desire in personal relationships—Lawrence countering the just previous Lawrence—hardly conceivable by Nietzsche.

The Nietzschean-Lawrencean Sensibility

Surely some of the conjunction between the two dark prophets can be put in other ways than the "influences" and related practices of Will to Power and Dionysian ideologizing that I have partly summarized. There are some striking similarities in their sensibilities. Both writers came out of provincial northern European puritanical-pietistic Christian backgrounds, enforced by domineering mothers. With Lawrence, far more explicitly avowed than with Nietzsche, it was not merely Oedipal dramatization but post–*Sons and Lovers* doctrine, as in "Education of the People": "If we are to save the ultimate sanity of our children, it is *down with mothers! A bas les meres!*" It has (in the same discussion) a pathetic personal dimension in a sense of incurable inadequacy put in a longing pagan analogy: "Would God a she-wolf had suckled and stood over me with her paps, and kicked me back into a rocky corner when she'd had enough of me. It might have made a man of me." And that, of course, also comes out as anti-idealist–misogynist doctrine, not only so often dramatized in the fictions but declared—"let spiritual, ideal self-conscious women be the most damned of all."[49]

Both Lawrence and Nietzsche rebelled against family, religion, and ethos, yet remain, I think, partly understandable in terms of radical Protestant individualism, including its extremes of moral righteousness, however intellectually inverted, that drove them to reactive conversions and revelations. They dramatically polemicized against Christianity: Zarathustra's "God is dead" and Lawrence's "the Almighty has vacated, abdicated, climbed down," and even more strident blasphemies.[50] They were hyperbolic, in savior as well as raging sorts of ways, in the violence of their mental warfare with the Christian heritage. Both were certainly acute in diagnosing the "idealistic" sensual perversions, moral nastiness, and metaphysical pathos in fungoid growth from that heritage. Both were consequently often brilliant at discovering dubious motives, especially in Christians and other idealists, and in, partly projective, discovering subversive impetuses. For both, the old repressions became inward perversions. Yet both insistently lusted after new-old gods and revived pagan demons in a desperate quest for noble values. This psychological-moral-transcendental struggle took on sometimes heroic, sometimes grotesque, proportions in which both overreached into megalomania—sometimes literally confusing themselves with the Crucified and the Dionysian, as they desperately sought to be the angry last prophets of decadent and destructive Western civilization.

Heroic, surely, and this is partly why we continue to make much of these often messy and confusing writers. But we also should not forget some of the grotesque context, such as the facts that our literary heroes were from childhood on frail, sickly, often grievously ill. They were also desperately unmanly. Both were finished—Nietzsche mad, Lawrence dead—by the age of forty-four, and neither (we old readers no doubt especially note) reached the full seasoning of the *amor fati* (Nietzsche) and the insouciance (Lawrence) they trumpeted. For the larger part of their productive years these invalided ex-teachers were compulsive wanderers after physical and spiritual solace, pilgriming in parallel "oscillations between north and south" (*Aaron's Rod*, p. 303; the biographies of both make emphatic the oscillations). That itself provided an insistent dialectic (and rather hyperbolic tropes) of cold northern versus responsive meridional cultures, and characters. Though physically weak, both glorified a harsh manliness—over-exalting the ruthless "blonde beast" (Nietzsche) and demonic dark lover (Lawrence), both at times expounding a crass Caesarism, and both almost comically defending a physical violence of which they were quite incapable. Such hero worship must be viewed as a mixture of

Lawrence's Nietzschean Matrix

the personally compensatory, the ambiguously homoerotic combined with an idealistic philia, and a rage against the smugly dominant bourgeois mediocrity of order which they wished to subvert with a made-up aesthetic-aristocratic utopianism of passionate heroism which had little tangible social reality. The shrill demands for the "aristocratic principle" and the "vital hero" (Lawrence), for the "*Übermensch*" and "nobility" (Nietzsche), and other tropes of ambiguous philosophy of the Will to Power (both), in demonic reversal of the God of Love, and his denatured ethic, often led to the horrendously contradictory. Such dark prophets deny all existent authority, often with a devastating insight into its falsity, while angrily demanding authority. The politics appears outrageously arbitrary. And right there may be its essential logic: if we are going to have "politics," "heroic leaders," and the rest of imposed order, let it be more candidly and grandly arbitrary. As Nietzsche contemptuously held of Bismarckian Germany, and Lawrence of Great War Britain, "The State is a dead ideal."[51] The appropriate response is antipolitics. Perhaps Nietzsche and Lawrence should be viewed in their moral politics as authoritarian anarchists—a paradox that understandably escapes many commentators.

It is in such large parallelisms that the relationship, not mere "influence," seems important. And, of course, I wouldn't want to override the differences as persons. To note a few: Nietzsche may have had an "abnormally low" sexual drive,[52] in spite of Wagner's *macho* suspicion that he masturbated too much. Indeed, he may long have been impotent. Lawrence was for long more insistently sexual (indeed, if we take as autobiographical, as many do, the account in the later part of *Mr. Noon*, he had multiple orgasms in a short time, however little that was adequate for his errant wife), and was apparently not fully impotent until his forties. So, naturally, positive sexuality takes a much fuller role in the Lawrencean view. The two also differed in class origins (minister's son versus coal-miner's son), in education (classical academic philology versus grammar school-teacher training), in social status during their main writing periods (nearly reclusive academic versus married writer in bohemia), in disease (syphilis? versus tuberculosis, though both suffered persistent breathing problems), in overt responsiveness (generally reticent versus mercurial), even in hirsuteness (overgrown military mustache versus trimmed full beard). Yet such fundamental similarities seem evident that we might speak of a *mentalité*.

As writers, in their obsessively energetic flow of words, they often seem inherently contradictory: poet-polemicists, antirationalist intellectuals, iconoclastic mythographers, visionaries full of antimoral moralizings. While it is commonplace in discussions of both to point to their extreme tropes as hyperbolic, that partly collapses the harder reality that both were not just exaggerating but attempting to reach beyond the accepted in their often powerful negations. For the responsive, I suspect, they are equally suggestive and irritating. Both sometimes wrote brilliantly, though often sliding into strident rhetoric of rage and murky abstractions. There are differences, too, of course: Nietzsche could be far better in argumentative writing—dialectical, complex, ironic—where Lawrence, especially in expository passages, tended to the fundamentalistic. But Nietzsche had little powerful sense of scene, dramatization, or, especially, human character and relationship.[53] Lawrence did, and, in spite of obvious faults, some of his poems, stories, parts of his novels, and other literary forms (such as his travel pieces) are highly realized. Not so with Nietzsche, who essentially only wrote fragments, which he called aphorisms. (Even his most sustained effort, *Zarathustra*, I suggest, could be rearranged in several different ways without great loss.) The art was often as perplexing as the extreme perspective. The trouble with approaching either from a conventional aesthetic or metaphysical perspective is that such methods take the hammer away, and the nails as well, genteel-izing the impassioned, angry truths. Their very awareness of how others tended to neutralize their views may be a prime cause of some of the extremity of their literary manners.

Nietzsche's and Lawrence's writings probably cannot be altogether separated from their feverish illnesses (damaged brain, damaged lungs, though both seem to have been plagued with bronchial troubles—they literally could hardly breathe in our world). Certainly both not only wrote out of illness, alternately pained and euphoric, but *wrote* their illnesses, as with their very "nausea" (for the "herd man" and the "mass"). There was not a little "grandiloquentizing" of various personal disabilities, including the sexual, and related affections. Both individualists had periods of rather disgusting sycophancy (Nietzsche with the Wagners, Lawrence with the Morrells, among others), and both soon took literary revenge. Grievously ill as children, each also obsessively retaliated against mothering women. While the slashing at women may have some charm (for some male readers, anyway, and apparently masochistic females), and Lawrence even paradoxically had great imaginative empathy with women (the majority of his protagonists, and not just the willful witches, are women), and Nietzsche's images of women are dominated by a juvenile and impotent cynicism, both are major modernist misogynists in their effects.[54] They had trouble with male friends, too, making great homoerotic demands, insisting that others be loving followers, then feeling betrayed. The Nietzschean-Lawrencean sexual ambivalences take on monumental shapes, heightened by exacerbated senses of alienation. Socially as well as psychologically, then, both wrote as therapy; or, as Lawrence admitted, "one sheds one's sickness in books."[55] Indeed, it seems plausible to view some of the literary extremes in each, such as the ranting for violence and the authoritarian fantasies, as not just hyperbole but self-curative verbal psychodrama.

The blatantly extreme disparities of tones, styles, and demands in Nietzsche and Lawrence rather obviate the moralistic warnings of critics against them—the linking with Hitlerism, and the like[56]—since the roller-coaster effects, swooping from sensitive tenderness to raging nastiness, often become self-cauterizing, reader-therapeutic effects. For in reading much of either prophet there is a strong sense of the pathetic, as in each proposing a utopia of personal friends, or in the compulsive wanderings, or in the puritanical little economies, or in the incompetence with liquor, or in the obscurantism about illness, or in the grandiloquent mythicizing and authoritarian posturing. The sad irritability, nastiness—for example, Nietzsche advocated whipping women, and other mediocrities; Lawrence recommended whipping children, and other convicts[57]—hardly qualified as the trumpeted "nobility" (Nietzsche) or superior "tenderness" (Lawrence). Their racial prejudices, demands sometimes for caste rule, sexual denunciations of others, often vicious anti-egalitarianism, and overt yearnings for apocalyptic destructions are not pretty. There is considerable crassness, bullying, and other ugliness in their writings—and, as seems repeatedly evident (not least from the contradictory writings on each), confusion. But bad motives, both would probably agree as well as demonstrate, at least as much as goodness and love (so often spurious, as well as camouflage for resentment) are essential parts of intelligence and art and understanding. Or (to deploy a favorite paradoxicality of Nietzsche's) the "false" has a kind of "truth," "evil" a kind of "good." They certainly must have a pragmatic value, or there would not be so much of them around, as also in the dark prophetic traditions grown around their writings and roles.

Lawrence and Nietzsche, I have suggested, partake of what we may now view as a perhaps vestigial but important archetype: the modern rebellious Protestant psychopath as intellectual artist. From whatever perspective one approaches them (except, of course, obtuse piety or righteous dismissal), much will appear obsessional, extreme, raging, ill, perverse. Is this the price that must be paid (to use a proper puritan moral metaphor) for some undeniable radical power of perception and style and thought? It would seem to be the price they had to pay (not alone among modernists), perhaps not just because insight is costly but because badness and ugliness also inhere in the quest for human meaning and life. Nietzsche and Lawrence, in their very demands for passionate life, for intensity and overreaching, were willing to risk it, which is a considerable intellectual heroism. "Man," Lawrence repeatedly insisted, "is a thought-adventurer. Man is a great venture in consciousness."[58]

A more abstract way of putting this might be that Lawrence and Nietzsche conjoin in being both nihilists and antinihilists. Nihilism, the denial of any enduring humanly meaningful order in the world, is the center of Nietzsche's philosophizing, and probably the center of his legacy taken up by Lawrence.[59] But both were extreme aye- as well as naysayers, though it may sometimes be difficult to be certain which is which. Both emphatically affirmed, against mechanistic and idealistic views, the passional—"passions must be further developed if life is to be further developed," Nietzsche insisted. Lawrence, of course, made erotic "consciousness" his most dramatic theme. But to develop such, much destruction is necessary—for a new passional conception of life you have "to plant seed," which requires one "to kill a great deal of weeds, and break much ground."[60] Or, as Nietzsche put it, one must "philosophize with a hammer." Historically put, Nietzsche and Lawrence were relatedly engaged in the attempt to give the irrational fuller human significance, a post-Enlightenment skepticism turned, rather desperately it seems, toward intense life affirmations. Lawrence clearly announced that he was a "religious man," and pursued tropes and rhetorics and fables of religious quest; Nietzsche, somewhat more skittishly, propounded what are essentially religious substitutes, such as *Übermensch* and Eternal Return. Both may be understood as attempting religious answers to nihilism. However, if one separates out the large affirmations from the nihilism (as a majority of the recent commentators on each tend to do), raising up the aye-sayer over the naysayer, much of the purpose and quality seem undercut. Lawrence and Nietzsche are most religious when being most nihilistic. Otherwise put, the dark prophets usually have a highly negative-conditioned positivity, nihilistic vitalism.

Opposition (polarity), antithesis within and without, struggle (perhaps with both rather over–social Darwinized—neither had much sense of the cooperative), conflict (not least in the erotic) were essential. In opposing traditional authority amd its meanings, they vehemently attacked prevailing Christianity, idealism and rationalism, bourgeois order and morality, and even their own pursuits of truth seeking and art forming, which resulted in rather slippery "process" philosophies. Both demanded counterauthority, the Will to Power, the legitimizations of new vitalities. No doubt ambiguities here were unavoidable, not least because neither ever commanded much of anything, not just in public roles but even with family, pupils, cultural esteem. Unlike the more overtly successful, such outsiders rarely feel the need to moderate or ameliorate their extremist views much in terms of ambiguous realities. Both piled up declarations for new authority to replace the slavish and mechanical which, as they insisted, dominated the leaders as well as the masses of modern societies. They demanded nothing less than new societies and new human beings—rather more than art and discourse can readily bear.

In brigading Lawrence and Nietzsche, there may be the unintended implication of simple equation. Rather obviously, I think, Nietzsche was the more acutely ranging historical mind and philosophical aphorist, and Lawrence at his best the superior artist and more intriguing man. But that is not the issue. Nor are many of the differences which nonetheless led them to similar concerns, destructive and affirmative, and to their dramaturgy of demystification of a nihilistic age as well as to their heroic *amor fati* of new being. The dark prophets are still importantly and appropriately with us.

A Note on Literary Traditionalism

But why pay so much attention to such a "tradition," legacy, influence-relationship? Even if it be so strong, as I have proposed in part, as to make what Lawrence was doing—deriving from the earlier figure, arguing lifelong with the Will to Power, reasserting the Dionysian, and so on—more understandable as a kind of English Nietzscheanism. Isn't this source-influence-parallelism pursuit mostly a learned, and often a one-upping, game? Still several other issues seem at stake, at least if the game is being well played. An obvious one is that many of the usual "influence" theories are too simple-minded or too doctrinaire (as in the influential psycho-theologizing of Harold Bloom). Not surprisingly, influence processes are often mixtures of self-definition, self-aggrandizement, self-disguise, and self-argument. (I will look at some other examples of these in chapter 4.)

Defiant Desire

In short, influence often results in a dialectical and counterdialectical series of ways.

Another issue, of course, is my longtime persistent interest in recognizing and responding to the nuclear reality of Lawrence, which I take to be, contra usually dominant Anglo-American academic intellectual gentility, his radicalness, his extremity, his nihilistic and prophetic sensibility. But instead of arguing yet again the interpretations of particular writings, perhaps part of the issue may be suggested by asking, What is our proper subject? Even when, more than a generation ago, I was partly a New Critic (as I was trained, writing "readings" which I later published of works by Milton and Melville, and others), I wrote in the foreword to my earlier book on Lawrence, *The Art of Perversity*, prefatory to explicating the shorter fictions, that it was an attempt at "engaging as the fundamental entity something larger than the specific work, which can only be adumbrated as 'the Lawrencean view' and remains always our ultimate subject." While still aiming in that direction, I certainly want to drop "ultimate," not least because I now believe that all definitions of subjects are not only provisional but tend to fallacies of misplaced concreteness and reifications, claiming an order of things that does not exist, and that often falsifies. (I take the argument from Nietzsche's perspectivism.)

Otherwise put, our appropriate interest should go beyond D. H. Lawrence and his particular literary works, and beyond Friedrich Nietzsche and his fragments, though not lose sight of the experiences of either. The pathetic biographies, as well as the canons, are arbitrary entities. They are convenient and useful, but partly misleading egoistic constructs. To go beyond them is not just to go to the explanatory context but to something else. While I am attempting to use the canon and the writer, I am also claiming other constructs, such as a tradition of "dark prophecy." The peculiar Protestant-psychopath one that I have suggested here might also be useful perspective on a number of other writers, ranging, say, from August Strindberg to Ken Kesey. Some writers have also emphatically combined Nietzsche and Lawrence (see the discussion of Henry Miller in a later chapter). But the use suggests a kind of awareness and a group of responses pertinent to but not sufficiently grasped in a group of writings or a writer. Granted, to call it "dark prophecy" is also arbitrary, and so I have also flagged it as modern Dionysian ideology, as nihilistic vitalism, and by several other markers. But, whatever, the dark prophetic bent, which I have tried to make specific in terms of works and arguments, remains crucially important. And not only for Nietzsche and Lawrence.

To reach toward that fuller passional intellectual experience suggests other constructs, other perspectives (as Nietzsche would say), than the singled-out writer or work inclines us to. (The ornately pretentious deconstructionists certainly have an appropriate point here in not trusting the texts as adequate to the experience and significance.) Neither Nietzsche nor Lawrence, or a work, is the "thing-itself." Nor is their relationship quite it. But, then, is there any "thing-itself"? We are perhaps also well reminded—a strong Nietzschean and Lawrencean emphasis—that *Ding-an-sich*'s are indeed dubious, and not least when called Nietzsche or Lawrence. Our concerns need to be with certain views of reality and intense qualities of life (sometimes quite ugly as well as enlivening) that the dark prophets point us toward. Provocation is where much of it ends as well as starts. No doubt, a dark vocation.

3

Problems of Desire in
Lady Chatterley's Lover

"The Words"

Less dark, and certainly more novelistically successful than *The Plumed Serpent*, is the next, and last, long fiction of the writer-prophet Lawrence. Indeed, given Lawrence's oppositional cast of mind, an important context for understanding *Lady Chatterley's Lover*[1] is revisionary Lawrenceanism, that is, the *Lady* is in considerable part his own countering to his own *Serpent*.

An important though much flawed parable of tender human regeneration in a "counterfeit" social order (and what seems for many readers a too-poignant or a too-irritating reading experience), the last novel no doubt deserves, as the cautious like to say, several kinds of consideration. A bit incautiously, as with the rest of this study, I want to emphasize here an ideological as well as critical sense of Lawrence's desire/negation dialectics and elaborate it around such underconsidered issues as the verbal and erotic peculiarities, the emphatic denial of social class hierarchy, and the green utopianism of the pastoral to negate modern society. My critical bent, of course, is again to insist on an appropriate radical view of Lawrence. (Some of the evident effects of his radicalism, such as rebellious influence, blasphemy, and later sexual ideology, I pursue in the following chapters when considering Lawrence as culture hero.) Granted, part of my impetus is that much of the critical-scholarly discussion intolerably ameliorates the Lawrencean, but the concern here is not mostly with the bland ideologues camouflaged as Lawrence specialists or as faddish theorists. I also see the last novel as partly a continuation of the earlier themes but, more importantly, as also partly a dialectical self-countering—indeed, a correction of parts of the dark prophecy.

Now as a tendentious narrative, an insistently ideological fiction—surely a broad range of views must grant this, whether for denigration or affirmation—Lawrence's *Lady* has some problems. Some of them may be seen as difficulties of language, not just the once middle-class literary shockers of *cunt/cock* (discussed later) but rather inconsistent efforts at a diction of candor and intimacy combined with large social and religious denunciations—a romance-cum-tract. The many passages of rage at "Mammon" and the worship of "greedy mechanism and mechanized greed . . . the vast evil thing," or at other aspects of "the industrial horror," or at the "hyena instinct of the mob against sex," may be seen as a somewhat self-defeating stridency. Lawrence's mixture of idioms—Midlands dialect and male vulgate in a yet sophisticated ambience; sardonic intellectual abstraction and its mockery; woozy passional prose amidst antiromantic rhetoric; heightened, vivid descriptive nature writing amidst an ugly scene; arch-literary commentary and quasi-fundamentalist neo-pagan metaphors; naturalistic detailing within a romance narrative—must come out problematic, unstable in tone. (I take it that these characteristics are so obvious to the informed reader as not to require much quotation, though some examples appear in this chapter.) Lawrence is also upsetting in a formal sense, including (in the section just quoted [*Lady*, chap. 10]) a mixed point of view of a male character (gamekeeper Mellors), a quite different female character (Lady Constance Chatterley), and of the alternately world-weary and raging intrusive author. Such confusing viewpoint, of course, appears repeatedly and problematically in Lawrence's novels, a formal disorder expressive of a tempermental disorder.

The violations of narrative and stylistic order are frequent, and not trivial. In a partly excusing way, I suppose, they can be attributed to Lawrence's social angers (including the probability that his book would not be regularly published), and to an effort to combine variant notions and materials (more modernist-experimental than usually granted). The incongruity is evident, and so is the implausibility in a considerably "realistic" fictional form, though sometimes provocative. For example, Lawrence's fervent sexual-body doctrine of the crucialness of "touch" is, quite improbably in tone and allusions and self-consciousness, sometimes given to Connie, as in her noted countering of Clifford's antisexual Platonizing (chap. 16, pp. 219–20):

"Give me the body. I believe the life of the body is a greater reality than the life of the mind: when the body is really wakened to
life. . . . The human body is only just coming to real life. With
the Greeks it gave a lovely flicker, then Plato and Aristotle killed
it, and Jesus finished it off. But now the body is coming really to
life, it is really rising from the tomb. . . . I feel that whatever
God there is has at last wakened up in my guts . . . and is rippling so happily there, like dawn.

Certainly one can sympathetically parse the neo-Nietzschean cultural history of desire and its Western (Christian and dualist idealism) denial, though
there may be difficulty with the trope of the rippling god and dawn in the
gut, and the "really" redundantly overinsistent manner, but Lawrencean
bellicose intellectualism hardly seems appropriate to the naive and simple
Lady Chatterley, as developed in romance and realistic senses, and whose
un-"oppositional" characterization (she is no Ursula even of "star polarity"
with her lover) is one of the dramatistic problems of the novel. There is
such considerable awkwardness of imposed words and doctrine, and the
reflective reader might acknowledge the limitation before moving on to
what else is there.

Perhaps part of the problem can now be most immediately grasped, in
this time of uncertain modes, as an issue of discourse: The lady has just
returned from a good sexual engagement in the woods with the gamekeeper
and, as she intellectually defies her husband in the manor, is recalling
Mellors's "It's the nicest, nicest woman's arse as is!" Arse and guts, Plato
and Jesus, traditional class figures and their violation, rebellious sexual
holism versus dualistic spirituality—Lawrence's attempt to violently conceit together antithetical modes of discourse runs into troubles beyond the
sardonic humor (often insuffcently acknowledged for Lawrence), magni-
fied by novelistic conventions of traditional (rather nineteenth-centuryish)
characters and old-fashioned narrative situations.

But there was good reason for the effort. Lawrence, it seems evident,
shared the typical iconoclastic, modernist (and now attenuated postmodern-
ist) search for authentic language against corrupted traditional public rhetoric. Consider the parallel with one of the best-known literary declamations
on the matter, which, not so incidentally, was probably written within some
months of Lawrence's:

I was always embarrassed by the words sacred, glorious, and sacrifice . . . had read them, on proclamations that were slapped up by billposters over other proclamations, now for a long time, and I had seen nothing sacred, and the things that were glorious had no glory and the sacrifices were like the stockyards at Chicago if nothing was done with the meat except to bury it. . . . Abstract words such as glory, honor, courage or hallow were obscene beside the concrete names. . . .[2]

Fairly early on in *Lady*, Lawrence announces:

All the great words, it seemed to Connie, were cancelled for her generation: love, joy, happiness, home, mother, father, husband, all these great, dynamic words were half dead now, and dying. . . . As for sex, the last of the great words, it was just a cocktail term. . . . It was as if the very material you were made of was cheap stuff, and was fraying out to nothing (*Lady*, p. 58).

Approximate contemporaries in several senses, Hemingway's Frederick Henry and Lawrence's Connie Chatterley, in these romances of negation of the early twentieth-century societies, reject the traditional language of values, which they find fractured and fraying, not only false but downright obscene. So they end up affirming direct and immediate sense responses, and an attempted more concrete language to emphasize it—words closer to the individual body experience, and sexually positive. Both even insist upon what Lawrence in the following paragraph names as a "stubborn stoicism" (though Lawrence partly attempts to go beyond it later in the novel). Now I don't just raise the comparison as part of what used to be called the "Climate of the Age" (though that certainly has its pertinence for the post–Great War period), nor simply as an adumbration of an essential iconoclastic purpose of modernist aesthetics (though certainly it was, and remains valid), nor as an excuse for either Lawrence's often formal awkwardness or Hemingway's often human flatness (both sometimes seem self-parodying in their insistently repetitive countering styles), but as part of a larger, and quite justified, perplexity in iconoclasm about literary discourse. The usual language—understood as vocabulary, decorum, and values—will not do. It drastically distorts, in its false abstractions of honor and duty and love and sex, tangible experience. What Lawrence angrily calls the "counterfeit" naming and feeling is too pervasive and destructive, and must be negated: Language against itself, style as antistyle, with rasping but probably necessary novelistic difficulties if one is to struggle with the real issues.

Surely this is one of the contexts in which to consider Lawrence's notorious use of sexual obscenity, which is one of the antistyles. Lawrence's *epater* by vulgarity (which, in spite of his later denial, it surely was[3]) no longer serves as much of an insult of the genteel-repressive, at least at the level of literary vocabulary, since by contemporary novelistic decorums it is rather limited in range as well as sparse in quantity. The first usage does not appear until the fourth chapter (p. 31) where a minor male character (one of Clifford's smugly "moderne"-intelligentsia, upper-class cronies) mildly puts down sexual concern by saying that he doesn't overeat or "over-fuck." Here, and throughout, Lawrence does *not* use *fuck* in the most usual way of male language for at least three generations, i.e., as an intensifier (frequently but by no means exclusively hostile—in *OED* [*Supplement*] terms, "as the coarsest equivalent of damn"). Mostly, Lawrence's *fuck* has the restrictive usage of direct copulation—and intentional violations, of course, of the politely repressive. But in Lawrence's context, it is sexually immediate, without much hostility, and mostly appropriate to character at the time (male, and primarily defiantly declassed Mellors) and sexual situation. Only those against "fucking" should find it a problem.

The usage of *cunt*, which appears fourteen times, most of which are distinctively positive in tone, may be taken as not quite the same issue. *Cunt*, whether as physiological designation, synecdoche for the female, or more generalized trope, most commentators treat as highly negative in tone, though not all common usage supports that.[4] (Perhaps some British usage— for example, as I have heard repeatedly in working-class pubs, one male denigratingly referring to another as a *cunt*, which seems somewhat less commonly American—may be more cumulatively insulting in tone.) In the past generation, some feminist ideology, attacking the verbal reduction of the female to sexual part and function, has insisted that the term is always degrading (example cited later). That seems arbitrary, and false to some usage. At least in considerable part, the word is as the word serves, and it certainly can be affectionate, though no doubt it depends on who is doing the talking, and the coupling.

Clearly, Lawrence's purpose is partly to brigade *cunt* with his announced emphasis on "tenderness," as more intimate and direct affirmation of sexuality in an affectionate and direct heterosexual relationship. In one of Mellors and Connie's trysts in the woods, in affectionate postcoital verbal play, Mellors says, partly using Midlands dialect: "Th'art good cunt, though, are'nt ter? Best bit o' cunt left on earth. When ter likes! When tha'rt willin'!" (*Lady*, p. 166). *Cunt* here seems to be used in the enlarged, and mostly positive, sense of willing female sexual responsiveness, though granted that assumes female vulnerability and acceptance, which may well be a male bias.

Shockingly, the lady in reply expresses extreme language and sexual näiveté (especially for a woman in her late twenties who has had at least four extended sexual relationships), by asking, "What is cunt?" Curiously, his answer employs even broader (and apparently rarer) usage: "An doesn't ter know? Cunt! It's thee down theer [this part is standard]; an what I get when I'm i'side thee, and what tha gets when I'm i'side thee; it's a' as it is, all on't." The state of "cunt", then, the allness, is high sexual being. Sensibly enough, she warmly responds, "All on't," she teased. "Cunt! It's like fuck then." (Hardly verbally liberated, this is the only time she—or any other woman—uses either taboo term in Lawrence.) Idiosyncratically, it seems to me, Mellors replies, "Nay nay! Fuck's only what you do. Animals fuck. But cunt's a lot more than that. It's thee, dost see . . . Cunt! Eh, that's the beauty o' thee, lass?" The state of true "cunt", then, is also gender ontology, ultimate affirmative female being. (I take the question mark as a typographical error.) The scene appropriately concludes with the woman's return to the manor from the pastoral eroticism in an ecstatic condition of sexual-emotional fulfillment, with the natural world taking on a new aliveness, vibrancy (*Lady*, p. 167). The feminists finally do have a point, but reversed—not Lawrence's use of *cunt* as denigration but as exaltation, which is positively discriminatory about women, though Lawrence had also just made with Mellors's dialogue the larger point that *cunt* was "all on't"—achieved female *and* male sexual immanence. Or, in another Mellors's passage, a good loving state with "a bit of cunt an' tenderness" (*Lady*, p. 230). The passional desire is the defining thing, even with the traditionally taboo words: "It is all this cold-hearted fucking that is death and idiocy" (*Lady*, p. 193). This may be a somewhat unusual, but not in context and tone impossible, usage: fucking-with-love, Lawrence's intended major theme.

Lawrence's use of other once-taboo words does not seem problematic, at least for the current intellectual reader. Their appearance is sparing, and the usage relatively conventional and appropriate *as speech* of the character in the situation. Mellors's use of *cock* (not a considerably hostile term, such as *prick*, which is not used) does not appear in its denigrative ways (and *balls*, for example, is used quite positively, either as testes colloquialism or traditional metaphor for manliness) nor broadened in meaning, as with his *cunt*. *Shit, piss*, and *arse*, and the few other vulgar emphases he sparingly uses, appear to be standard enough, at least in speech though, of course, also scoring a point of countermanners when applied in print to a Lady (or a lady), in emphasizing common physical humanity. That they were, and to a lesser degree somewhat remain, offensive to Anglo-American petty bourgeois sensibilities (an issue considerably of class manners, in as well as out of the academic) is not of much literary or moral interest. Granted, Lawrence cannot be said to obviate that all languages attempting to catch sexual experience are at best problematic, alienating, since they object-fix intense flows of subjectivity. That may well remind us of the more general insufficiency of language to catch and contain nonverbal experiences adequately. This is a recurrent issue of Lawrence's forced language, as with the repetitiously insistent and overreaching erotic prose of heat and darkness and transcendence.

What has aroused more interest in this generation (at least with intellectual commentators)[5] is Lawrence's nonuse of obscenity, his failure of courage at indiscretion of vocabulary. I refer to the now notorious apparent anal sodomizing of the lady by the gamekeeper—the "night of sensual passion" in the cottage in the woods before she leaves for Venice (chap. 16). The description has the curious overreach of euphemism, the exaggeration of the oblique, with its "shameless sensuality," explicitly "not voluptuousness," "not really love," but "burning out the shames, the deepest, oldest shames, in the most secret places." Abelard-Heloise, unspecified scenes on Greek vases, the imposed "phallic hunt," and the woman's role as a "passive, consenting thing, like a slave, a physical slave," are all called upon in the large claim that Lady Chatterley was transformed by the submission, which "made a different woman of her" (*Lady*, pp. 231–32). The case for reading this to include anal penetration is appropriately reinforced by Clifford reporting the scandal from Mellors's wife of his having practiced sex in the Cellini "Italian manner" (p. 250), and by Lawrence's fervid concern in other works (as in *Women in Love*, cited earlier) with the "dark" sensuality at "the base of the loins." That Lawrence did not have his lady more explicitly penetrated in the anus is not, I suggest (counter to some commentators), because of the common-law crime or sexual taboo of buggery—all of the double-adulterous sex between the lady and the servant was, of course, illegal as well as socially taboo—nor because it by definition violates the theme of "tenderness" which is still partly there in the concern. (And not just in Lawrence—compare John Updike's Harry Angstrom, for example, who rather tenderly has anal intercourse with Thelma in *Rabbit Is Rich,* or contrast the hostile sodomizing of women in several Norman Mailer fictions, or note the intense interest in heterosexual sodomy in Joyce, Naipul, Roth, and others.)[6] Certainly Lawrence's repressed and possibly displaced homosexuality or regressive anality (in the Freudian argument) may be an element as, surely, was his puritanical sense of taboo, evident in the indirection of language and, therefore, some sense of violation however therapeutic for the lady.[7] (We are also not told if, as first experience, she found it painful, as usually reported, which suggests further male bias.) Lawrence in *Lady Chatterley* was inconsistent, timorous in language and theme, not nearly as explicit as he should have been, given his materials and purposes. The lack of a fuller play of the erotic, in language and behavior (not much sexual variety—no oral sex in what was then known as the "French manner," not much humor, not more varied phallic responses) certainly limits the writing. So does his vagueness on the variable sexuality which he was implicitly propounding as essential part of fully physical being. In sum, Lawrence's use of taboo terms was not only rather limited and restricted—and in the case of *cunt* somewhat highfalutin unusual—but he may reasonably be criticized for not being "obscene" enough. Lawrence's struggle towards a more polymorphous sexual consciousness (his intermittent but not directly acknowledged large purpose, as I read him) was not altogether successful, and insufficient obscenity may thus point to the real literary difficulty.

Sexual Peculiarity?

Since Lawrence, and especially in this last novel, is taken as a sexual prophet—and surely he wanted to be (as also confirmed in the concurrent essays)—we should pursue a bit further some of what is at issue in what he calls "real sex." With some of Lawrence's peculiarly broadened use of *cunt* there may also rise to consciousness what I take to be a real Lawrence obscenity (in the sense of nastiness): an angrily restrictive definition of proper female sexuality. Inadequately emphasized in most discussions (male, of course) of *Lady Chatterley's Lover*, it is a major and insistent element, first raised on the third page of the novel. Women, we are told in authorial pronouncement around a summary of Connie's early sexual experience, can, as a "power play", resist in orgasmic submission to the male. "For she only had to hold herself back in sexual intercourse, and let him finish and expend himself without her coming to the crisis: and then she could prolong the connection and achieve her orgasm and her crisis while he was merely her tool." Lawrence obsessively returns to the point, in Mellors's statements, Michaelis's declarations, and in what must be read as editorializing intrusions (pp. 7, 28, 51, 189–91, etc.). Because of this, we are not dealing with just character Mellors's opinions of women but the overall book's view, which we may appropriately abbreviate as the Lawrencean.[8]

Take the extended discussion by Mellors of his sexual history to Connie (chap. 16)—plausible subject for the lovers but peculiar in its male rage in a loving situation—in which he gives his account of his conflict with two antisexual women, no doubt selectively drawing on Lawrence's own experiences (the first was literary and intense but antisexual—Jessie Chambers?; the second was musical and amorous but again antisexual, even into hatred—lesbian-inclined Helen Corke?).[9] Then Mellors discusses his sex with the "common" Bertha Coutts, which was a part of his young, rebellious, intentional declassing (from clerk to pit blacksmith, from proper English to speaking "broad,")—"a woman who *wanted* me to fuck her." After he married her, however, she willfully put him off sexually, and even when they conjoined at her caprice, "she'd never come off when I did." Instead, she would actively use the post-orgasm male, "tear, tear, tear"-ing at him in "blind beakishness," aggressively forcing clitoral gratification against the expended, gritting man. Mellors-Lawrence crassly interprets such female gratification, and her inability to have orgasm in any other manner, as not a likely failure of his own premature ejaculation or other limitation but as the "low" way of "old whores" (factually improbable since it is usually reported that experienced prostitutes generally avoid orgasm with clients) and "a raving sort of self-will." It is, then, an issue of ego and power. Here is a tangible focus of Lawrence's obsessional attack on female "will" throughout his writings. The following couple of pages make that "false" female orgasm the centerpiece of a line of bad female sex and the defeat of male desire. There is the "old-fashioned" submissive but unresponsive female, and the "sly" woman who just pretends desire and orgasm, and the not "natural" ones who "make you go off when you're *not* in the only place you should be," and the ones who are unresponsively "dead inside," and the ones who force the male out and clitorally gratify themselves. (The typology seems true enough, though one may be surprised that Lawrence had the variety of experience, or other evidence, to arrive at it.) In sum, says Mellors-Lawrence, it seems that most women are, "consciously or unconsciously," "nearly all Lesbians," and "I could kill them." And there wasn't left any "woman who'd really 'come' naturally with a man: except black women, and, somehow, well, we're white men: and they're a bit like mud."

I cite that last bit not only to acknowledge the gross (and, it appears to me from other literature, conventionally British for the time) bigotry (including the fantasized greater sensuality of the "muddy" black), which isn't just confined to this character, and that intermittently appears in Lawrence,[10] but to note that, as so often seems true, the several bigotries cluster together. The character is corporately speaking for white men, as also apparently in his contempt for quite a variety of female sexual response, the hatred for lesbianism, and the narrow male definition of what constitutes what he calls "real sex." Several partly separable issues might be considered here. One is some obvious inconsistency, such as Mellors's claim here to "the only place" the male organ should be put with his shortly later insistence on anal intercourse with Connie. A conflict of doctrine and actual desire which may be seen as more extensive? This seems evident not just in middle-aged and sexually uncertain Mellors nonetheless climaxing three times with Connie in apparently about an hour (chap. 12), but also the hyperfervent rhetoric connected with it—"the sons of god with the daughters of men." And, again, we have the treatment of the woman's sexual response as a conversion experience, a rebirth—orgasmic Connie is "born: a woman" (p. 163). Now there is religion for you![11] It repeats, of course, the key conversion experience I have noted in a number of Lawrence's earlier fictions. But, as with most religious claims, there is the temptation to violate and go beyond the tangible experience, though not into the extensive falsification, objectification into a cult, of *The Plumed Serpent*.

Certainly there is some wobbly perspective on sexual meaning, varying from the "natural" to the threatened male, and the racially bigoted to the religious. Another is Lawrence's usual nasty, and no doubt defensive, rage against anything suggesting homosexuality, or merely clitoral gratification which makes the male at best instrumental if not irrelevant even in heterosexual relationships, except when he is doing the lady an enlightenment favor by way of her *arse*. But the more poignant, if still doctrinaire, issue is the one I started with here: only certain kinds of female sexual response are acceptable. The main one affirmed seems to be that the woman is to be passive but not detached (Connie "willed herself into this separateness" [*Lady*, p. 117] during one intercourse in the hut, and in consequence finds much of the sexual performance "ridiculous," and her response nonorgasmic and generally negative). The ideal, Mellors repeatedly makes clear, is simultaneous orgasm—hardly an odds-on situation with temperamentally different people some years apart, and one requiring the submission of one person's rhythms to another's. As Lawrence sets up the situation, that submission must be the woman's effort to accord her more "chooseable" sexual condition to the man's somewhat precarious gratification. Now a woman can endlessly delay, as we are told in the early description of Connie's sex life, or as seems forced upon her in her intercourse with short-lasting Michaelis (chap. 3 and 5), or endlessly refuse (as with the wanting but repeatedly raped Dolly of "The Princess"), or submissively and unstrivingly submit to the possibility of it happening, or more probably settle for less (as with Kate in *The Plumed Serpent*). In sum (without relentlessly multiplying Lawrencean examples, not all of which are clear), Lawrence seems to make a distinction (as do traditional Freudians, updating a nineteenth-century mythology) between "clitoral" and "vaginal," or here his "beaked" and "deep," female orgasms. By the time at least of the "Aphrodite of the foam" passage in *The Plumed Serpent* and certainly by the narrator's and Mellors's discussions in *Lady Chatterley*, the clitoral is bad and wrong. However, it seems that current clinical material on female sexuality (on which I am not fully expert) emphatically denies the distinction, insisting that all female orgasms engage the clitoris. Granted, the clinical evidence may override practical differences in female sexual responses, especially emotionally heightened "all-over" sensations, as well as possible conditions of psychic mergence, both of which Lawrence seems to repeatedly emphasize. The clinical reports also do not much distinguish styles and degrees of aggressiveness, particularly in the direction of female "power" and relatedness, which may not be separable from much human sexual experience.[12] But why does Lawrence make so much of it? In both of Connie's adulterous affairs, the quite different men express great resentment of women who "grind their own coffee," whose sexual rhythms seem to selfishly not accord with the males. Quite possibly, this may sadly point to the threatened male's sexual inadequacy, not inappropriate to the indicated sexual-psychological weaknesses of both Michaelis and Mellors (and quite possibly of Lawrence and his probable impotence [see the cited Meyers, Spilka, et al.] which I am not going to biographically pursue). Can there now be any doubt that Lawrencean sexuality is partly problematic?

However, I suggest sympathy with the problem and sexual style—not just out of tolerance but because it may also highlight some fundamental male/female sexual disparity (contrary to many sexologists, such as Alex Comfort, who assume fundamental full compatibility, given appropriate situation and technique). Lawrence's emphasized male/female sexual disparity may be widespread, perhaps (I have no very certain way of knowing) even fundamental: if there are the extreme, oppositional, gender differences he was always insisting upon, it would probably have to be. Widespread assumptions of male/female sexual accord may be an ideological imposition (especially a "romantic" one in modern times?) on some common reality, some perhaps basic gender disparity. But we should also grant that Lawrence's handling of it is both excessively negative and nastily prejudiced. Certainly Lawrence also repeatedly relates the aggressive, direct, clitoral female pursuit with women's "willful" power—often described in an obviously displaced way as "bullying"—and hence arrogant domination, which may not have a necessary connection, even for Lawrence's own perceptions. Mrs. Bolton, for example, who is presented as having had a warmly positive sexual relation with her dead miner husband, appears with him, and later with the regressive Clifford, to control by ostensible submission. And, indeed, Connie's sexual transformation from the manipulative-clitoral to the conversion response in which she was "gone in the flood" (*Lady*, p. 163) partly undercuts the righteousness of Lawrence's sexual argument. Given the right circumstances, the longtime clitoral-manipulative lady can arrive at the sexual redemption of good *cunt*, though she may have paid a self-subordinating price for it. Lawrence emphasizes, as usual, the *impersonality* of intercourse, for *both* male and female ("The man, the individual, let him not dare intrude. He was but a temple servant, the bearer and keeper of the bright phallos . . ." [p. 127]—supposedly the woman's thoughts). The now usually lambasted treatment of the other as "sex object," is for Lawrence both male and female, and desirable. Such impassioned sex— primordial experience of engaging woman and man rather than individual

81

Defiant Desire

personality, and conflicting-separating egos—also may undercut the demand for the sympathetic responsiveness of orgasmic accord. Really good sex is not readily come by.

This is certainly Lawrence's long insistent theme (and indeed a large one in literature more generally, however euphemistically, I suggest). But Lawrence has in this novel finally made his emphasized disparity between male and female—as we saw in the high rhetoric of the "oppositional" in *Women in Love* and the essays—into the specifically sexual. Most women, it seems to suggest, not only have a different sexual demand than the male but often refuse to accord with his sexual needs and rhythms and desires. Here, to recall *The Rainbow* earlier generation, we have a specific locus for the "deep, deep hidden rage of unsatisfied men against women." Curiously, in *Lady Chatterley* the "oppositional" does not much appear in the relation of Connie to Mellors (mostly a weakness in her characterization?) but is displaced on to the other characters and the society, in pure negation. Connie is rather easily converted to male desire, and gratified with staying eagerly still and passive and accepting, front or back, and responding ecstatically. Lawrence insists that such can be achieved only by an abeyance of individual will, which then allows the primordial to take over, though that seems suspiciously like negative willing.

Some of the crucial sexual views so righteously emphasized in *Lady Chatterley* may have some commonness—possibly there are widespread biological-sexual as well as emotional disparities between male and female—but one may be also uncertain as to how universal or normative they are. However, the pro-feminist commentators (including such males as Robert Scholes and Mark Spilka) may do a disservice in not recognizing either partial or possibly fundamental gender disparities. Once again the apparent idiosyncracy of Lawrence's views of desire may be suggestive in their intensification and anguish but sometimes are righteously, precariously, misengaged. The novelist, then, negates some of the dimensions of desire which his theme should be defending, and this leads to some of the compensatorily strident declarations and muddled prose and point of view which weakens the novel. This also (I suggest in the context with other lines of argument developed in this study) may be seen as finally not just sexual but metaphysical, the desperate effort to find overweening meaning in and through sexual desire in a cosmos mostly denuded of other meanings. Antipassion in sex, represented by (but not limited to) willful female clitoral manipulation, is negation of the primary, deeper (and thus by metaphoric

82

leap, deep orgasm) passion which is so essential. "And when passion is dead . . . then the magnificent throb of beauty is incomprehensible and even a little despicable . . ." (*Lady*, p. 117). A "good fuck," an achieved state of "cunt" allness, is a teleos, but apparently, Lawrence wishes to claim, something beyond personal will. Hence the metaphysical anger against clitoral manipulation (and elsewhere, the intolerant rejection of male masturbation) and a pious hope for "deeper" and more total orgasm, more superlative, polymorphously encompassing sexuality. "Good fucking," I would agree, is an admirable goal, but Lawrence wants much more.

The Conditions of Passion

Good, impassioned sex may be essential, at some time or other, for authentic awareness, but it is not enough, especially in a "counterfeit" and otherwise bad society, for the Lawrencean. Here I want to consider some social issues especially raised by the extant three different versions of the last novel, eventually published (not part of Lawrence's intention), and rather arbitrarily named, as *The First Lady Chatterley, John Thomas and Lady Jane*, and, as the final and in several senses truer version, the one I have been considering. Lawrence's rather odd method of composition, which produced the three almost alternate versions between 1926 and 1928, may be partly explained by his ostensible aesthetic.[13] This was the position he attempted to take in many of his writings on the novel, with the exalted purpose of catching the "spontaneous flow," the sympathetic record, of the authentic physical-emotional relatedness of persons and places. Indeed, one of the most noted statements of the emphasis appears in the final version of *Lady Chatterley*. Connie is, rather improbably, intellectualizing the gossip of Mrs. Bolton—the miner's widow who in middle age has become nurse-companion to war-crippled Clifford Chatterley, and who is probably the most persuasively realized character, in the traditional realistic sense, in the novel:

> She ought not to listen with this queer rabid curiosity. After all, one may hear the most private affairs of other people, but only in a spirit of respect for the struggling, battered thing which any human soul is, and in a spirit of fine, discriminative sympathy. For even satire is a form of sympathy. It is the way our sympathy flows and recoils that really determines our lives. And here lies

the real importance of the novel, properly handled. It can inform and lead into new places the flow of our sympathetic conciousness, and it can lead our sympathy away in recoil from things gone dead. Therefore, the novel, properly handled, can reveal the most secret places of life: for it is in the *passional* secret places of life, above all, that the tide of sensitive awareness needs to ebb and flow, cleansing and freshening. (*Lady*, p. 94)

Lawrence, who has as so often only loosely hooked his reflections on to the consciousness of his character Connie, goes on to condemn Mrs. Bolton's kind of gossip, and by extension the "popular" novel, for its "vicious, conventional channeling of sympathy," instead of into the "passional secret places" (such as those I have just been discussing). The double play of argument—sympathy/recoil, the novel as the record of either "sensitivity" or the "vicious conventional"—constantly marks the distinctive Lawrenceanism, the dialectical cast of mind so crassly missed or distorted by so many commentators, yet which gives him much of his literary edge and intellectual power.

Now the satire-as-sympathy, most commentators seem to agree, was certainly increased in the final version of *Lady Chatterley* but apparently with considerable spontaneousness, as in the mockery of the "mental-lifer" attitude. This is mostly pronounced by a rather artificial self-mocking spokesman for it, General Tommy Dukes, who does not appear in earlier versions (and soon disappears from the last one—essentially a limited sage-commentator, like Hemingway's Count Greffi). The failure of the mental-lifer to fuse body and thought, to live and act directly, Lawrence saw as one of the terrible results of Western dualism, in Christianity, Greek thought (see the earlier quote), and modern rationalism. But, in social context, "mental life" also seems to serve as just a summary statement of the bent of the "intelligentsia" who often seem "rooted in spite and envy" (*Lady*, p. 35). The view is more asserted than dramatized, but then it is considerably self-evident to the sophisticated reader.

The dilemma of the gap between "mental" and responsive physical life often required, contra the given self and accepted thinking, that one has a kind of conversion experience (William James's "twice-born"), to emotional heightening and wholeness, as Connie does sexually. As I adumbrated earlier, such erotic-conversion experiences, which depend on heightened desire with negation of the old and conventional self, provide the cruxes in much of Lawrence's work, and are the counterings to the "willful" and "self-consciousness"—the modern mental diseases—including manipulative sex (sometimes labeled "sex-in-the-head") and various kinds of power and dominance.

What does this have to do with writing novels? Willful consciousness also marks artistic warping, the elaborate self-consciousness, for example, of Proust, specifically mocked by Connie (though much admired by her crippled, impotent husband) as boring and dead for his excessive concern with "streams of words" and "self-important mentalities" (*Lady*, p. 182). Elsewhere, Lawrence makes similar comments about other major moderns, such as Mann and Joyce. Art concentrating on itself and its own importance less reveals the ebb and flow of feelings and "true and vivid relationships" than it reveals the willful egotism and manipulative distortions which constitute artistic "immorality."[14]

To be a moral novelist, by which Lawrence mostly meant a vitalistic recorder with impassioned prophetic-conversion purposes, one must be relatively unself-conscious, responding with intensity and immediacy to the flow and feeling of the fictional experience, pursuing its physical and emotional realities rather than rhetorical extensions. In the practice of novelistic craft, this meant avoiding clever involution, verbal ornateness, labyrinthine orderings, parodistic formalism, the dissolution of humane purpose, and the other self-aware probing and play so characteristic of some of his modernist contemporaries (and even more, it seems, of postmodernism.) It also meant, at least as confirmed by the results, a good bit of awkwardness, loose ends, redundancy, tonal lapses, mixed if not muddled point of view, and other roughness. For Lawrence, one should write, as it were, straight on (as he apparently did this novel, fraily sitting under a tree with his pad in the Tuscany countryside). One tends thus to deal with uncertainties by replacing rather than revising. While the evidence, in letters and manuscripts, suggests that Lawrence often did not resist some of the usual sort of detailed revision and elaboration (are they not pretty much inevitable in writing?), he believed in doing so. In principle as well as temperament, he rejected the tortured search for the *mot juste* (as we can see, for example, anguishedly reported in Flaubert's letters to Louise Colet) and the artistically elaborated manner (Proust, Joyce, et al.). Apparently better, as Lawrence saw it, to come back fresh to the vivid relationships, the scenes and the passions and the rages—the process of desire and negation—than to polish up and otherwise manipulate the verbal by-product. This can be viewed as having a strong element of a puritan iconoclastic aesthetic. It is certainly opposed to the idolatry of art, as so often in modernist ideology. Art should not be a precious image-object but the sensitive entry into a crucial larger, and socially and spiritually righteous, experience of redemptive importance.

The three versions of his final novel, then, are overlapping alternate attempts to determine the right response, the appropriate discriminative sympathy and satire, to the regenerative love affair and its relation to the larger society. Thus we have revision by replacement (writing teachers might take due note of this for some temperaments). Several of the directions of the replacements, such as the declassing of the protagonist and the increased harshness towards the prevailing social order, seem to me important in confirming the purpose and meaning of the final version, and Lawrence more generally. But first a dialectical qualification. Modernist sensibility, which Lawrence with his quick atunements to the world around him so obviously had in many ways, was not so easily set aside, particularly as a serious writer. The self-aware and self-aggrandizing artist—really, the self-condemned mental lifer—was at least with some inevitability in his specialized labors, as Lawrence's were, producing for an anonymous audience a processed cultural artifact, a "modernist" one which would both engage audience sympathies yet strike at its limitations. In spite of his claimed desire and aesthetic of "spontaneous flow," Lawrence the novelist was not just responding from direct experience and in direct contact with a sensitive auditor. He was writing, partly with commercial purposes, for conventional publishing to at least partly conventional bourgeois audiences. The last novel, as with a number of his later works, often shows him insistently "literary," waspishly argumentative, manipulatively self-aware. To read in close proximity the three published versions of the last novel in the order of writing is to see demonstrated Lawrence's own exacerbation of the accursed self-consciousness, mental life.[15]

For instance, the final version shows a condemnatory social anger much increased over its predecessors, as in the repeated descriptions of the society as "sickness" and "insanity," and the angry attack on Midlands England as the ugliness of the "insentient iron world and the Mammon of mechanized greed" (*Lady*, p. 111). Also in partial magnification of rage from the earlier ones, the last version of the novel treats many of its characters—Clifford Chatterley, Connie's sister Hilda, the artist-friend Duncan Forbes—unsympathetically to the point of savage caricatures, not just of themselves but of the general state of intellectual gentry, willful women, and modernist, abstracting artists.

Sir Clifford Chatterley seems especially burdened with a variety of satiric purposes. In "*A Propos Lady Chatterley's Lover*," Lawrence's long, digressive, and freewheeling editorializing essay written after publication of the final version of the novel, he insists that he did not start out with the intention of making Clifford's crippling and sexual impotence "symbolic" of the condition of dominant modern man. Perhaps not, but the portentous moral crippling of Clifford expanded in each rewriting. His role, for example, as a ruthless engineer and capitalist modernizing his coal mines— and with the dehumanized instrumentalism characteristic of many modern technologues (an extension of Gerald Crich's doctrine in *Woman in Love*)— comes late and relatively undeveloped in *John Thomas and Lady Jane* but earlier and in greater proportion in *Lady Chatterley's Lover*. Aptly enough, Lawrence makes the point that as a human being the advanced industrial financier had become a "crustacean" with "a hard efficient shell of an exterior and a pulpy interior" (*Lady*, p. 102). But the specific development of Clifford in his industrialist role is rather cursory (generalized summary paragraphs), and not very relevant since already, by class character, he is a sexual and moral crustacean. It may also be hard to altogether align with Lawrence's own acute insight that "industry had a will of its own," which may not even be that of its ostensible owners (*Lady*, p. 147), such as Clifford, and it is such institutional dominance by impersonal forces (versus the primary passional impersonal) which is so much of the horror.

Even more bothersome is Lawrence's addition of other roles for Clifford in the final version, such as his having become, early in the novel, a clever writer of nastily empty stories, a bit of a commercial as well as critical literary success. For the rather rigid and retiring country gentleman and mine-owning engineer to have quickly become a successful writer of maliciously gossipy, fashionable social fiction may not be very persuasive. We certainly do not novelistically see much of Clifford's "malicious" analysis of people. Part of Lawrence's point, of course, is that dehumanized manipulation applies as much to literature as to the industrial and social realms. Morally, the issue seems well taken, but it lacks plausibility and presence in the novel because an inappropriate loading on.

In this third version, Lawrence also added another writer, Michaelis (identified by the biographers with the Armenian-American popular fictionist Michael Arlen—therefore, as usual with Lawrence's defensive-bellicose personal relations, to be treated mockingly), and he is as an aggrandizing and mannered arriviste popular playwright. He also becomes the aggrandizingly doggish and inadequate but resentful (with premature ejaculation) lover of Constance Chatterley. Since Clifford is literally crippled, the addition of this writer-seducer seems to represent the manipulative society's resentful eroticism as well as the lady's desperation. Dramatically, the husband should have had that role, but Lawrence is relentlessly scoring off the literary life, and uses Michaelis to harshly comment on the dominance of the "bitch-goddess of success" (*Lady*, p. 58; a repeated phrase he attributes to Henry James, though he probably got it from the less stranglingly genteel William)—the deity of counterfeit culture. Proper point, but is this (as with various comments on Clifford's brittle stories and London success) not the involuted self-conscious nastiness which Lawrence objected to in other modernist writers?

When Lawrence reconceived the Chatterley story, his angers expanded into the social-cultural world, and in consequence he loads Clifford, and some of the lesser characters as well, with new negative functions. Can Clifford carry the roles of not only being an impotent and obtuse husband but of being a fashionable fatuous writer, an arrogant country gentleman, a dogmatic authoritarian snob, a cultural traditionalist (exalting Racine and Proust), a compulsive gambler, and much else? He is also an obscenely regressive case nuzzling the breasts of his nurse Mrs. Bolton (the inverted emotional price of his ruthless dealings with the industrial world—in Lawrence's intolerant view, disapproving of any pleasure for the poor crustacean-cripple). Conjoining with his worship of technology, from Lawrence's point of view, Clifford appropriately becomes an early mass media addict (compulsively listening to the radio). In all versions, Clifford is presented as ardent defender of class privilege and authority (in some of the best-realized satiric scenes, as when he glories in his power and then his motorized wheelchair bogs down and has to be pushed by the frail servant-lover and the angered wife). In all versions, he is also the recurrent Lawrencean villainous ideologue, the Platonic-spiritualist-gentry intellectual who puts down the body and tangible life, and its social spirit of "sympathy." The negatively burdened nasty baronet-artist-industrialist-idealist-cripple-pathological case seems also to have led Lawrence to eliminate in the final version some of the more positively sympathetic qualities of the earlier portrayals, as with Clifford bravely, if somewhat grotesquely, learning to swing along his crippled legs on crutches, supposedly to please his wife; was this too bodily human for the final mechanical emphasis? Lawrence's final all-purpose villain, though often a focus for astute psychological and ideological satire of emotionally crippled but cleverly functional modern people, seems an overdone grotesque, rather heavily disproportionate in the intermittently emphasized social realism.

Some similar burdened effects develop in the rewriting of other characters and motifs. While in all versions Lawrence and his gamekeeper demand sexually submissive, passive women, the raging specifics (such as the anticlitoral quoted earlier in the chapter) are peculiar to the final version, and partly twist sexual regeneration into misogynistic sexual righteousness. Other commentators have objected to such scenes, unique to the final version, as Constance Chatterley's gentleman-artist father sniggeringly discussing his daughter's sexuality with her gamekeeper-lover. Lawrence may again have slipped out of character in somewhat defiantly justifying the sexual action, and fantasizing parental erotic acceptance, for his repressive middle-class audience. The ideological rhetoric shows some similar heightening: what had been an emphasis on the largely unconscious power of sensate and responsive "touch" in the first version has become an avowed politics in the final version, a quaint argument (given to Connie by Dukes) for "a democracy of touch, instead of a democracy of pocket" (*Lady*, p. 70). In rewriting, then, even though in complete versions to maintain the aesthetic and vivid-life "flow," Lawrence slipped into self-consciously strident art that pulled "down the balance" of the fiction toward his angers and idiosyncrasies—forcing the artist, who is not to be trusted, over the tale (to employ Lawrence's own famous warning in *Studies in Classic American Literature:* "Never trust the artist, trust the tale."). The last novel thus partly became, by Lawrence's own avowed standards, artistic "immorality."

Yet it would be wrong, I believe, to argue from this (and I have been putting some emphasis on the negative case) that the earlier versions of the novel are better. This has repeatedly been done but often seems to depend on obtuse readings of the larger purposes of the fiction and why Lawrence rewrote it a couple of times.[16] That requires a different sense of the commanding tropes, the delineation of the protagonist, and awareness of some of the implications of Lawrence' defiant social perspective. The Lawrencean change moves towards a profound social response, and provides a key self-discovery of negation.

Defiant Desire

Outside with the Pastoral Lover

Lady Chatterley's Lover should be recognized as in significant part an alienated intellectual's pastoral utopian credo. Sick and exasperated Lawrence only gradually arrived at the recognition of that purpose for his last novel. I suggest that the personal incitements for that change (such as personal satire or possible impotence and dying) are less interesting than the ideological results of it. The early extant version, published as *The First Lady Chatterley*, a rough and incomplete work, may reasonably be viewed as more simply poignant than the others. The second version, published under a title of folkish sexual euphemisms that Lawrence several times played with, *John Thomas and Lady Jane* (also used a couple of times in the final version [pp. 196 and 283]),[17] was considerably longer and more socially detailed than the first and last, and it may be experienced as less idiosyncratically and ideologically irritating. But there are essential and often justifiable reasons for many of the changes Lawrence made and for the partly different focus of the final version. As I have just argued, the last doing of the Lady Chatterley story seems seriously flawed, and partly so in ways not in the earlier conceptions. But Lawrence also, with proper artistic imperative and social wisdom, changed the story and treatment in its crucial awareness and regenerative parable, and not just in idiosyncratic concerns and strident self-consciousness.[18] One way of summarizing this is to say that the history of the three versions shows not only an increase in prophetic rage against the society and its culture but also an increase in awareness which resulted in the considerable shift from "proletarian" to "pastoral" fiction and from a socially dissident view to a prophetic view.

The pastoral romance, unlike, say, the sonnet or epic or tragedy, has little agreed-upon lineaments or formal definition, though obviously some related materials and attitudes have been widely recurrent in Western literature. Some characteristics, traceable back to Renaissance pastoral and its classic origins, appear fairly common. The pattern tends to be one of upper-class lovers retreating from a falsely sophisticated world to an ostensibly more simple, erotic, and "natural" interlude in a *locus amoenus*.[19] The European conventions (in contrast, for instance, to nineteenth-century American pastoral, which usually lacked many of the heterosexual dimensions) provide an idyllic and regenerative "sacred" place for loving, such as a grove or other rural retreat, whose description carries pagan religious meanings. (Granted, the pastoral is not the only literary mode which appears to have carried on paganism more or less covertly against the vicious repressions of Christianity.) *Lady Chatterley's Lover* insists, far more than the earlier versions, on pagan associations as well as specific avowals by Mellors of Lawrence's "phallic consciousness" neo-paganism. Pagan religiousness, of course, characterizes Mellors and Connie dancing nakedly in the spring rain and twining flowers in their pubic hair— hardly to be viewed as a "realistic" scene, as some readers report with a misplaced irritation at such ritual action. (But note also that here the ritual, unlike those in *The Plumed Serpent*, is not institutionalized, cultized, and resentfully and dominatingly imposed on others—Lawrence's wise, libertarian, change.)

The regeneratively erotic sacred wood lacks full dimension when sundered from the Golden Age mythos.[20] Still, as with Lawrence, the pastoral scene is less a world of its own than a brief sanctuary of religious dimensions which points to a different way of life. The lovers less identify with rustic life in itself—the playing swain and maid performing ritual actions— than pursue an arcadian model of the return to a prelapsarian emotional wholeness, away from the corrupting civilization which, however, continues to provide the basic consciousness of characters, author, and readers— the pervasive pastoral irony. The pastoral may be viewed as a pagan withdrawal-and-return pattern, a religious-erotic renewal or conversion of personal life, but one pointedly conditioned by an antipastoral order.[21] The apparent primitivist reversion is really a sophisticated purification.

In all three of the versions of the novel, the pastoral scene as polarity is central: the gamekeeper's cottage (and, even more poetically, the pheasant hut where the seduction takes place) in Wragby Wood, which is a vestigial part of ancient Sherwood Forest, with some pagan wood worship and perhaps Robin Hood-ish socially rebellious resonances. It repeatedly serves as emotional and moral contrast to Wragby Hall, the cold and dreary manor house of social power (however crippled and impotent the baronet-artist-industrialist master), and several times to Tevershall, the grimly ugly industrial-mining town from which Wragby Hall draws its wealth, as well as the urban scenes and their resorts (London and Venice in the final version, Paris and a Spanish resort in *John Thomas and Lady Jane*). Lawrence rhetorically elaborates the contrasts, often using such images as gray iron and blackened buildings, and greening sunniness and forest and flowers, which go back to a pastoral basic myth of a Golden Age which has declined into an Iron Age.

As the second version also expounds the contrasts of woods and towns, gold and iron, spring flowers and coal works, the counterings connect with "two main sorts of energy." One is the "frictional," characteristic of machines, modern competitive social intercourse, and reductive, superficial (clitoral?) sexuality. The other is "forest energy . . . frail bud-tips and gentle finger-ends of awareness" which fuses the lovers in mutual orgasm, the fecund natural scene, and a vision of a transformed order.[22] Such pastoral energy, of course, should not be sensed as either literally or tropistically wild but, rather, as one with a *cultivated* nature, neatly cleared and humanly improved and tended (as with the park woods), scene and relations marked with their own civility, responsiveness, ancient ritual, rich eroticism, and tender awareness. The embittered gamekeeper and the despairing lady are appropriately regenerated. And a significantly different way of life seems to follow.

But before considering the postpastoral, note that in the first two versions Lawrence was also attempting something else, a version of "proletarian fiction." Here that is simply definable as stories centering on the working class, and with a self-conscious ideology affirming such origins, virtues, and powers. Parkin, the gamekeeper in *The First Lady Chatterley*, gets his identity from his working-class origins (a coal-mining family without, in contrast to the Morels of *Sons and Lovers*, other pretensions), in development (he had been a pit blacksmith, then a common soldier, then a hand in a steel mill), in speech (he prefers speaking Midlands dialect, and crudely), in friends and manners (quite specifically including his ways of eating, dressing, and sex), in social attitudes and even, at the end of the novel, as devoted secretary of the local Sheffield factory "Communist League." That last must strike one as especially inappropriate for Lawrence, who obviously knew little about such a role except as a metaphor for proletarian revolution after 1917, and it is trivially presented.[23] This disappears in the second version for a more vague and romantic socialism in the William Morris tradition, and in the final version for a rather different utopian politics. (Nowhere do we have the authoritarinism of *The Plumed Serpent*, now rejected by Lawrence.) But in the two earlier versions the protagonist's proletarian identification is strong. There Lawrence may be seen as rebelling against the genteel and aspiring respectability of his own early years and affirming origins—his father's values—that he had rejected when quite young.

In all versions of the novel, Lady Constance Chatterley comes from a wealthy gentry-artist background—"well-to-do intelligentsia"—and has been mildly upper-bohemian in development, and then the wife of a wealthy, landed, and mine-owning, cultivated aristocrat. Therefore much of the story must center on differences in social class. Can the cultivated lady love and live with the proletarian? For Lawrence, reasonably enough, the answer finally must be that she cannot. In the first two versions, the issue seems unresolvable, though the dominant direction of the first is that the lady will have to be proletarianized, and of the second that the world will hardly allow their continuing love. But even as the *First*'s Parkin puts it, the sensitive lady cannot really make the choice of proletarian life: A working-class existence "means drudging and dragging and being worn out wi' doin' things—an' bein' *under*." For Lawrence, that is no choice at all, no matter what the flight from bourgeois respectability or upper-class futility, not even with sexual regeneration. Aptly enough, Lawrence sees that a cross-class love tale can only be resolved for the long-term when at least one of the lovers essentially changes social class. After all, that, as Lawrence dramatizes in so many stories, is where social class gets part of its emotional power.

John Thomas and Lady Jane seems transitional in terms of changing social class. Where Parkin, of the first version, appears insistently proletarian when out of the pastoral woods, Seivers (the name change from Parkin midway in the novel), of the second version, shows an added romantic tenderness and sophistication, and a clear inability to continue in a working-class way of life when out in the larger society.[24] Mellors, of the last version, has become largely declassed. Declassing the protagonist and de-proletarianizing the tale seems to be the artistic-intellectual destiny Lawrence struggled towards. It is a strong social-political statement for marginal man, a more modest version of the overman than in the authoritarian mythology of the preceding novels.

The details of this evolving conception prove crucial to the rewriting: they are not only various and emphatic but this larger conception overrides merely novelistic craft—excellent scenes and details are dropped to accord with the de-proletarianizing. For example, in the first and second versions there appears a poignantly drawn-out scene of social class disparity in which the lady and lover go to tea with the working-class family friends of the gamekeeper. Though moving as well as socially insightful on the differences between working-class and educated gentry on taste and rituals, it is entirely dropped in the final version. As in his personal style, Lawrence's direction was beyond class delineations to a declassed and deracinated bohemianism (though considerably on the upper-middle-class margins).

A couple more significant examples: Parkin (in the first) and Seivers (in the second) engage in fistfights and lose a couple of teeth (not replaced)— a rather important image of lower-class appearance for the fastidious Paul Morel-ish Lawrence. But Mellors in the final version does not behave or look that way. Both Parkin and Seivers go to work in a factory (the latter unsuccessfully) when fired by Clifford as gamekeepers; Mellors does not, and never even contemplates doing so. Lawrence worked hard, twice around, to combine the pastoral with the proletarian. But in the final version the working-class scenes and characterizations are largely eliminated or muted (Connie, in a much lighter scene, does go to a more informal tea with a working-class woman, Mrs. Flint [chap. 10], but never Mellors). All classes, not just the middle-class—"ladylike prigs with half a ball each"; "rotten as high game . . . arse lickin till their tongues are tough" (*Lady*, p. 203)—and the domineering gentry and the depressed working classes are rejected. From his perspective demanding radical social change, Lawrence, of course, has turned out to be historically correct—none of the traditional classes (I am one of those who also hold, contra traditional leftism) has been the crucial bearer of radical consciousness against the prevailing order.

Mellors, the final version of the gamekeeper, came up from the army ranks to be a commissioned officer in the colonies, reads serious books, and can pass, unlike Parkin and Seivers, as a gentleman (even in a club) in London, though not pleased with the temporary role. He speaks working-class dialect only in erotic or mocking situations, and expresses (unlike his forerunners) more complex, fanciful, and, almost inevitably for radical intellectual Lawrence (and consistent with earlier characters such as Annable and Birkin), more apocalyptic-misanthropic ideas. His politics are neither the first version's rather vague working-class ideology nor the second's loosely romantic socialism but the utopian views of the late Lawrence, a kind of elitist anarchism. The final protagonist is de-proletarianized but less embourgeoised or gentrified than declassed, which apparently offends patronizing Marxianizing and conservative readers.

By paring away the proletarian identification of his protagonist (except for the passional impetus and defiance from his origins), Lawrence tended to define him as he defined himself—that peculiar would-be "aristocrat" of modernism, the outcast intellectual and counterculturist. In the form of the story as well as specific invective within it, the author announces that the whole "class thing" is outmoded, irrelevant, as well as wrong. There can be no upper class in any moral sense in an order in which authority is impersonally functional, technocratized and "media-ized" (as with Clifford), endlessly manipulative and arbitrary. The modern pastoral figures must be outside of class, heroically marginalized in their otherness. Neither the degradation and parochialism of the proletariat—Lawrence knows better from his origins as well as radical sensibility than to sentimentalize it like middle-class Marxists—nor the vestigial and crippled upper class is pertinent to a different vision of society. Both ends of the social scale, he says, are "emotionally dead." Like the Tolstoy he ambivalently admired (and, of course, mocked) and whose *Anna Karenina* lies distantly behind this novel (though socially and sexually reversed), he never had much admiration or sympathy for what came between in the now omnivorous embourgeoisement.

Constance Chatterley, too, breaks with class, not only in her erotic passion but in her newfound repulsion towards the manor world, the industrial scenes (her embittered Lawrencean views of the hellish collieries and the spreading towns, as in the obvious Lawrence tour in chap. 10), the social manipulation, and most of her previous life. The earlier versions of the story harshly rejected Sir Clifford but not the secondary gentry. The final version of Hilda, Connie's sister, has become a satiric portrait of one of Lawrence's *bêtes noirs*, antisexual "willful woman." Where Connie's upper-class artist friend, Duncan Forbes, had been a sympathetic friend in the first version, by the last version he had become a hysterically hostile invert. Originally, he had served as a bridging figure between classes, and had said to Parkin, not quite accurately, "You're one of the odd ones that doesn't fit in any class."[25] But when Lawrence finally presents the gamekeeper outside of all classes, the class-bridging artist is no longer relevant and gets harshly rejected. We no longer find "good" and "bad" people within a class (as usual in the novel of manners tradition, from Jane Austen on), but instead, people who are within a class, any class, and those who are profoundly outside. Lawrence's tendentiousness, of course, is less in attacking social class, and its pseudohierarchies in modern society, than in mostly allowing good sex only to those outside. Class is "fucked-up."

Defiant Desire

Utopian Perplexity

With the decisive rejection of social class—the de-proletarianized ex-gamekeeper refuses most embourgeoisement and gentrification (and the lady publicly pregnant by a servant has certainly lost her ladyship, though she retains a moderate trust fund from her late mother)—putting the characters into an orderly continuing relation with society becomes difficult. Where shall they go when they leave, as they must, the pastoral sanctuary?

Constance had said that "she would be content with this little house [the gamekeeper's cottage in the woods] if only it were in a world of its own." But Lawrence fully dramatizes that it cannot be a self-sufficient world. From the wartime cutting down of the last great oaks (as with contemporary Ford's Tietjens, a postwar image of the end of the "olde" England) to the inescapable scream of the coal pit whistles and the red-glaring of the sky and sooting of the air, from the grotesque intrusion of Mellors sexually revenging wife to the impotently mean power of official owner Clifford, the pastoral world is rent by hostilities from below and above. By its very premise, of course, the pastoral erotic interlude and the redemptive sanctuary cannot last.

In the final version, in contrast with the earlier two, Lawrence self-consciously retaliates, at it were, by arguing that the answer to the pastoral-destroying order is to re-pastoralize the society. In a couple of properly noted passages given to Mellors, Lawrence adumbrates his vision of the good society around a rather quaintly Elizabethan trope of a community where the men all wore "close bright scarlet" trousers (*Lady*, pp. 205, 279 ff.). It can be taken as a rather Pre-Raphaelite image (from their influence on Lawrence's youth, evident in *The White Peacock;* the scarlet trousers also appear in both early and late essays), and a perennial reversion, as it were, to flower children in red tights, but also as an attenuated reassertion of Lawrence's recurrent positive utopianism (which he had been intermittently proposing—"Rananim"—to friends from 1915 on, as we can see in the letters). His countersociety, in brief notation of *Lady Chatterley*, includes the dominance of handicraft production (specifically against early twentieth-century industrialism), autonomous small communities (as against mass society, for patently as every pastoralizer and other sensitive person knows, our "world is overcrowded," though less than half as badly in Lawrence's time than in ours), rural-natural conditions (as against megalopolis), egalitarian-exchange economics (as against traditional class exploitation, and modern money-market economies which Lawrence, as also in many of the essays previously cited, was always attacking), communal arts such as "the old group dances" (as against modern mass media, such as Clifford's radio), and sensually positive pagan worship such as of "the great god Pan" (as against Christianity and other oppressively moralized "higher cults"). Generally, this but annotates what is arguably the main line of Western utopianism of several millennia (which I have elsewhere analyzed as "primatopianism").[26]

The tone and function of such passages in *Lady Chatterley* is wistfully earnest. The social anger running throughout the novel is not (contra a good many critics) mere irascibility of the dying (and sexually defeated) Lawrence but the radical rage that goes with a large and countering social view. Lawrence demands that the pastoral regenerative eroticism be viewed as going beyond personal experience and a mere arcadian interlude to a large ecotopian alternative. And, of course, the knowledgeable reader will recognize pagan and Golden Age mythological elements, Renaissance pastoral images, the English anti-industrial heritage (William Morris, et al.), and the ideas of the artful community and impassioned life which are a radical countering of Western civilization's technocracy, in Lawrence's time, and since. I am arguing that we should take Lawrence's final social vision seriously.

Perhaps there is a watershed line in consciousness between those who do and those who don't recognize the fundamental awareness that, as Lawrence-Mellors puts it near the end, "if there's got to be a future for humanity, there'll have to be a very big change from what now is" (*Lady*, p. 259). While *Lady Chatterley's Lover* often seems responded to now as a nearly antique tale of a couple of generations ago, what with its earlier scene of coal-and-iron industrialism ("utter, soulless ugliness"), of more overt erotic repression (even of the little sexual words), of more traditional class distinctions (the lady and the servant snobbery), and so forth, it is more, not less, appropriate to recognize that our "civilized society is insane" (*Lady*, p. 90, and repeated) and that it is even more appropriate to "contemplate the extermination of the human species" (*Lady*, p. 259), which in the present environmentally destructive order seems nearly inevitable. Whether one sympathizes or not with that ideological perspective, I suggest, is considerably determining of how one responds to *Lady Chatterley's Lover*. Instead of finding the Lawrencean view quaint, as a number of sophisticated commentators trivializingly seem to do, it might well be proper to see it as a forerunner of an increasingly widespread radical ecological view, the vision of the human turning, intimately and socially, to posttechnocratic, biologically suitable, drastically limited place and aspirations. Lawrence's use of the pastoral is less quaintly yearning literary device than commitment to a biocentric vision, an explicitly (if perhaps insufficiently developed) ecotopianism.

However, the tangible hopes of Mellors, and his author, were also more bleakly, practically, realistic. In Mellors's concluding letter to Connie, most of it unique to the final version of the novel, puritan-pagan religiousness and pastoral-utopian community are mostly reduced to a somewhat forlorn personal resolution. Both will divorce their meanly resistant spouses (the ostensible reason for their separation); she will have the child conceived in the sacred grove; and the family will withdraw to a small farm in Scotland.[27] (Mellors is apprenticing to a farmer as he writes; her inheritance will buy the place—a rich-uncle resolution rejected with workingman's machismo in the preceding version.) The hoped-for resolving image of the distant farm and family attempts to adapt the pastoral, somewhat anachronistically (and with no dramatized consultation with, much less resistance from, Connie) into the actual society. The expatriate farm—in Scotland, Italy (*The Lost Girl*), Canada ("Daughters of the Vicar"), New Mexico (his own life as well as his fictions such as *St. Mawr*), even Africa (*The Captain's Doll*)—provided a favorite concluding metaphor for Lawrence's marriage tales, early and late (as I previously discussed). Marriage is generally treated negatively by the late Lawrence. In the somewhat skittish tone and situation with which it is presented in *Lady Chatterley*, it might be viewed as less a persuasive resolution and exemplary social choice than as a rather desperate refusal to give up the redemptive pastoral-utopian vision. But Lawrence has nonetheless clearly concluded—as he did with his nonmarriage late tales (heroine Lou Witt's regenerative retreat to the American desert in *St. Mawr*, or the Christ figure in *The Man Who Died* ending as the mythic seasonal wanderer)—by opting out of a society which Mellors-Lawrence saw as "doomed" as well as unacceptable. Nothing less than the radical transformation of the social order, to nonclass organic communities in a drastically reduced and less technocratic human world, could bring the pastorally "twice-born" back in. The Green World. but in the meantime, the marginal refuge.

In several times redoing his pastoral romance, Lawrence seems to have been inexorably driven to declassing his characters who had been awakened to and through passionate desire. Hence the insistence on the class-decorum violations of the taboo words, though they did not come broadly and fluently to the author. Even if his resolution be seen as a reactive one of individual escape and a rather pyrrhic hopefulness for a utopian-pastoral world, it has, I suggest, some crucial truth not only about erotic regeneration but about society, including the one that was to come. Appropriate to the passional is a radical vision of culture and society, a break, however marginalized the autonomy, with the collective disciplines and prohibitions and aspirations and manias. Such social negation is absolutely crucial to his view of continuing desire.[28] That is the proper implication of intensely responsive awareness and richer quality of being. Probably such pastoral wisdom can neither avoid stridency nor perplexity in our "insane" social order of antihuman and antinatural proportions. Yet not to struggle to maintain the regenerative consciousness and more humane ordering would be to give up the fullness of the primal human, which Lawrence, with whatever difficulty of art, saw more as a matter of living truth than literary artistry, was not about to do.

The artistic and ideological limitations, to which I have certainly given due emphasis, do not, however, mean that I am holding that *Lady Chatterley's Lover* is a bad literary work. Any consideration not heavily loaded by an antagonistic ideology (however disguised as an issue of class manners and language, or sectarian sexual politics, or moral prejudice subsumed under aesthetic formalism, or anti-utopian acquiescence to a counterfeit and vicious social ordering) would have to grant that it is probably one of Lawrence's three best novel-length works, and arguably the best, the truest, of all. In broader perspective, it would seem to require (we might put it tongue in cheek), short-listing as important English fiction among those of at least his generation in Anglo-American literature. Anyway, having perused hundreds of discussions of it, I can find no appropriate contrary case which responds to what is there. It is an ideological work, of course, and the antagonism is mostly unadmitted contrary ideology, contrary, too, to my qualified ideological affirmation. Lawrence's moving struggle for intensified desire and the requisite social negation of green utopianism, however sometimes idiosyncratic and strident, should be allowed its proper claim on us.

4

Lawrence's Desiring and Negating American Progeny: Henry Miller, Norman Mailer, and Some Melvilleans

Some of the more striking heritages of D. H. Lawrence may be found in ways only tangential to the dark prophecy of Lawrencean Nietzscheanism that I discussed earlier, and, indeed, tangential to much of what Lawrence did, though nonetheless strong responses. For major example, there is a tradition of American insurgent writers who took the British figure as cynosure of sexual sensibility, prophet of Dionysian religiousness, and apocalyptic artist-rebel. Part of his attraction seems to have been his powers of both present negation and promised desire. Two of the best-known writers in this Lawrenceanism, a generation apart but overlapping, were Henry Miller and Norman Mailer. To my social as well as reading eye, there appear to be quite a number of others of lesser note. There has also been a tradition of interpreters of Herman Melville who drew prophetic lessons from Lawrence on Melville. While these two inheritances provide only part of Lawrence's effect on American literature and other responses, they do seem to appropriately illustrate Lawrence's cultural role.

Many of these writers seem to have identified with Lawrenceanism from defiant bohemian and later socially marginalist erotic perspectives, in spite of arch-ideologues (such as Norman O. Brown and Susan Sontag, and then some variety of feminists) emphasizing that Lawrence was sexually reactionary. Perhaps the rebellious writers did not primarily respond to Lawrence that way because as often notorious "bad boys" of American letters, they needed Lawrence as a defiant sexual precursor. Though literary practitioners, they also did not primarily respond to Lawrence as novelist, tale teller, and poet. Instead, Lawrence for them was a shamanistic, though often also perplexing, culture hero. To take him up and on was to cast one's self in a role of high defiance as sexual ideologue and apocalyptic artist. The mantle was that of passion's prophet.

Henry Miller, Buffoon with the Apocalyptic

The last book Henry Miller supervised the publication of, and which appeared a few weeks after his death in 1980, was *The World of Lawrence, A Passionate Appreciation*.[1] It was also, as a manuscript, one of his earliest books (the subtitle was probably a late, and rather defensive, addition). Half a century before, Miller, but little published, had been an enthusiast of not only some of Lawrence's writings but of what he took to be the Lawrencean *Weltanschauung*, which he partly saw in terms of an earlier enthusiasm for Nietzsche, and the extension of that into Oswald Spengler's *Declines of the West*. He was apparently looking for an updating of such prophecies. When Miller's first book to be published was accepted (by Obelisk Press, Paris, in 1932—the process is summarized in the editors' introduction to *The World of Lawrence*), he was asked to write a small book (Miller elsewhere refers to it as a "brochure") on a favorite, serious and reputable author, Lawrence, which would be published before, and pave the way to possible literary acceptance of, *Tropic of Cancer*. He was encouraged in this by a deep and dear friend who was an admirer of the subject, Anaïs Nin; she had just completed *D. H. Lawrence: An Unprofessional Study*.[2] Nin (as is evident in her *Diary*) not only encouraged Miller's Lawrence project but discussed the issues and provided books unknown to Miller, such as the especially crucial, to the American, essays of *Reflections on the Death of a Porcupine*, which he seems to have taken to as "wisdom literature."[3] Miller worked obsessively on his Lawrence project, which grew increasingly ambitious, through most of 1933 (eight hundred pages of manuscript, he later reported to Bradley Smith)[4] but did not have a publishable book before *Tropic of Cancer* (1934). He did later publish as essays some revised parts of the Lawrence manuscript, which he seems to have intermittently worked on in the following years: "Creative Death" in a periodical, then as the lead piece in *Wisdom of the Heart* (1941), which also included another essay around Lawrence (as essentially Jesus Christ), "Into the Future"; "Shadowy Monomania" appeared in *Sunday After the War* (1944), which one critic argued was the most coherent and insightful of his many otherwise usually poor literary discussions; and "The Universe of Death" (in a Paris collection in 1938, then in America in *The Cosmological Eye* [1939]), which a noted and influential critic of the postwar period, Philip Rahv, called "a truly inspired piece of criticism."[5] In a later letter to Nin, Miller suggested, with usual loose portentousness, that his finishing the Lawrence book would be the final summation of his writing life and its meaning (in *World of Lawrence*, p. 22). The Lorenzo phoenix had already risen again in a rather odd way.

However peculiar Miller's obsession with Lawrence, for more than a decade the dead contemporary (Miller was only six years younger) appears crucial to him. There are also citations to Lawrence in a number of other Miller writings (as, typically, with Lawrence as victim-of-the age artist in *Black Spring*)[6] and allusions and imitations in a number of other places. It has been cogently contended that Miller's indiscriminate effusions making up his pseudo-mystical travel book on Greece, *The Colossus of Maroussi* (1941), is a muddled but ecstatic parody of Lawrence's Italian travel writings.[7] Certainly it pursues the passional spirit of place in some of Lawrence's senses, though rather murkily emphasizing Miller's feelings rather than much sense of person or place or time. It is offensive only in the poor writing.

Other Lawrencean elements in Miller may be seen as rather the parody of a parody, as he adapts what he repeatedly claims to be his favorite American author, Sherwood Anderson, in sensual self-discovery and social breakout, in which Anderson was much influenced by Lawrence. (This is discussed in Miller's *Books in My Life*, and repeated early and late, though apparently more for the self-mythicizing Anderson of *A Story Teller's Story* than for the most influential, poignantly awkward sketches of *Winesburg, Ohio* or the would-be Lawrencean sensualism of *Dark Laughter*.)[8] Miller in an Anderson-cum-Lawrence way was to obsessively create his own conversion self-discovery mythology (as in the books collectively entitled *The Rosy Crucifixion*). More specifically, late Lawrence provided sanctions for Miller's emphasis on sexuality, including the use of obscene language. Indeed, Miller took the bellicosely unbalanced view of *Lady Chatterley's Lover* that "only wherein it is obscene is it magnificent; in its obscenity lies its great purity, its miraculous, its sacred quality. The rest, that padding, that cotton-wool in which the visions are often wrapped, is the dead weight . . ." (Miller, *World of Lawrence*, p. 176). It is unclear whether the Lawrence "padding" consists of *Chatterley* turning sexuality towards romance and family and utopianism, or in a number of respects subordinating obscenity

102

in the order of traditional fiction. Fractured Miller generally had little sense of the novel as a reading experience, and also of Lawrence as a utopian social critic. And, of course, Miller's obscenity, in its genially alienated, lower-class colloquialism of the streets, which some plausibly argue is his main contribution to American literature,[9] is that of the "cunt-happy" American Joes dallying with whores (and each other) which Miller reports so effectively, and the adaption of surreal extremity into American hyperbole (as in "The Land of Fuck").[10] Both are distant, indeed, from Lawrence's sacral, tender and pastoral-ritualistic eroticism (though sometimes bitter and contentious, as previously discussed) in *Lady Chatterley's Lover*. Norman Mailer was right in his essays around Miller (especially in his anthology, *Genius and Lust*)[11] to emphasize that Millerean sexuality was above all emphatic "male lust" in contrast to the far more feminine and transforming Lawrence.

The earlier writer also had rather more ambivalent and restrictive views of obscenity.[12] Millerean obscenity is often lustily comic and hyperbolically fantastic, not transcendent in its claims. The analogous censoring of *Chatterley* and the *Tropics* may for a generation have confused for some the drastic differences. Miller certainly recognized it, as in poignantly noting in a would-be erotic letter written in his eighties (to a sexually skittish young woman who was using him as a grandfatherly patron): "I wish God had given me the gift of writing about sex like D. H. Lawrence."[13] Lawrence, but hardly ever Miller, however much he admired it, wrote about sexuality as part of a passionate eroticism of transforming religious dimensions. Not Miller, and many other would-be Lawrenceans.

The rather different, fascinating and repellant, sides of Lawrence that Miller could use (perhaps unconsciously), seem evident later in the portrait of Moricand (the long "Devil in Paradise" section of *Big Sur and the Oranges of Hieronymous Bosch*),[14] which has striking parallels to Lawrence's introduction to Maurice Magnus's *Memoirs of the Foreign Legion*[15] (and which, noted later, Miller had appreciatively read). Yet other influences include, it seems strongly probable, the sanction of Lawrence's example of the literary artist as subjective metaphysical essayist, which was shortly after his early works to become a dominant, though not very successful, quasi-genre for Miller (many of the essays in *The Wisdom of the Heart*, *The Cosmological Eye*, and other collections.). But it was above all Lawrence as victim-artist and prophetic culture hero which dominates Miller's conscious responses to him.

Yet, oddly, when Miller comes to write an absurd list of "The Hundred Books Which Influenced Me Most,"[16] there is no mention of Lawrence. One of his favorite artist-thinkers at what most (including Miller) agree was the high point of his writing career, and the one literary canon which he had deeply—indeed, by his own account, obsessively—pursued, has been eliminated. Part of the reason may be that Lawrence's reputation in the decades after his death was limited (until the late 1950s), part may be a process of rejection. Here (and not alone for an erratic sensibility such as Miller's) is one of the curious anomalies of literary heritage and ideological influence: the process of using *and* dismissing a predecessor in drastic self-revisionism and self-mythologizing, partly to accord with literary fashion, partly to assert one's now-achieved self-importance.

In a brief prefatory note to the reprinting of a Lawrence essay ("The Universe of Death,"), Miller suggested that he hadn't finished the Lawrence opus because of "utter confusion."[17] Apparently some take this as referring to the state of the manuscript around another, and uncongenially unegoistic, subject. But both internal and external evidence suggests that the very meaning and effect of Lawrence for Miller was personal justification, which had become increasingly contradictory because of Miller's personal satisfaction with his sense of his literary self-importance. Indeed, such ambivalence may be a considerable part of the significance and heritage of Lawrence, and not just for Miller. A heritage, of course, is often what one revises and rebels against while expending and exploiting it.

Miller apparently started his book on Lawrence with both intellectual and practical enthusiasms, and became so engaged in the subject, as he wrote years later, "for months, I was truly possessed" with Lawrence.[18] As he also commented while reconsidering his Lawrence opus in the last year of his life, "The [Lawrence] book was virtually dictated to me by the 'guy upstairs' or someone of that order."[19] But the divine dictator apparently also had problems, for as Miller told an earlier interviewer, "I made the sad discovery that my idol [Lawrence] was not the writer I had imagined him to be."[20] And that may be the most interesting issue of *The World of Lawrence*—from Lawrence as cynosure of rebellion to something to be itself rebelled against, negated, and as an influence to be gotten over. (While I won't probe here many other examples, the same pattern seems to often apply to other sometime Lawrenceans as well.) To rather fully know, whatever one's perspective, Lawrence often makes it quite difficult to simply have an affirmative view of him and his writings—a point, of course, that I have been making in various contexts.

Miller's apparently later concluding ruminations to the early book as published were this: "The world of Lawrence now seems to me like a strange island on which for a number of years I was stranded" (*World of Lawrence*, p. 259). Miller acknowledges having "changed" over the years away from Lawrence (p. 260), and concludes almost embarrassedly that Lawrence "made foolish errors, he conducted himself unwisely, he contradicted himself, he diminished himself, he was a bad friend now and then, and a bad husband and lover too. He wrote some bad books, atrocious nonsense too" (p. 263). This may make sense beyond projected self-accusation as he looks back at a predecessor who seems no longer useful. Lawrence, as Miller insistently declared several times in the book, tried to become God, a savior, and failed *as a man* in this ideal pursuit, yet heroically posited a "transfigured life" (p. 263).

Now the process by which Miller, a deeply muddled and fractured egoistic sensibility (which is much of his appeal to many readers), got to this conclusion is not quite clear. But part of it can be followed in the later sections of the book as a revulsion to Lawrence's "femininity": "A potent figure of a man he was not" (*World*, p. 255). Or a bit earlier: "He was an artist, a minor artist with a minor soul," though Lawrence "was one of the few artists of our time who possessed a soul at all," but "a great life-adventurer he was not" (p. 227). A partial underlying cause for this negative side throughout Miller's "passionate appreciation" of Lawrence seems to be the secondary literature of the early period. The reverse hagiography, such as that of John Middleton Murry (his first of three Lawrence studies, *Son of Woman*) and Mable Dodge Luhan (*Lorenzo in Taos*), Miller started out to revise, but he ended up by being strongly influenced by them and their contemning view of Lawrence.[21] In sum, Lawrence was a negative man as well as artist.

Actually, a conflicted view of Lawrence seems evident from the start of Miller's study. He wanted to confirm a very large "visionary" Lawrence, an "aristocrat of the spirit, like Plato, like Jesus, like Buddha," but could hardly help also seeing a different figure, "a modern Don Quixote tilting against the windmills of white idealism" (*World*, p. 37), and a man full of "hatred" who was often "pathetic—*ridiculous*" (p. 39). Not that all the hatred was bad, for some of it confirms Miller's own misogyny (especially directed at American women) since Lawrence was the kind of "mystic genius whom woman always rallies round, vulgarizes, sullies and degrades." The women "don't give a real fuck for the man's philosophy, only as it effects their tickling or would be tickling cunts. They are the real vultures of the age" (*World*, p. 42). In various passages, Miller both accords with and mocks Lawence's harsh treatment of women. But Miller, of course, quite lacked Lawrence's empathy with women (as we see in Lawrence's portrayals of Ursula Brangwen, Alvina Houghton, Lou Witt, Connie Chatterley, et al., to which there are no parallels in Miller's writings). Indeed, this very incapacity of Miller's might be properly summarized by the wry passage in *Tropic of Cancer* in which, fantasizing during a concert, he tries to imagine what it would feel like to be a woman during sexual intercourse, and concludes that all he feels is "a pain in the groin."[22]

But for Miller, the woman-ravaged age, as Lawrence so thoroughly expresses it, is a painfully bad and declining one. Miller's Lawrence (as with the justification for much of his early work) is by way of notions from Nietzsche and from Oswald Spengler's *Decline of the West*, which he constantly paraphrases in his supposed discussion of Lawrence, partly because those sweeping condemnations justify his own alienation and failure, which he is attempting to bootstrap into a self-pitying-rebel literary victory, and which he thought he would also find in Lawrence. But Lawrence was not just aggrandizing himself, or artists, for whom he had little idolatry. He was after more radical denials and a revitalizing vision of the world.

Miller's Lawrence is a womanish antiwoman "religious genius" whose main works are *Reflections on the Death of a Porcupine* (the murky long essay "The Crown" is "Lawrence's mystical best"; "he never surpassed this utterance" [*World*, p. 212]), *Apocalypse*, *Studies in Classic American Literature* (especially the Poe and Whitman studies—Miller doesn't seem to know Melville, which study might also support his perspective [see the following discussion]), the brilliantly harsh introduction to the Magnus *Memoir*, and only incidental passages from the novels. *Sons and Lovers* (mentioned four times) is mostly, following Murry, just the psychological problem with the mother, repeated with Miriam. The briefly cited *Rainbow* and *Women in Love* are, to Miller, attempts to resolve man-woman relationships ("the former showing the disintegrative powers of corruption and the later the creative powers" [*World*, p. 120], which seem to reverse the usual readings, though other Miller allusions seem to reverse the reversal).

Miller, Mailer, and Some Melvilleans

Aaron's Rod ("one of the most important novels Lawrence wrote" [*World*, p. 61]) shows him turning away from his inferiors, women, as part of his self-revelation as "a narcissist of the first water" (*World*, p. 68), a condition Miller well knows.[23] *Kangaroo*, with pathetic absurdity, shows Lawrence turning to males and violent claims to authority (*World*, p. 123), as does *The Plumed Serpent* (*World*, p. 130). Miller never cites the stories or novellas (which some have taken as Lawrence's most achieved art) but does incorporate a few brief points from the poetry and the Italian sketches.

Miller's Lawrence becomes primarily a psychological failure who in compensation became a religious savior: "His hope is to save the world. Art has been only a means to promulgate his ideas." Failing in relationships, partly because of his early blighting, and "forced into isolation, Lawrence makes himself god. He achieves his individual, private union with the cosmos" (*World*, p. 120). Finally Lawrence was dedicated to "Revolt! Only revolt!" (*World*, p. 122). "Unable to save himself he tries to save the world. The savior type is the essentially religious man who has an unusual portion of femininity in his character which comes to represent his spiritual nature" (*World*, p. 127).

In his claims to male authority, Miller says, Lawrence can only miserably and inadequately "bully-rag" his wife and other women. "It is not to criticize him I say this, but to point out the limitations of the . . . savior type" (*World*, p. 132). Indeed, this is also Lawrence's greatness, and made him one with the other intellectual megalomaniacs—"Jesus certainly, and Nietzsche, and Whitman and Dostoevski. All the poets of life, who in denouncing civilization contributed most heavily to the lie of civilization" (*World*, p. 136). I would guess that he means that the defiers enshrinement of the opposed civilization continued its irrelevant importance. In this metapsychological interpretation, we arrive at the ironically positive role of the great negators. Lawrence, and the others, took culture too seriously, instead of buffoonishly thumbing their nose at it, as with *Tropic of Cancer*.

However, Miller's ambivalence about Lawrence allows for a partial identification with this redeemer and his "devouring hunger for life" and "ultimate intensity of experience" (*World*, p. 54), while yet rejecting Lawrence for becoming "filled with hatred. He searches frantically for symbols of destruction; he admits of no solutions other than his own . . . this scourge and avenger" (*World*, p. 84). "*He becomes a traitor to the human race*" (*World*, p. 140). That is, given Miller's usual hyperbole, not a very good person in the world. This "neurotic-savior" sadly and "unfortunately had

107

not enough stamina to develop his ideas rigorously" (*World*, p. 191), or he might have resolved his male-female, and other radical, dualisms, proclaims the self-fractured, bumptious American.

Proclaims Miller: "Here is the picture I am trying to paint of Lawrence: the tragic picture of that last man of genius, that last individual rebel, that lone spirit, insisting on having his say" (*World*, p. 174). Lawrence awaits a better age. For modernism is the time of the literature of cancer (Miller's just expounded trope in his first book), of the mortuary "head-culture" of Joyce, Proust, Eliot, Pound, of the "world-as-disease," in which the "Revolution of the Word" (Joyce, a major influence on *Cancer*) is the proper literary "outcome of this sterile dance of death" based in "a profound hatred of humanity" (*World*, pp. 94, 100, 103, 106). Lawrence was also against all that, though finally caught up in it, too. Continuing the prophetic tradition, the "artist-philosopher" (the related Nietzsche was the "philosopher-artist") is "the logical culmination, the apotheosis of two thousand years of Christian idealism, now gone over to its opposite" emphasis on the flesh and intense immediate experience (*World*, p. 199). Miller, I suggest, has a strong insight into Lawrence here, including the emphasis on his insistent effort to "make the world religious and [yet] godless," and to continue the radically prophetic tradition, including an earnest utopianism of changing the world (which idealism Miller cannot abide). In the process, Miller had also pretty much discovered that he cannot abide much of Lawrence's actual "art": The "lesserworks" which will fade away (*World*, p. 233), only the "visionary" caught in "creative death" will remain. There "is something lacking, something sterile and artificial about his characters and novels; they do not sum up his ideas" adequately (*World*, p. 223). Though Miller does not specifically say so, much of Lawrence's art, especially his sometimes old-fashioned sense of the novel and style, were antithetical to one who had identified his artistic and personal liberation with dadaistic burlesque and surrealistic fragmentation and other rhetorical pyrotechnics.

Lawrence, cosmic rebel but not artistic vanguardist, was the archetypal and revolting visionary "artist," overreaching and misunderstood. Such turned out to be Miller's real, and self-justifying, subject. And so much of his redundant essay consists of rather pretentious, free-floating abstractions about the "artist" in uncongenial times, and his defiance of the age. Miller's Lawrence "spent himself in an effort to restore a feeling, a [religious] view of the world, which in this age it seems impossible to summon" (*World*, p. 246).

In sum, Miller had ended up both identifying with Lawrence in his artist-prophet role (and even ambivalently in his hatred of woman, that "vulture," "black widow spider," and "praying mantis"), and in his rejection of the inadequacy of the very Joycean "head-culture" of the word which had so influenced Miller, as well as in his cultural negation and revolt, and yet rejecting both the art and the man. As Miller aptly notes toward the end of his study, "It seems as if an appreciation of Lawrence must always be half-antagonistic. Perhaps the reason for this is that conflict is what he himself best expressed" (*World*, p. 203). For "Lawrence's whole life was a struggle and his philosophy of life was based on a sense of struggle. This is the Dionysian view of truth apprehended not through the intellect, but through passionate experience" (*World*, p. 211). Surely this point is well taken. Lawrence's essentially oppositional nature—his own male/female polarity as well as polarity with the world—was finally for Miller the intriguing power of him, reasonably enough. But Miller really wanted something easier, a self-justification by excusing all in art (which at some points he dubiously attributes to Lawrence [*World*, p. 255]). Or Miller wanted amoral acceptance (as in *Tropic of Cancer*), with a kind of Nietzschean "converting the fatality itself into . . . the highest form of self-creation" (*World*, p. 230). Or he wanted an easy subjectivist religiosity, with which he concludes the book, though he more wisely noted earlier that "when we eliminate God by becoming God [as Miller was clearly to do in many of his later works] there is no longer any struggle" into art or thought (*World*, p. 234). More simply put, Miller's immersion in Lawrence strongly influenced him while simultaneously encouraging him and repelling him. He could thus make use of Lawrence—a Lawrence less of the best art than as a superior but failed "visionary"—but in rather un-Lawrencean ways.

Miller had started with a slight acquaintance with the literature and a sense of Lawrence as the prophetic artist and life-affirmative countermodernist. As he swam himself in the subject, he found Lawrenceanism more encompassingly perplexed, destructive, and oppositional, even to him. The perplexity may have been discouraging, even threatening, since the immersion in Lawrence, and the attempt to write a whole book about him, was probably the single largest and most organized intellectual effort Miller ever attempted. Seeking both ideological and personal self-justification, rebel-buffoon Miller realized that he was at sea with Lawrence, who had gone beyond such personal solace, and so Miller turned back to the land of his bumptious American egotism and optimistic vagaries, though the immersion had permanently soaked him, and become an inevitable part not only of the Millerean but of the larger heritage of Lawrenceanism as the heroically passionate.

Norman Mailer as Lawrencean Ideologue

More than a generation later, Mailer, American cosmopolitan and exhibitionistic man-of-letters, who took on some variety of roles as American provocateur and exploitative self-publicist with a striking mixture of vivacious intellectual perception and gross silliness, also hardly appears to be a "natural" Lawrencean, yet was to insist that he was. On the basis of Mailer's early fictions, I do not see much significant connection with Lawrence. Indeed, *The Naked and the Dead* and *Barbary Shore*, with their "progressive" ideology and predominantly naturalistic fictional mode, around the American Pacific campaign in World War II and postwar New Yorker intellectual politics, seem to have little of the Lawrencean.

That applies to the public persona as well.[24] It is hard to see much of frail and self-exiled Lawrence in Mailer's aggrandizing roles in the mass media, New York and protest politics, and, for example, rather literal theologizing of professional boxing. For two decades Mailer went in for shock effects, flamboyant identifications, belligerent stances rather for his own sake—though he often combined them with considerable earnestness (this was what may have most shocked clever intellectual snobs)—to produce, as he himself labeled it, *Advertisements for Myself* (1959). Mailer rather spoiled his taste as provocateur-defier, whether practiced in awkward novels or other literary and subliterary forms, by cloying it with adolescent sweets or exploitative popular goodies. He simultaneously wanted to be a charming middle-aged rebel, a celebrity who was yet grand artist, and a serious ideologue who was also big business. Apparently he turned over a lot of money. Dying Lawrence, of course, did spend himself peddling *Lady Chatterley's Lover* and somewhat self-parodying journalistic bits (though when one looks through the notebooks he kept in the 1920s, with expenditures listed in the pence, one sees the true son of an English petty bourgeois mother).[25] But perhaps only in America could one claim, as Mailer did, radical social criticism yet identify with the empty political style of John

Miller, Mailer, and Some Melvilleans

Kennedy, pose as sexual revolutionary yet elaborate lusting fantasies about manipulative cold or schizophrenic public women (Jackie Kennedy, Marilyn Monroe), and indulge in a wide variety of narcissistic power ploys and profit plays. But he did so not without some self-mockery: "You can't grow up in America without thinking once in a while about becoming president. But since I'm an anarchist, I try not to think about that too much."[26] Horatio Alger as revolutionist of sensibility. This is pretty Americanism, the simultaneous lust for power and for liberation.

But perhaps the Lawrence influence was indirect, other than "literary." I note that partly because Jeffrey Meyers, in his compact but ranging and researched introduction to a collection of studies on Lawrence's influence, quotes a letter to him (1985) from Mailer which includes the claim that he read *Lady Chatterley's Lover* in 1941 at Harvard and that it long powerfully influenced him with its "hypothesis" that "one could not have sex without love, or love without sex." And he says that he admired Lawrence's other works (though no specifications of which or when he read them) and thinks that with them he was a "great writer," "but *Lady Chatterley* changed my life."[27] By this, he seems to mean his "sex life" rather more than his literary life, exemplified no doubt in his many marriages. I suspect that Lawrence's influence on styles and feelings of sexual love, which after all was part of his purpose, has been considerable, though it is something hard to demonstrate in textual examples.

My concern here is primarily with Mailer's writings, though of course we may grant their dependence on his erotic experiences, and problems. The influence of other, and quite different, writers than Lawrence (Dos Passos, for example) is evident on Mailer's early fiction, and the announced lineage from Lawrence may be a later self-reconstruction. (I am not criticizing the possible discrepancy, for I think some of it inevitable, and that most do it.) Yet glomming on to the Lawrence heritage seems to have been of increasing ideological importance to Mailer as he searched for a radical role. With his ideologizing from the mid-1950s on, we can plausibly note linkages. I suppose we might see a bit of Lawrencean sexuality (per the sodomy scene in *Lady Chatterley's Lover*) in the story "The Time of Her Time" in which the Mailerean protagonist, "messiah of the one-night stand," brings enlightenment to an arch-woman by buggering her, part of an ornate commentary on sexual power plays, perhaps properly updated, however ostensibly reversed, Lawrencean concern.[28] But more importantly, it would be hard for the knowledgeable not to relate Mailer to Lawrence in some ways because of the religious sexuality of apocalyptic proportions and the emphasis on extreme polarities. For the Mailer of this period, sexual actions become "the revelation of meaning through the passionate intercourse of opposites."[29] First expressed in his demonic-decadent Hollywood saga, *The Deer Park*, it receives even more extreme articulation in his fervent speculative essay, "The White Negro," especially in the discussion of "the apocalyptic orgasm."[30] Mailer specifically alludes there to Lawrence's "blood consciousness" (probably with something else in mind than *Lady Chatterley*) in his definitions of the millennial black hipster with his ecstatic potency. He also insists on a Lawrence-like male/female polarity, and an analogous quest for a primal libidinal energy and for radical social change.

In positing his hipster, a combination of megalopolitan black with the bohemian and delinquent, as liberating figure of revolt, Mailer has a fantasy figure of analogous compensatory power to Lawrence's Mexican revolutionary leaders in *The Plumed Serpent* (I am not suggesting any direct influence). Through mystical dispossession of the self, and protective detachment ("cool"), violence, and superlative impersonal libidinousness, the hipster can overcome prevailing confusion, impotence, and emptiness. To insist on localizing the impetus in an American black sophisticate here seems a displaced literalizing for demonic powers, but isn't that also true for Lawrence's Ramon and Cipriano? With a heavy "neo-Marxian calculus" (in place of Lawrence's Nietzscheanized Aztec-mythology-cum-Methodism), Mailer theorizes a socially revolutionary underclass and a psychopathic type as the vanguard for radical change. (More realistically, of course, such types usually turn to ambitious conformities and authoritarian compulsions.) What elsewhere was the virility of the primitivistic or the proletarian became the explosive power of the declassed hipster. While both Mailer and Lawrence made large revolutionary claims, the declassing and demonic mythicizing exalted marginality. It was obviously outside any literal politics. We might well grant Mailer's realistic point that individual barbarism is "always to be preferred to the collective violence of the state" (not least since in its necessarily untechnocratic way it is likely less), but the synthetic black psychopath (or synthetic-primitive Mexican one) seems a dubious image of the rebellious barbarian. While the dark imagery demonically reverses the white-willed denaturing of the flesh and feeling, and the apocalyptic-orgiastic defies the rationalized religion of "science, factology and committee,"[31] in control it would probably be even nastier because less functionally rationalized. Mailer's ambitious mystic-toned rebellion against the dominant manipulators and the re-creation of a religious intensification of experience becomes but manipulation in blackface with defiance reduced to crass power rather than a return to the mysterious sources of existence.

Judiciously, a number of Mailer's notions and tropes may be linked to another Mailer source than Lawrence at the time, the more literal-minded, fantastic-therapeutic sexual cosmology of Wilhelm Reich (widespread with litterateurs in that period—Saul Bellow, Isaac Rosenfield, Paul Goodman, et al.—and sometimes incongruously brigaded with Lawrence).[32] Reichean sexual literalism appealed to Mailer both in its claims for better orgasm and for the cure of disease ("cancer biopathy"). Whether left-Freudian or Lawrencean, the sources helped provide sanctions for what Mailer calls a "mysticism of the flesh."[33] It may be pushing matters a bit to see, as one commentator does, "remarkable similarities between Mailer's mythicized hipster . . . and Lawrence's mythicized instinctual heroes."[34] The violent, megalopolitan, underground hipster is a long way from gamekeeper Mellors, and other of Lawrence's withdrawn and contumacious surrogates. Surely the Mailer and Lawrence contexts and tones are drastically different. Still, there may be broad ideological analogues in the role for each of extreme sexual prophet.

Mailer's best writings of the 1960s, such as the high reportage of *Armies of the Night*, has little evident direct connection with the Lawrencean, except in broad rages against technocracy—as crucial concern—and perhaps in the insistent view of women as "witches."[35] But Mailer's melodramas of the period—*An American Dream* and *Why Are We in Vietnam?*—may be seen as analogous with Lawrence in large mythical ways. The forced sodomy, wife murdering, and absurdist heroics of Mailer's megalomaniac protagonists, as well as the ecstatic sexuality and irascible ideologizing of these two fictions, may keep appropriate company with *The Woman Who Rode Away* and *The Plumed Serpent*. Both sets of fictions project not only nastily vengeant fantasies but result in a fervently heightened bad poetry. Influences can also be ugly things. The writer who doted on wife-murdering fantasies, and who sometimes named his penis "the avenger," was hardly predisposed to be judicious, much less critical, with some of Lawrence's nastiest fantasies. Perhaps the linkage of the two writers is less a matter of literal influence than of similarly exacerbated sensibility, analogous extreme literary "thought experiments," and the now-evident continuation of a tradition of public defiance which had, plausibly enough, become a central part of the Lawrence heritage.

But it wasn't until well into middle-age and late in his career, and as his ideologizing became more defensive, that Mailer turned to a spirited apologetic for Lawrence. Ironically, the impetus may have been less his than that of vociferous feminist critics linking his with Lawrence's perceived misogyny (such as Germaine Greer, et al., but especially with Kate Millet, my discussion of whom in the next chapter I will not repeat here). Mailer's defense of Lawrence, following his defense of Henry Miller, in *The Prisoner of Sex* (1971), was partly self-defense.[36] But it went beyond that in the exaltation of Lawrence as the majestic portrayer of "man and woman fucking with love"—by the "sacramental poet of a sacramental act" (*Prisoner*, p. 98).

Mailer's primary text, of course, was *Lady Chatterley's Lover*, less taken as a whole than for some key sexual passages (he opens and closes the main section of his argument by quoting them). However, he also analyzes a key passage of the Birkin-Ursula polar conflict in *Women in Love* (*Prisoner*, pp. 105–7), comments on several passages of Lawrence's explosive "rage against the will of women" and on his sickly "male love affair" in *Aaron's Rod* (pp. 112–14), makes passing but apt references to *The Rainbow*, *Sons and Lovers*, and *Kangaroo*, and affirmatively utilizes the notorious "Aphrodite of the foam" passage against female orgasm in *The Plumed Serpent* (pp. 108–10). Mailer has certainly done his scholarly-critical homework (as so often, he seems to be writing for and against the professorate). His prophet, in sharp antithesis to Henry Miller's Lawrence, is primarily drawn from the novels, though nonetheless also with an emphatic ideological purpose.

But perhaps most crucial to the conception is Mailer's perception of Lawrence as a product "of the classic family stuff out of which homosexuals are made" (*Prisoner*, p. 111), resulting in an anguished man "with the soul of a beautiful woman" (p. 110), though also Oedipally burdened with "that intolerable masculine pressure to command." As with Miller, Mailer's Lawrence centers on ambivalent masculinity (though treated far more positively in his feminine empathies), a death-obsessed figure not just of gender and life dualisms but of even greater extremities, for "he contained a cauldron of boiling opposites" (p. 100). Such a figure becomes heroically desperate in his "tendencies towards the absolute domination of women by

114

men, mystical worship of the male will," and consequent "detestation of democracy." However, such social politics (always a Mailer concern, unlike the politically obtuse Miller) should not be taken literally. "Lawrence was not only trying to sell dictatorial theorems, he was trying to rid himself of them" (p. 101). This does accord with Lawrence's own acknowledgement, and even more evident practices, that he was using his books to "shed" his illnesses, and with his late rejection of his earlier authoritarianism.

Yet Mailer also takes with great seriousness Lawrence's erotic politics, which he sees as his "deepest messages of sex" which are that male/female love is rightly constituted by total and threatening engagements (*Prisoner*, p. 107). "Lawrence saw every serious love affair as fundamentally do-or-die" (p. 112)—and that it could destroy or that "sex could heal." Indeed, impassioned sex may be the only positive "nostrum" in our horrendously destructive society—for Mailer, a technocracy of lunatic proportions. As defiant erotic prophet, Lawrence is a culture hero.

Mailer's case for Lawrence was made in the context of a counterattack against feminists who had attacked Mailer (and Miller and Lawrence). Some of his arguments are perceptively paradoxical, such as that Lawrence must be treated complexly because he was both a "great writer" and one who often wrote "abominably" (an awareness that marks most of the better responses to Lawrence). He was a man burning "with tender love" though often sunk in humorless tyrannical fantasies. Lawrence, he aptly notes, was also an extreme ideologue yet frequently marked by a "profound British skepticism." He grants the feminists that Lawrence was a "counter-revolutionary sexual politician" who shows "unmistakable tendencies towards the absolute domination of women by men." He also rather dubiously thinks he has answered the anti-Lawrence arguments by showing that they poorly analyze the texts (playing the professor again), and that they fail to recognize that Lawrence appeals to women readers because he wrote with wonderful intimacy about them and so they love his work because they recognize that he is a "sacramental poet" of male/female relations.

But, Mailer insists, one must recognize Lawrence's heroic effort in several ways. For one way, his demand on the erotic: He is "saying again and again, people can win at love only when they lose everything they bring to it of ego, position, or identity" (*Prisoner*, p. 99). Quoting Birkin from *Women in Love*, to reach erotic truth people "have to deliver themselves over to the unknown" (p. 101). Lawrence was also making an heroic demand on himself because the heightened eroticism was underlain by both personal desperation, a "tortured" struggle for manhood of an Oedipal case whose "psyche was originally shaped to be homosexual," and by a not-so-slowly-dying man's quest for transcendence. With heterosexual heroics, and against the limitations of the novel form in *Lady Chatterley's Lover*, Lawrence achieved a final affirmation of man/woman love. Crucially, he did it against the grain of his consciousness as a "beautiful, imperious, and passionate woman" (pp. 110, 113). Now others have noted that Lawrence "was a woman in a man's skin" (Daleski), or "womanish" in sensibility (Miller), or especially "sympathetic" to female consciousness (Nin), but hardly as a major weapon against what Mailer takes to be lesbian views (he shares Lawrence's extreme hostility there). Would-be he-man Mailer has made Lawrence into a she-man companion-in-arms of heroic proportions.

Mailer's provocative interpretation seems especially apt in positively presenting Lawrence as a peculiar sensibility, rather than, as in the majority of literary discussions, strapping him into the merely normative. But Mailer's Lawrence is also used for rather diabolical dogmatics, including against not only feminists rightly dubious about his effects on fairness and equality—or even mere decency—but also, like Lawrence, for denunciations of masturbation and contraception, to which Mailer nastily adds abortion (I can find no comment of Lawrence's on that last, to go with his vehemence against masturbation and contraception). Modern heroizing, of course, is a dubious business, and here, it seems to me, Mailer is driven to using Lawrence for his own existential absurdities. Mailer exploits certain rather inconsistent prejudices in Lawrence who was generally negative on "unnatural" contraception (and sexually—fearfully?—turned off by it). Yet Lawrence, (unlike Mailer, with numerous offspring), was repeatedly insistent on limiting children and our insane overpopulation. Mailer distorts Lawrence for his own rantings against contraception and abortion. Sick stuff.

For both Lawrence and Mailer, such antinatal practices give women too much autonomy from their vulnerability to males, and allow them to escape from the melodrama of sex. But Mailer has, taking off from Lawrence, a much larger argument. To give the largest and most intense "meaning to sex," which is to give primal meaning to life, there must be an innate metaphysics of "fucking." In a magical embryology (*Prisoner*, pp. 142, 152), Mailer insists on finally viewing intercourse less as pleasure and therapy than as portentous affirmation with apparently purposive sperm and eggs. There must, must be a larger meaning in the erotic, and "conception could not be empty of it." Even in tone, it is a sexual metaphysics of desperation. In the right mating, the teleological embryos may even choose their own gender (p. 97). The magical egg is given the power taken away from the mere female person. Male/female sex thus becomes religious dramaturgy in which the polarized genders, as Lawrence certainly emphasized, confront the primal "unknown" in an extreme antithesis of something larger than themselves. The quality of their passion becomes metabiology, and that is really dark revelation for resolving the unresolvable, thus the ultimate paradoxes of the "separate and joined," with which Mailer concludes (p. 115). "Fucking" is no mere play but a productive and portentous melodrama of transcendental proportions. Sex, which would otherwise be feministically ameliorated (really, androgynized) has thus regained conflictful drama, high excitement, and ostensible supra-individual meaning.

Mailerism-cum-Lawrenceanism is appropriately sex as religion. Both reached a nihilistic awareness of the loss of human meaning—traditionally, socially, cosmically—for which they sought replacement with erotic primal meaning (and, apparently, compensatory sexual experience). The Lawrencean sexual metaphysics seems to promise a pervasive sense of erotic intensification, and one rather beyond good and evil. Thus it is only a secondary consideration that it engenders polarization, male/female conflict, including the mystery and threat of pregnancy, and mere injustice and indecency. Just more drama, struggle, purpose. Lesser lusty goats such as Henry Miller, though also attracted to adaptable Lawrence gender doctrine in the insistent American he-man overassertion, apparently recognized some of this as "atrocious nonsense," and turned away. But in some senses, so too did Mailer. There is little that seems directly Lawrencean in, say, the sexual fantasies of *Marilyn* (1973) or *Tough Guys Don't Dance* (1984; including Mailer's movie melodrama of that name), except possibly a general erotic intensity, though one Lawrence would certainly have found repulsive in its rococo heightening and sex-in-the-head fantasizing, and some ambivalent worship-revenge against women. Perhaps, though, a case could be made for something analogous to the Lawrencean in the nihilistic romance in *The Executioner's Song* (1979). The obsessive, more-than-a-thousand pages, of lavish documentary-novel devoted to the life and loves, and murders and execution, of Gary Gilmore not only takes the ordinary, thuggish, with high intensity but discovers in it a total love and death romanticism, though one appropriately corrupted and annihilated by ordinary America.

And perhaps there shows through also a larger sense of Mailer's relation

Defiant Desire

to Lawrenceanism. In spite of his avowal (previously quoted) of the early, and continuing, powerful significance of Lawrence to him, and in spite of his use of elements of Lawrence (in his sexual-apocalyptic hipster philoso-phizing), and in spite of his fervent and insightful exposition of Lawrence as central to his own sexual ideology (in *The Prisoner of Sex)*, and in spite of a more broad similarity of concern, indeed obsession, with such Lawrencean themes as male/female conflict in polarity, existential erotic metaphysics, and a role of social and cultural defiance, oh-so-American Mailer had other fishy things to fry. The vulgar metaphor seems necessary to direct emphasis to the very large qualification that whatever Mailer was using, and writing, was partly subordinated, though never quite submerged, in his very American aggrandizement. The intellectual positions seem overwhelmed by vanity and money. Mailer had to play Mr. Big in the New York intellectual scene, and in the pantheon of American fictionists in spite of not being at his best as a novelist (the repeated sparring comparisons with Hemingway, and others). Much was self-promotion (*Advertisements*, he made clear, was partly engendered by his resentment, as a previous critical and commercial success, at not getting the attention he thought he deserved for *The Deer Park*). He exploited the most crass kinds of self-aggrandizement: running for mayor of New York, getting arrested early at the Pentagon protest in hopes of making it to an important party of the noted, again and again taking up fat writing contracts for front-page newspa-per topics such as presidential campaigns and space rockets and famous suicides and executions, or enviously identifying with celebrities in boxing and film and politics, or chairing writers' conferences and attending MLA conventions, or taking up the misogynist cudgels for D. H. Lawrence. Not to strongly qualify everything of Mailer's, including his Lawrenceanism, with an awareness of the extreme self-aggrandizing context would seem to be intellectually dishonest. And after all, to be the contemporary American Lawrencean—a role variously tried on by Sherwood Anderson and Henry Miller and Tennesee Williams (and numerous less well-known figures)—would seem to be appropriate stance for the rebellious but ambitious litter-ateur.

Where Henry Miller, at a shrewd pornographic publisher's suggestion, and with the support of a lover and several friends (Anaïs Nin and Walter Lowenfels who had already written on Lawrence, and others) took up writing a book on Lawrence to give some serious intellectual, artistic coloration to the forthcoming *Tropic of Cancer* (which is not to deny that

118

the subject was already of enthusiastic post-Nietzschean interest for him, and that he intermittently pursued it for years beyond that unsuccessful plan), so we may see ulterior motives affecting Mailer's use of and apologetic for Lawrence. Lawrence, to adapt current cant, was a role model for the literary, rebellious, sexual ideologue. Miller had to partly be led into his somewhat uncongenial use of the model; Mailer, a generation later (and with the enlargement of Lawrence's intellectual and popular reputation), probably did not need outside encouragement to do the quick-witted and *au courant* use of Lawrence (and of Henry Miller, then at the height of his inevitably declining reputation). Such, in significant part, are how literary and other intellectual influences are often manufactured and marketed in contemporary America.

Granted, Lawrenceanism also provided an intensified and demanding responsiveness for these rebelliously assertive as well as crassly aggrandizing American males and their barbaric yawps. Lawrenceanism helped provide, at crucial stages, defiant self-sanctions in an overreaching sexual ideology. But it also seems that it was perplexed and difficult to enduringly live with and by. Lawrence was useful, but finally not all that useful, for the aggrandizing Americans. Such writers were in rebellion both for and against the Lawrencean—perhaps the most appropriate heritage for the prophet of passion.

The critical reader might plausibly object that not only were Miller and Mailer dissimilar (Mailer, according to his enthusiastic excursus on Miller in *Genius and Lust*, does not agree, though he is obviously the far more intelligent, accomplished, and interesting writer), but that both were far, indeed, from Lawrence. Were not the usages, then, by the Brooklyn buffoon and the intellectual hipster just idiosyncratic as well as exploitative? (Pretentious theories of influence, such as Harold Bloom's, quite ignore most of this cultural reality.) I also suggest that Miller and Mailer were not just being idiosyncratic and exploitative, for they did in their ways perceive true things about the Lawrencean, not least the deep spirit of gender struggle, erotic transformation, and social revolt, and Lawrence against himself.

The Curious Melville Interpreters by Way of Lawrence

Much other use of Lawrence has also been idiosyncratic, yet pertinent, too. Take an apparently quite different example of Lawrence influence,

119

British yet un-English in not stockily placing him in romantic naturism and Midlands working-class purposes. In an early, and one of her witty best, fictions, the British novelist of intellectual moral manners, Iris Murdoch, deploys a major motif in *A Severed Head* which must quite consciously come from Lawrence.[37] This is the "dark gods"—that favorite Lawrence metaphor—who are linked, both in authorial mind and in that of her would-be romantic lover (Martin Lynch-Gibbon), with the enigmatic central figure of Honor Klein. A compound totemic figure—mythic, alien dark Jewess; incestuous anthropologist with a samurai sword to sever consciousness with primitive powers; an unbeautiful but intense creature with the "searing presence of a god"—she becomes the object of a transformation experience. The result is an erotic conversion into something "deeper than ordinary knowledge," leading not to mere "happiness" but to primal struggle and new identity. Shockingly placed in the polished confines of a cultivated London upper–middle class, and the prevailing cult of psychoanalysis (deliciously mocked for its endless regressions and manipulative reductions), it is also a game of sexual musical chairs (a kind of positive redoing of *Les Liasons Dangereuse*). With almost endless ironies, it is quite un-Lawrencean in its witty dallying, yet curiously is Lawrencean in its affirmation of his central mythology of sundering dark eros.

Examples of such strange yet confirming use of Lawrence could be multiplied. To just note in passing a more recent one: Martin Amis in *London Fields* (1989) gives his reversed femme fatale an unexpected "weakness" for her favorite writer, D. H. Lawrence, though "he can be a complete embarrassment. But the *expressiveness* is the thing."[38] And the awed puzzlement in extremity is the way to it.

However, I want to return to my concern here with the quite different (partly because less class-defined) sea changes of the rebellious Americanization of Lawrence by briefly pursuing some of the odd history of Lawrence as progenitor of the modernist American Melville. Apparently Lawrence fortuitously read a friend's copy of *Moby Dick* in 1916.[39] As part of his rejection of his provincial origins, and probably further encouraged by his rage against Britain and the Great War, Lawrence was reaching out for various other writings and values (as he had earlier with Nietzsche, as previously discussed), and his purposes might be described as prophetic. By 1918 Lawrence was publishing versions of a group of essays he had sketched out on nineteenth-century American literature—the interest had turned into a project—though he did not publish in a periodical, unlike some of the others, the one he had apparently done on *Moby Dick*. In 1922 he had completed rewritings of the pieces and published them in what was to be his most influential literary commentaries, *Studies in Classic American Literature*. Prior to his final revisions of the Melville essays, he had evidently read American scholar Raymond M. Weaver's *Herman Melville: Mariner and Mystic* (1921), the rather unprobing study sometimes credited with the "Melville Revival," since he echoes several of its points.[40] Weaver, however, neither started nor much shaped Lawrence's apocalyptic view of Melville. Lawrence's critically taking up the in many ways uncongenial Melville at such an unfashionable time, and in such a high manner, is certainly striking, and another credit to Lawrence's often distinctive sensibility and role.

Lawrence's sharply iconoclastic essays on American literature are not, of course, scholarly in purpose or tone nor are they, in most conventional senses, literary criticism. Rather, they are a curious combination of personal essay, jeering broad polemic, and prophetic religious rumination which became somewhat hysterically wisecracking in the critic's exacerbated revisions while living in America—compare *Studies* with the earlier versions now published as *The Symbolic Meaning*.[41] While the *Studies* seem to have had but little public response in Lawrence's time, in the World War II period, long before Lawrence's revival, a doyen of American literary and cultural criticism, Edmund Wilson, impressed, and impressively, reprinted them in their entirety.[42] In the postwar years, they were readily available and often cited in their provocative role. But I will suggest some provocation from the start.

For Lawrence in *Studies*, America's nineteenth-century writers "reached the pitch of extreme consciousness" (p. 2), which is a radicalness of view hardly congenial to most patriotic commentators. Aware of this, and of the repressive order of the writers' times, Lawrence holds that they self-consciously used "subterfuge" and "double meanings" which now need to be exposed. (Here was a program for what was to become an interpretive industry.) Consequently, in a brief survey chapter, "The Spirit of Place," Lawrence insists on countering the duplicity by "saving the American tale from the American artist" (*Studies*, p. 13) since the story rightly interpreted can reveal the truth often defensively obscured by the lying American writer in his national pose of innocence, optimism, and freedom—characteristics that the bitterly war-disenchanted and socially-culturally negating Lawrence would not accept. In sad fact, according to Lawrence, Americans exist in terrible isolation in their purely negative freedom from authority and community. (This is the period of Lawrence's most desperately authoritarian "leadership" novels and essays.) Thus Americans come out less as a new hummankind than as recreant Europeans, quite lacking positive freedom in their flight from ancient authority and community. In this disenchanted perspective, Americans necessarily lack full and rich humanity, and are anxiously in search of it.

This holds especially pertinent to Melville. In the first of his two chapters on Melville, primarily on *Typee* and *Omoo*, Lawrence finds the underlying Melville antihuman, expressive of the "Viking" and "Northern" antilife values in contrast with warmer-blooded Mediterranean culture and people. Whatever its applicability to Melville, this contrast had been emphasized much earlier, as in Lawrence's prewar Italian sketches (*Twilight in Italy*) and in his middle-period novels, as with the ending of *Women in Love*, and the scenic action of *The Lost Girl* and *Aaron's Rod,* as well as in his self-exiling preferences. The contrast of Northern and Mediterranean sensibilities has, of course, a long European history, many intellectual formulations (perhaps with its nineteenth-century culmination in Nietzsche), and holds a significant place in other twentieth-century modernist writers (Forster and Ford, Giono and Camus), and even plays a significant role in Pound and Faulkner) As Lawrence wanted to see it, the dominating Northern European recreant Americans, who negatively fled European culture, developed an extreme Northern fear of sensuality and human responsiveness. So with Lawrence's Melville: "Never did a man instinctively hate human life, our human life . . . more than Melville did" (*Studies*, p. 145). Melville's South Sea adventures were a desperate and faltering attempt to escape the Northern puritanism, a search for the paradisiacally ideal in the primitive. But Lawrence also identifies with this desperate quest, with good reason; however, "We can't go back. And Melville couldn't" (p. 149).

Lawrence's Melville also tried in the picaresque *Omoo* to identify with the rebelliously roguish but was afraid of it. Bound to the antilife American pursuit of the "ideal" (for some time idealism-as-repression had been Lawrence's ideological *bête noir*, as evident in a long range of essays and fictions, previously discussed), Melville was trapped in religious moralism and restriction, including conventional marriage and a life of disillusionment, after he dallied in his early fictions with fleeing it. Lawrence, of course, had long been fleeing his own repressive and puritanical-provincial upbringing. Citing Melville's *Pierre* (probably second-handedly from

Weaver, since he shows no other sense of it), Lawrence insists that Melville reveals that "the old pure ideal in itself becomes an impure thing of evil" (*Studies*, p. 154). Even without the bad *Pierre*, Lawrence views Melville as "writhing" all his life because of his demands for the ideal in morality, marriage, friendship, and belief. Thus Melville denied rich, tangible human responsiveness—"he refused life" (p. 155).

However extremely he put it, surely Lawrence perceived something importantly Melvillean. While many have noted of Melville his drastic inadequacy in presenting male/female relationships, and the often guiltily punitive and anxiously forlorn emphasis, it was only later seen as significantly homoerotic.[43] But Lawrence is preoccupied with another issue—his persisting existential attack on Christianity and the essentialist idealism related to it. In viewing Western idealism as a fundamental falsity—dualistic, rationalistic, antisensual, unholistic, conservative—he sees Melville as caught up in the same issues. Lawrence repeatedly announces that he has himself given up on idealism, but concludes that Melville had not. In his sweeping comments, then, he sees Melville as a symptomatic victim of the duplicitous American form of diseased Western consciousness.

Lawrence's longer chapter on *Moby Dick* takes a more exalted view of Melville's struggles of consciousness. He relishes quoting at length some of the novel's better representative passages because it is "a great book," a "surpassingly beautiful book." But at the same time he is the hard-nosed critic: "Nobody can be more clownish, more clumsy and sententiously in bad taste, than Herman Melville even in a great book like *Moby-Dick*" (*Studies*, p. 157). Lawrence reasonably senses that Melville is often "not sure of himself," "amateurishly" pontificating, sometimes a "solemn ass," and quite unable to deal with "human contacts" (p. 158). Part of the appeal of Lawrence as a literary commentator is just such full, extreme responsiveness.

Curiously but typically, Lawrence turns some of his negative criticism into the positive. Melville's very lack of full human dimensions—the abstractionism in *Moby Dick*—provides his power in profoundly recording "the extreme transitions of the isolated, far-driven soul" (*Studies*, p. 159). Such explorations, of course, confirm Lawrence's theme of the radically peculiar and alienating characteristics of American culture. Lawrence is also strongly aware of the strange but representative American-ness of *Moby Dick* in its combination of the documentary and the metaphysical. He notes the exaggerated efficiency of "American industry" (whaling) combined with an antithetical poetic overreaching—"all this practicality in the service of a mad, mad chase" (p. 162). Lawrence makes other suggestive points as well. He is, so far as I can find, the first to emphasize the "phallicism" of "The Cassock" chapter around the whale's penis. He also praises Melville's powerful poetry of nonhuman, non-anthropomorphized, nature—so different from romantic subjectivism and Victorian sentimentalization—which was the direction in which Lawrence's own nature descriptions had been moving, what now would be called a biocentric rather than anthrocentric view of the natural world. Melville, in sum, was the great poet in American prose.

The heart of the poem of *Moby Dick*, as Lawrence recognized it, shows the destructively "extended consciousness" of "northern monomania," with the *Pequod* as the "symbol of this civilized world of ours" (*Studies*, p. 172). Melville's deeper purpose is to reveal our—not just his—"fatality," the "doom of our white day." The American imagination, despite its guise of energetic innocence, reveals the furthest apocalyptic reaches of this doomed Western civilization.

"What then is Moby Dick? He is the deepest blood-being of the white race." Ahab's quest is to destroy that being, guided "by the maniacal fanaticism of our white mental consciousness" (*Studies*, p. 173). As Lawrence's concluding elliptical interpretation adds, "Jesus, the Redeemer, was Cetus, Leviathan. And all the Christians his little fishes" (p. 174). Apparently, then, Melville pursuing his whale subterfuge was out God killing—properly so, since our great white father is the enemy of sensual and psychic wholeness. Melville thus exposed, for those willing to see through the tale's very American subterfuges, the necessary nihilism (in the Nietzschean sense) of humanly abstracting and falsifying Western civilization.

Lawrence's interpretation may not be altogether consistent; for example, the white whale is both deepest "blood-being" and white Christian God— antithetical terms in Lawrence. But such commentary less aims to be systematic than suggestive and provocative. (Otherwise it would turn into the viciously dehumanized structure of a symbolist or archetypal philosophy—something, I think, Lawrence often dallied with but never quite submited to.) The main suggestion seems to be that Melville, in spite of his terrible idealistic self-defeat, struggles into a tale revealing the nuclear conflict of white American consciousness, its abstracting doom. And what of America since its prophet? As Lawrence mockingly noted earlier, with a quite un-American sense of fixity, it is just mostly "post-mortem effects" (*Studies*, p. 173).

Lawrence's Melville, of course, has been drastically selected to somewhat hyperbolically emphasize only a few key issues in the early novels and *Moby Dick*. His fascination with significant parts of American culture was purposeful, but not personally literary. Surveying all of Lawrence's novels, tales, and essays, I am not aware of any significant allusion to Melville. Nor did he take on the portentous documentary manner of *Moby Dick*, never elaborating any "industry" or parallel way of life (not even coal mining or gamekeeping). Nor did he have much sympathy with the Melvillean imitation of Shakespearean tragedy. (Anyway, Lawrence had a considerably negative view of Shakespeare and bardolatry, as we see early in the discussion of *Hamlet* in *Twilight in Italy* or late in the verses "When Reading Shakespeare.")[44] The usual issues of literary "influence" do not seem pertinent. What he did instead was make a large statement about American consciousness by way of an apocalyptic mythology with Melville as culture hero.

That last may have had "influence" in future directions. A few brief examples follow. Hart Crane, a half-generation younger, seems to have admiringly read Lawrence's *Studies* (indicated in his letters, as noted by earlier commentators).[45] However, Crane may well have read *Moby Dick* before he read Lawrence's essay. Becharmed with Melville's ornate style and portentous symbolism, reinforced by such readings as Lawrence's, he came to see the white whale as "a metaphysical image of the universe."[46] Crane used Melville several times in his poems, making him his American sea-culture hero, most notably in a sixteen-line elegy, "At Melville's Tomb," which is one of his strange poetic arguments for a visionary reach without a recognizable vision.[47] But as Lawrence had in effect predicted, Crane's transcendental yearnings "came a cropper"; the America of bridging sacramental mythos turned out to be machined fakes leading to a "dead conclusion" in the despairing rage of the alienated wanderer (as in Crane's crucial "Key West").[48] Lawrence, all I am suggesting, may have contributed in several senses to the use of Melville and the exaltation-disillusionment of the mystical-romantic Hart Crane.

Another, and rather more emphatic, example, is Charles Olson, New England poet, legendary progenitor of the "Black Mountain school," Melville scholar-critic, admirer of D. H. Lawrence (see, for example, the gnomic "The Escaped Cock, Notes on Lawrence and the Real,") and self-defined "mythographer" of a peculiarly American imagination. Olson seems to have consciously continued the Lawrencean approach to Melville.[49] In his noted small volume *Call Me Ishmael*, he elliptically combined dry-influence scholarship (Melville's reading of Shakespeare and whaling narratives) with gnomic and ecstatic pronouncements: "I am willing to ride Melville's image of man, whale and ocean to find in him prophecies, lessons he himself would not have spelled out." This Lawrencean method aims to discover primal American meanings in a "myth, *Moby-Dick*, for a people of Ishmaels."[50]

The method and purpose may be similar to Lawrence's, but some of Olson's insightful points are partly of the cast of a later time. He views the whaling industry as a way of projecting the America that was developing, a maniacal commercial-technological society. Unlike Lawrence, however, he emphasizes that the *Pequod*, with its mixture of races and human types, provides an image of democracy, yet with its rigid hierarchy, tyrannical captain, and exploited labor, it also provides an image of democracy's defeat. The very conquest of vastness (in a kind of Hegelian turning of quantity into quality)—the whales, the Pacific, the American space—also led to a defeat of the traditional consciousness which was the basis of America. Melville may not have been aware of the change he recorded, but it is there for the mythically imaginative reader.

For Olson, Melville's use of Shakespearean tragedies not only gave an Elizabethan breadth to a simple whaling tale, thus expressing his "disillusion in the treacherous world" (*Call Me Ishmael*, p. 44), but also gave recognition to the tragedy of the American impetus to dominate the world. However, as one of the more learned commentators on Olson sensibly concludes, he ignores much of *Moby Dick* "because Melville's work is only a means to his own visionary pronouncements."[51] So it had been with Lawrence.

And so with the sense of an American religious-psychic torment. Melville "wanted a God" and thus made "his whale . . . his God" because he "was agonized over paternity. . . . He demanded to know the father" (*Call Me Ishmael*, p. 82). That does make provocative sense of the biography. Following Lawrence, Olson sees a Melville overwhelmed by a familial and larger guilt—"the ethical and northern Melville" (p. 92)—which came to dominate his life and writings. Surrounded by conventional guilty Christianity, he "surrendered to it"; "the result was creatively a stifling of the myth power in him" (p. 102). Melville's later writings (which Lawrence did not know) are failures that but compound his *isolato* silence. Olson not only notes the absence of heterosexual love in Melville, as Lawrence and others had, but also the failure of homosexual love since from *Pierre* to *Billy Budd*, the love males are only pale and passive images. A despairing Melville without virility and love is but a victim of the American ethos.

Although Olson yokes the Melville of *Moby Dick* with Homer and Dante, taking it with Lawrence as supernal American myth, we have, as with Hart Crane, a visionary without a specific vision, though Olson may be said to have gone beyond Crane in seeing Melville as a major figure of defeat by an uncongenial society and religious culture. Stock commentary, Olson repeatedly charges, ignores that, and falsifies Melville's later (*Billy Budd*) failure.[52] Only D. H. Lawrence, Olson wrote in a later essay, had an honest and profound understanding of Melville.[53] The lineaments of Olson's version of that understanding, including an antirationalistic psychology and some sort of cosmic organicism, are far from clear (nor are they in his multivolume *Maximus Poems*, a Pound-Williams style pastiche of details about Gloucester, with exotic free associations of an essentially fractured and idiosyncratic sensibility), but his mythic view of Melville seems to have affected a generation's responses. It is also a provocative example of the personal-prophetic as an alternative to other modes of literary awareness—a continuation of Lawrence's contribution.

Rather less charming are the somewhat related efforts of Olson's onetime editor-mentor, Edward Dahlberg. A devotee of Lawrence while he was still living, Dahlberg inveigled Lawrence to write a preface (and probably, as some later remarks of Dahlberg's indicate, give him some money besides) for his naturalistic-autobiographical novel *Bottom Dogs* (1929).[54] In his preface, Lawrence mostly comments, in usual prophetic vein, on how the obduracy of the American experience with the wilderness destroyed the "sympathetic" consciousness and real human warmth so that the "will-to-success and will-to-produce became clean and indomitable" in the American character. This resulted not only in the "most brutal egoistic self-interest" but in a hygiene-obsessed "physical revulsion." Dahlberg's document of the consequent lack of human feeling, the "psychic disintegration," is negatively useful in presenting the consequent "repulsive consciousness, consciousness in a state of repulsion." Some introduction!

Dahlberg (after writing some proletarian fictions in the 1930s) seems to have finally taken Lawrence's response to heart and converted into a would-be prophetic writer of poetic prose, redoing *Bottom Dogs* into the ornate

Because I Was Flesh (1963).[55] In giving himself a somewhat Lawrencean cast, he also attempted rewriting the mythos of American literature in *Do These Bones Live* (1941; I am using his yet again revision, *Can These Bones Live*, 1960).[56] Obviously influenced not only by the Lawrence of *Studies* but by Lawrenceanizing Charles Olson (whom he took in hand after his break with the academic, and published his first Melville study with Twice-a-Year Press), Dahlberg makes Melville a key American prophet. Conflating Melville, in his fractured dithyrambic and imitation Elizabethan ruminations, with Old Testament prophets, Shakespeare (from Olson), Cervantes, Dostoyevsky, classical mythology, and others, Dahlberg presents Melville-Ishmael as the prototype of the alienated American artist, such as himself (*Can These Bones*, p. 45). (Dahlberg was as egomaniacal and self-pitying as Henry Miller.) Dahlberg's Melville, like Lawrence's, was at war with northern American puritanism, using his white whale as a "spermal demon" with "ejaculatory blasphemies" (pp. 122–23). While Melville longed for a larger sexuality, in his early work he mostly created "arrested phantoms of sensuality" (p. 129), to end in *Billy Budd* with a Christianized sodomistic fantasy. Melville, yet again, is prophetic for American culture mostly as a victim of it.

Dahlberg again recast his version of Melville more harshly in "*Moby-Dick*: An Hamatic Dream."[57] He confesses that "I once loved this cyclops" of a Melville ("Hamatic Dream," p. 170) but have come to reject him because of his dangerous lack of manly sexuality. The theme of the meandering comments ornately presented is that Melville's works are the fantasies of a repressed homosexual, including a consequent ugly "misogyny" (pp. 173, 191). Because of Melville's repression, "*Moby-Dick*, a verbose and tractarian fable of whaling, is a book of monotonous and unrelenting gloom" (p. 175). (All of those I am discussing here, including Lawrence, seem peculiarly immune to Melville's humor.) Dahlberg also now decides that the book is "shabbily written" (p. 181), with inadequate character development, repetitious rhetoric and disconnected metaphors (all characteristics of Dahlberg's own style), and thus the prophecy must be shabby, too.

Dahlberg, of course, practices an art at least as old as Enlightenment biblical criticism in his newfound iconoclasm toward a prophetic text gone sour (he had also developed an animus towards Olson, and perhaps towards Lawrence). "I must impugn *Moby-Dick* as inhuman literature" ("Hamatic Dream," p. 194). The rest of the case deploys mythological pedantry in which he plays on Melville as Ishmael and Ishmael as the descendant of Ham, supposedly the first sodomite. In creating the white whale, Melville was projecting a "Titanic sodomite serpent" (p. 176). After this (and early cannibalistic sexuality, incest fantasies, and so on), he ended with the "perverted Christian" homosexual spiritualization of *Billy Budd* (p. 196). But Melville also hated his homoeroticism, and the "tawdry writing . . . is to some extent willful self-hatred" (p. 197). Melville, then, is doubly perverse, a "Pauline invert" who puritanically made *Moby Dick* "the bestial Bible of modern Ham" in the "worship of the male sperm" (pp. 200–201). Thus, according to Dahlberg, Melville is a dangerous source of modern homosexual mythology, and an incentive to the perversion now undermining heterosexual manliness and fuller humanity in America.

Certainly Melville's sexuality should be recognized as more peculiar than often acknowledged, and no doubt some of popular as well as learned modern responses to Melville might well be seen as homoerotically cultish (especially those to Budd as the "Handsome Sailor," and the apologetic for lovingly vicious Vere), but Dahlberg's case seems overdone and personally askew. It does give more specific restatement, however twisted by sexual rancor, to Lawrence's point that Melville was full of "hate" for our human life, though Dahlberg no longer has the positive sides of Lawrence's responses to the "great" author of *Moby Dick*.

It may also be salutary to recognize, though rarely done by pietists of mythological readings, that mythicizing cuts both ways; that which can be mythically exalted, as was done by a number of writers following Lawrence, can readily be demonized by the same hyperbolic impetus. Holy texts can easily be turned to scurrilous tracts. Only a slight twist in perspective is needed for larger-than-life heroism to become a threatening antilife evil. What hath Lawrence engendered?

My examples of the three modernist American writers—Crane, Olson and Dahlberg—combining Melville and Lawrence are only a small part of the story of the influence of *Studies*. There were large academic-critical effects, which might reasonably be represented by Leslie Fiedler's preface to his iconoclastic scholarly-critical *Love and Death in the American Novel*:

> Of all the literary critics who have written about American books, the one who has seemed to me closest to the truth . . . and who has brought to his subject an appropriate passion and style, is, of course, D. H. Lawrence. His *Studies in Classic American Litera-*

ture attempted for the first time the kind of explication which does not betray the complexity or perilousness of its theme; and in the pages of that little book I found confirmation of my own suspicions that it is duplicity and outrageousness which determines the quality of those American books. . . .[58]

It has been taken up by others, often less rebellious.

But my intention here is not to provide any fulsome history of influence, only to illustrate how some of Lawrence's influence went, and worked. Not incidentally, most of the figures I have discussed—not just Miller and Mailer, but Crane and Olson, Dahlberg and Fiedler—were in revolt against what they saw as the prevailing genteel culture, which they sought to negate in terms of more admitted desire. Lawrence, though an alienated, mocking, and outrageous, as well as outraged, visitor to America, was appropriate nucleus and impetus to that. Curiously, the British Midlands provincial, autobiographical writer had become in several senses an American litterateur and ideologist. Those who view Lawrence and Lawrenceanism as mostly British not only miss a good many points of interweaving, and intermeaning, but much of the reality of the Anglo-American's cultural role. American Lawrenceanism is an essential part of the legacy. It can also be seen as centrally engaging the distinctively counterfeit and sexually ambiguous nature of American culture.

5

Desirable and Negative Legacy of Lawrence as Dissident Culture Hero

In several contexts, I have been pointing up Lawrence's role as a culture hero, necessarily characterizing it in dual and often oddly aslant ways. Much of the way he is now responded to—indeed, the way his works are often read and interpreted—depends on seeing him less as the author of, say, *Sons and Lovers*, or *Women in Love*, or culminating as a novelist in *Lady Chatterley's Lover*, or the poems, or the best short fictions, or the other particular writings, as we scholarly critics often ostensibly do, than as a rather noumenal figure who fundamentally but often peculiarly represents certain defiantly impassioned responses to life. One often takes Lawrence up, or puts him down, according to an explicit or an implied stance towards not only literature, narrowly conceived, but to crucial broader desires and negations. These include, of course, such matters as censorship and other social censuring, gender and other sexual ideologies, and utopian and apocalyptic longings. Otherwise put, Lawrenceanism is important as social-cultural phenomena that goes beyond literature in many limited senses, and that poses such exacerbated issues as blasphemy and antifeminism, heightened erotic consciousness and societal nihilism—radical responses to nature, society, and self. But, I conclude after exploring a bit some variety of affirmations of Lawrence, who has had more of a nonacademic role than a number of modernist writers, it may be less his doctrines on those matters (or the ostensible role of his novels), than the very impassioned responsiveness which radiates the dissident and subversive images of Lawrenceanism.

Lawrence not only raises but has been taken as answering questions of how and why one should live, and not live. So he often intended. Part of my existential literary subject here, then, is the literature of the "extraliterary" role. With the indulgence of the "professional" reader, I wish to draw on some diversely representative statements, including not least the anecdotal (I insist that such is properly responsive literary-intellectual material), in the attempt to adumbrate the role of Lawrenceanism.

Censoring Blasphemy

Let me start with an old, but apparently never quite finished, issue, the censorship and censuring. I combine them because in historical Anglo-American reality, literary censorship has not been very effective and in fact is mostly a public form of censuring. Almost every year we are reminded—by way of the furor over a "blasphemous" movie, threats against an impious/perverted writer, righteous rhetoric for an antiobscenity arts funding initiative, and the like—that such a cluster of angers is perennial, if not, as I suspect of our cultural matrix, essential. Something else than mere "bad" words or images is at issue. In Western traditions, from at least Euripides and Diogenes on, some of the crucial arts of the word self-consciously defy the accepted and provoke outrage. It seems an essential impetus and role, traditionally known as blasphemy. (Since blasphemy is constitutionally legal in the U.S., and its prosecution defunct in Britain, official censorship has been the substitute; blasphemy, of course, is more than Western—an Islamic scholar once advised me of the dire wrongness of Lawrence.) Lawrence's porcupinish social politics (as discussed in my first chapter, and on) are only understandable in significant part, I think, as carrying on the blasphemous vocation. And so were his taboo words, which are not appropriately understood, as I previously argued, as simply sexual candor.

There are several curious reversals in the history of Lawrence's relation to what he contemptuously called the "censor-morons," beyond his being both the victim of censorship and a defender of some censorship (as emphasized in his somewhat obfuscating attack on "dirt for dirt's sake" in "Pornography and Obscenity," and related puritanical responses which he never quite lost).[1] For example, even at this late date of his cultural enshrinement, some variety of contemporary feminists have inclined to a censuring view of Lawrence's writings (including the directive that he be eliminated from the academic canon), which sometimes seems close to traditional censorship, as a streamer of their liberation. An anecdotal example: Germaine Greer, noted feminist writer and contentiously performing media personality, vehemently denounced me at a large social gathering for having quoted someone with a witticism that had the word *cunt* in it. *Any* use of the word *cunt* for a woman or her parts was male degradation and insult, Greer accusingly announced to the company at large. Since I had been discussing teaching (including Lawrence), I mildly countered, "Even when tenderly used by a gamekeeper?" Quick Greer returned, "Precisely, you Lawrencean prick," and went on with some skillfully used male-degrading obscenities to properly place Lawrence and his apologist.[2]

I tried to argue (as I have in chapter 3, above) that Lawrence's use of that obscenity was both to defy hypocritical prudery and to positively turn obscenity, as usually defined, to poetic service of sacral-direct eroticism. Context and tone and special usage were determining. But that had little persuasive effect on Greer and her epigones. There was, of course, on both sides, as soon become evident, a larger ideological issue. Greer had mocked Lawrence in *The Female Eunuch*, and was to later announce that Lawrence's erotic heightening was false: women should now "recognize that we are not so sexy as we thought we were. The Lawrentian myth has been exploded."[3] (So had Germaine's sometimes flaunted sexiness.) The real issue, then, was what it has usually been—the significance of the erotic, and domination by way of it.

When sometime later I told the story to a rather literal-minded psychoanalytic Lawrencean scholar he, too, reacted negatively to the language, on which he held that "those may have been his [Lawrence's] intentions, but he didn't succeed—not at all. Those were and still are foul terms. Pure hostility!" Such censuring views, probably important to contemporary feminist and other limited erotic ideologies, may be widely current as displaced censoring impetus that defeats not only the text but a certain kind of blasphemous role.

Curiously, then, part of the Lawrence obscenity issue still seems to be in dispute. That is puzzling because Lawrence's obscene language in his late work is, in current comparative terms, limited, and (with the exception previously cited of one brief bit of dialogue by Constance Chatterley) confined to male characters, and even then of less than usual variety and frequency. I suggested earlier that Lawrence's use of obscenity was certainly restricted and even rather prudish. This in spite of the obscenity being consciously defiant (patently evident in Lawrence's private publication and considerable efforts to defend and promote the book). It could be argued that a weakness of the novel's theme of turning a lady into a woman appears in the lack of female obscenity, but I cannot find in print any such feminist objection. It could also be argued, however, that for the late-1920s Lawrence was literarily brave in even his limited use of obscenity, and so it was taken (as shortly by the Henry Miller whose enthusiastic response was previously cited, and by numerous defenders since). It may also be noted that the very seriousness of Lawrence's other themes—such as erotic redemption, and apocalyptic antimodernism—raise difficulties for some readers who do not, in effect, find obscenity obscene except when yoked with the serious or more or less sacred. The disapproval, I take it, may be the very negation that much good obscenity is really about. Disputed obscenity is often less about arousal than impiety.

While the objections to Lawrence's language have continued for more than two generations, in spite of ostensible large changes in language taboos, the grounds appear to have shifted. For example, *cunt*, whether as anatomical nomenclature or feminine synecdoche or erotic poeticism, now condemned for sexist denigration, was previously denounced as language serving "lewd and lascivious intent," or "appealing to prurient interest," or revealing a "tendency to deprave and corrupt."[4] Such key phrases in the obscenity laws seem not the same as the "feminist" and other "taste" charges currently leveled. Lascivious arousal and insulting put-down are taken as considerably antithetical. But are they? There may be an only partly covert antisexuality (as in my anecdote), as well as discomfort at blasphemy, connecting the historic shifts in taboos about obscenity, whether old moralist or new feminist. "Good fucking" as well as "right thinking" are still at issue.

Some contemporary feminism, anxiously petty bourgeois and merely transposing old restrictions, tends to indiscriminately treat whatever is identified as male sexual as sexist, including conventionally tabooed language, and therefore to be censured. There has even been a historic movement, including by some official feminist groups, from a "progressive" anticensorship stance to a desperate (because superficial and misplaced in terms of equality) procensorship of "pornography."[5] As usual, "pornography" tends to include the "obscene" since the difference between, say, the Sadean and the Lawrencean, though perhaps seeming obvious to the discriminating reader and central to Lawrence's writings on censorship, is hardly programmable. At a slightly fancier level, there has also been a proclaimed effort to remove Lawrence from the emphasized official literary canons, which comes close to *pre*censorship.[6] (Granted, this is but a byway in a larger doctrinaire movement for political correctness.) Yet, so far as I am aware, there is not currently much Anglo-American direct censorship of Lawrence, and that seems to be partly the result of an odd, and probably distorting, history.

The old censorship dispute may merit a little further reflection, in line here with considering Lawrenceanism's cultural role. By a curious historical twist, recognized serious novels—and it is now widely accepted that *Lady Chatterley's Lover* is one of those because by an otherwise reputably "serious" writer (partly the Leavisite effect)—acquired a "literary exemption," even if partly obscene. That redefinition of censorable material considerably developed out of a larger history of what were considered sexually errant heroines—not just Constance Chatterley but Emma Bovary, Sister Carrie, Fanny Hill, and others—and took some generations to develop and then decline in Western countries. Lawrence served as a crucial figure in that history. That his long-censored last novel is no longer given stock treatment in public as "depraving and corrupting" is, as they too readily say, due to a substantial change in verbal and sexual mores as well as changes in case and constitutional law. However, it may also reflect a changed role in the social-cultural function of the novel for its middle-class audience and its demand for proper education and entertainment. The roles of the critical novels and their errant ladies have been partly displaced by other forms. A less central form is less a focus of contention, and we may now see more generally the defiantly critical novel, especially in its modernist modes, as peculiar in insistently attacking the values of the middle-class audience it ostensibly aimed to titillate and edify.

Before briefly considering some of the trials of errant Lady Chatterley, it might be pertinent to recall some of Lawrence's other "obscenity" problems. Some sexual candor was apparently edited out of *Sons and Lovers* by a friendly editor wishing to meet conventional decorum.[7] However practically helpful, it was really precensorship. His next novel, *The Rainbow*, was legally suppressed and withdrawn in 1915 in Great Britain. In spite of efforts in its defense by influential connections of Lawrence's (he had licked his way into important cultivated social circles), the censoring was maintained then but not renewed or extended later. That is peculiar. The usual interpretation of this somewhat obscure short-circuited censoring has been that the punishment was for "obscenity," probably the Ursula-Winifred lesbian relationship, though that is not described with any obscene language or with much direct detail. A later, and rather obscenity-disapproving scholar (Emile Delavenay), after examining the unclear records, argued that the suppression of *The Rainbow* was political, that is, punishment for Lawrence's strong antiwar views in the early Great War period. While that does fit the pathological patriotism of World War I (as Delavenay does not note), the consensus of Lawrence commentators seems to be that he was primarily being punished for what was taken as the obscenity of fictionalizing deviant sexuality, lesbian and premarital. However, a recent biographer (Jeffrey Meyers) shrewdly argues that "pacifism and sexual morality were closely connected" in official as well as other public views at the time, as were religious heresy and antipatriotism.[8] The underlying issue, then, was blasphemy.

Lawrence seems to have been outraged and embittered by the treatment of his very earnest novel (as we see in his letters), which may be one source of his decade-later self-conscious defiance of obscenity taboos (including a more specific sexual attack on lesbianism in *Lady Chatterley* than in *The Rainbow*). Perhaps the continuing effects can also be seen in some later efforts at self-censorship, including his own suppression of the "Prologue to *Women in Love*," which fervently discussed Birkin-Lawrence's homosexual feelings, and which are ritualistically symbolized in a number of works—same awkwardly defiant impetus? Other symptoms of self-censorship by a writer who aimed to both attack his audience and make a living from it include two published endings of the story "Sun," with a slightly more pointed sexual description in the small press edition.[9] In his penultimate novella, *The Virgin and the Gipsy*, he surprisingly left the bedding-down scene of the young middle-class virago of desire and the older alien dark outcast stranger—a tabooed, threatening subject—quite vague (even in manuscript), which has allowed some repressive moralistic commentators to foolishly hold that the relationship was not sexual, against the whole thrust of the story and the insistently repeated role of Lawrencean desire.[10]

The self-censorship in *Lady Chatterley*—in spite of private publication, Lawrence was eager to reach a financially significant audience (who paid a hefty price for that time)—may be seen to include the elliptical way he treated the anal sex. In his final novella, and testament of death-revivified desire, *The Man Who Died*, his purposes were obviously obscene blasphemy, but he went to elaborate punning stratagems with an escaped rooster cock as a marker of virility, erection as resurrection, etc., as well as a rather fervently heavy Black Mass coitus on an altar of his Christ and a pagan priestess. But he avoided direct obscene language and much sexual detail.

Lawrence as Dissident Culture Hero

His artistically crude but only mildly sexual paintings (though most seem to have a male sexual organ visible somewhere, and a lot of emphasized buttocks) were, of course, officially prohibited in Britain, and otherwise treated as obscene. And he wrote polemical essays and verse squibs attacking censorship (yet also defensively attacking other kinds of obscene writing). Censorship of obscenity—sometimes pooh-poohed as unimportant, minor, by the archly cultivated—certainly has its repeated effects on Lawrence's writings.

Obscenity issues, then, are not just incidental to Lawrence's works or to his public role. Censoring and precensoring may have had a strong, and, I would suggest, often deleterious effect on his style. Thus there is a too-heavy sexual ritualization (called "symbolism" by formalist readers) for the erotic displacements in the wheat-shocking scene in *The Rainbow*, the wrestling scene in *Women in Love*, the massaging scene in *Aaron's Rod*, and the erotic regeneration scene in *The Man Who Died*. Through much of Lawrence's fiction there is also a coitus-like repetition, a bit ingenuously and obscenely defended by Lawrence in the foreword to *Women in Love*, writing of his repetitious language: "natural . . . passion or understanding comes from this pulsing, frictional to-and-fro which works up to culmination." This is stylistic imitative fallacy. And there are the sometimes overblown erotic metaphors as a substitute for the appropriate detail and obscenity (what Lawrence-admiring W. H. Auden called his "woozy" passional prose, and what I partly described earlier as his oxymorons around desire). This, along with the scandalous public banning of *Lady Chatterley's Lover*, which Lawrence assumed in his private publication, for more than thirty years, was in considerable part defining of Lawrence's broad identification. But that had its positive side, too, for his fame and his defiant effectiveness as a blasphemer of sexual and other decorums.

Lawrence was most immediately identifiable for more than a generation as the author of that forbidden "dirty book," which was, however, widely available (in the 1940s and 1950s I easily obtained copies for only moderately high prices in a couple of provincial cities). The "dirt" consisted of less than a hundred (total usage) common "obscene" words, along with a middling degree of description of not unusual heterosexual actions in about a dozen scenes (I can find no printed mention of the buggery or the attack on clitoral orgasm before those of the postcensorship 1960s which I cited in chapter 3). The censoring furor, of course, was grossly disproportionate.

Defiant Desire

No doubt that is partly because censorship, like also the feminist sort of censuring, is usually considerably about something else than the ostensible object, such as the taboo words.

But then statist actions often are by the nature of their source disproportionate. Furthermore, trial transcripts and other public discussions indicate that the obscene words and coital descriptions almost always importantly yoked with some other issues, including, of course, the fear of an exalted view of sexual desire. Another is multiple adultery, however quaint that may now sound. Inconstant Constance has two extramarital affairs in the novel, out of a kind of necessity it is usually pointed out (her impotent husband is not very helpful—for reasons of doctrine as well as disability— and he obviously could have provided her with variant sexual gratification, confirmed as common parapalegic practice by anthropologist Robert F. Murphy in *The Body Silent*). Mellors, though separated from his wife, is also bitterly married throughout the story. However commonplace for the best part of a millennium in love romances, prosecutors (in and out of law courts) emphasized the "illicit" for obvious conventional reasons, plus that Lawrence was not just presenting guiltily furtive eroticism but explicitly propounding—indeed, exalting—his adulterers as engaged in redemptive mating. The prosecutors were factually right.

In the condemnatory discussions, the crime of adultery is compounded by class violations—the aristocratic lady is having sex with her husband's *servant*. Obviously that supposed degradation, clearly part of Lawrence's social defiance, has been made more of in England than in America (though to suggest to American students the analogy of a suburban doctor's daughter running off with a Mexican gardener does draw some parallel discomfort in California). Discomfort at a cultivated, upper-class woman subordinating herself to a sometimes surly and crude "working man" does seem to inform some discussions of the novel, though Lawrence's final version made Mellors the lady's intellectual superior and declassed him, which seems to offend some (such as Marxists and conservatives) while heroic to others (such as bohemian and other "marginal" sorts). In spite of Lawrence's vehement arguments for aristocracy, his influence seems to have been as anticlass cynosure on the social margins. That more or less upper-class ladies need liberation, sexually and socially and ideologically, may be viewed as a recurrent conceit of Lawrence's (from his social origins as well as personal romance), and seems to be part of his perhaps perverse appeal to certain kinds of women readers.

138

Lawrence as Dissident Culture Hero

But such issues do not directly enter the crude American censoring cases, though perhaps indirectly as moral bias, or moral seriousness. Charles Rembar, the publisher's leading attorney in the juridical U.S. Post Office Hearing on the banning of Lawrence's novel (and main defense attorney of record in the following federal district court and appellate court cases in 1959), held that he obviated many of the old issues when he pursued new legal grounds in obtaining the sanction of Lawrence's obscenity by "literary merit."[11] It was not the obscenity itself which had such "value"—that would be a more interesting argument (and one available since Justice William O. Douglas had made a mild version of it in his dissent in the standard-setting *Roth* decision)—but that the "lustful" was conjoined in the work with "literary quality," which, "considering the work as a whole," gave the book (but not the obscenity itself) "redeeming social significance" by way of being literary art. Thus the obscene is rather more excused than justified.

Given the legal history of censorship in the past century—derived out of English common law, developed into the restrictive "Hicklin rule" in British courts in the mid-nineteenth century, variously extended by the vicious religious-moralistic Comstock Act of the U.S. Congress later in the century, modified in the 1930s by the Woolsey (and Hand) decisions on *Ulysses*, etc., and then in the 1950s by the *Roth* decision of the Supreme Court—there were several continuing problems because literary value, not just the value of obscenity, was not a primary concern in law. The tests that had to then be met, such as that the "sexual interest" in the literature could be held as "normal" and "positive" rather than "morbid" and "salacious," and that the treatment of sex did not violate "contemporary community standards" (rather unknowable in societies tending to the anomic), were ambiguous qualifications of freedom of speech and publication. The case now presented for Lawrence emphasized a rather teetering argument between what was generally accepted and the special "literary" recognition accorded to the writing. With the Lawrence issue, for the first time in major U.S. censorship cases, the emphasis was put on "expert" witnesses testifying as to literary value. Malcolm Cowley and Alfred Kazin spoke for the defense at length, and supporting material from positive contemporary reviews of Lawrence was put into the record (prefatory material by Archibald MacLeish and Mark Schorer was already part of the Grove Press edition).[12] It was a social success story for the authority of literary scholar-critics, however questionable their qualities and arguments, and the novel was freed. Moderate judicial liberality, in effect, went along with arguments for enlarged official freedom of expression, if the recognized professional litterateurs accepted the book (really, the author) as morally serious and important. Lawrence now qualified in law as he already had in a sophisticated part of the larger culture.

Rembar was also the lead attorney in some following cases in the next few years that went through trial and appellate courts in the United States—Henry Miller's *Tropic of Cancer* and, in a quaint throwback, John Cleland's *Memoirs of a Woman of Pleasure* ("Fanny Hill")—quite un-Lawrencean works. The combined history of such cases, which considerably started with the *Lady Chatterley* (post-*Roth*), meant a drastically modified definition of obscenity so that (in the words of Supreme Court Justice William Brennan), "a book cannot be proscribed unless it is found to be utterly without redeeming social value," an indeed sweeping standard. But the focus on "book" here was, and somewhat remains, restrictive on other formats and media. The special recognition for the published novel came about at the time such artifacts were taking proportionately lesser roles as the medium of entertainment and edification. It could be noted, too, that now allowable literary critics (institutionalized figures, of course, not only as prestige academics but as persons with histories of commercial relations with trade publishers) would be likely, for reasons of market taste as well as anticensoring ideology, to find some purveyable "redeeming" value in a very wide range of works. And such happened in the following decade.

Libertarians who are against all institutional censorship (I am one) should recognize some ironies in the process. Lawrenceans should also recognize some distortion and inflation of Lawrence beyond literary and ideological pertinence. Following the trials, millions of copies of *Lady Chatterley's Lover* were sold in the United States. If there is a good case for literary censorship, it might well be that any writing used to make much money (including the activities of the Lawrence estate agents and the prestige publishers), using sexual writing for intellectual whoring, which will then distort and falsify the effects, should be restricted and punished. But, of course, the Lawrence case is but small part of a more pervasive cultural prostitution, which Lawrence ended up ironically serving, and which deserves rather more radical answers than censorship and censure.

As the key attorney in the chain of cases starting with Lawrence, Rembar suggested several conclusions for America. "So far as writers are concerned, there is no longer a law of obscenity."[13] A bit overstated, that means for books, and for national distribution (school administrators and boards, as well as certain other custodial bureaucrats, have managed to maintain other standards in hundreds of places, as, of course, have the electronic media). Obscenity, itself a displaced issue, is also not the only basis for restriction of speech, pre- or postpublication. Above all, now the very processing of writing, whether for literary marketplaces, television programming or academic presses—often censorship by format—provides its own order of persisting and exploitative controls and denaturing restrictions.[14]

Rembar also concludes with the hopeful prediction (in 1968) that American society is on the way, and not just in the legal sense, to a time when "obscenity will soon be gone."[15] That seems to mean that once the censoring furors and enticements are over, the very impetus to obscenity will disappear. While the official actions of direct sexual censorship have drastically abated—and Lawrence's writings and role significantly contributed to that development—one can doubt that what Lawrence saw as the real obscenity, what Mellors labeled "cold-hearted fucking" confirming a false culture and destructive society, is gone. Nor, one hopes, is the obscene-sayer as blasphemer gone, which is certainly part of the Lawrencean role.

In the year after the Lawrence case in the United States, Lady Chatterley went on trial in Great Britain. As had previously been evident, the London response much more insistently emphasized adulterous ways, including class misbehavior. Is this the kind of book, asked the crown prosecutor, "that you would want your wife or servants to read?"[16] Unlike the American trials, the British trial was a jury proceeding, and perhaps some jurors didn't, but they apparently freed the book on other grounds. American attorney Rembar complains that the British defense attorneys, in spite of having the good fortune of his briefs and transcripts from the earlier American trial, provided only a "low parody" of free speech legal concerns—their "issue was morality" rather than any "question of freedom."[17] Strange separation. To counter the charges, the British defense was out to prove the lady's virtue—and Lawrence's—and proceeded to lengthy and legally loose public determinations of "what the law ought to be" in a moral sense. However, a more disinterested reader of the transcripts from both countries might note, besides parochial procedural differences (with the British more loose, and perhaps more capricious) that Lawrence's literary and ideological virtue were at issue in both. Some shift of emphasis was due, perhaps oddly, to the apparently more progressive British statute (the Obscene Publications Act of 1959), which more drastically than the American equiv-

141

alent (*Roth*) old-fashionedly defined "obscenity" as a work's "tendency to deprave and corrupt," but also gave a clearer escape hatch than the pre-Chatterley American law because of the possible exemption of material "justified for the public good on the ground that it is in the interests of science, literature, art, or learning, or other objects of general concern." The prosecution went after several "obscenity" issues, including the lady's crass adulterous behavior as well as "her lover's four-letter words," and the defense's various exemption claims, such as situational ethics, spiritual sexuality, the libidinous countering of mechanization, appropriate example for sexual counseling, and other large moral-therapeutic concerns. It is unclear, but also unlikely, that the Lawrence defense won on any free-obscenity issue with twelve men and women all too good and true blue, but they did apparently win on the literary and moral issues, especially when relayed though noted and notable witnesses, which was the real defense.

Even the British prosecutor generally conceded that Lawrence was a "great writer," just that he wasn't in his last novel—a view that can find support in a considerable number of the literary critics of the time, and some still.[18] Hence both literary notables and lawyers practiced considerable applied criticism of the text with, not surprisingly, mixed results, evident in the uncertainty even about the heavy redundancy which is one of obsessive Lawrence's frequent weaknesses as a writer. The defense presented thirty-five expert witnesses (the prosecution none, depending mostly on cross-examination), including quite an array of literary notables, who seem to go over better in Britain (E. M. Forster, C. Day Lewis, Rebecca West, among others), scholar-critics (Helen Gardner, Walter Allen, Richard Hoggart, Raymond Williams, Kenneth Muir, Noel Annan, among others), theologians and Anglican pastors, a member of Parliament, a distinguished publisher, a legal scholar, and "a sweet young lady." The case was heavily made that D. H. Lawrence was a great, nationally valuable, and morally worthy writer, leavened by some qualifications about erratic style and conception in his last novel, and by some negative insertions of the prosecution (such as part of the typically bigoted antisexual tirade against the book by Katherine Anne Porter). So was confirmed in a legal forum the approximate high cultural evaluation of Lawrence more generally, leading to the British sales of hundreds of thousands of additional copies of *Lady Chatterley's Lover*.

A good many noncommercial issues, however, remained murky, critically and morally. In both the English and American trials, "literary value" was at issue but hardly examined in any adequate intellectual way (though the British did a bit better). Even at best, the logic tended to the narrowly circular (this was a good book because it was by Lawrence who was a good writer). As a participant in a number of court cases soon learns to his or her exasperation, legal proceedings and broader intellectual concerns are often fundamentally incompatible. The simplifications of adversarial posturings, the usual reduction of issues to yes/no and simplified factual answers, the legalistic game playing of attorneys and judges, the pseudo-qualification of "expert" witnesses by public positions (including myself in related cases), the heavily ritualistic ambience, the cultural ignorance of many of the participants, and the punitive consequences hanging over all, among other conditions, increase the disparities between good intellectual discourse and court proceedings. Some of it may be, as lawyers often defensively insist, inherent in the operations of judicial systems, inevitable constraints on truth for institutional procedures based in adversarial advantage taking and state coercion, but it produces substantial falsifications of artistic and intellectual qualities. The crass realities of courtrooms in intellectual matters may provide the most pragmatic argument against any kind of official censorship. Even at their possible best (and the Lawrence cases were far from the worst), such processes under statist authority work out arbitrary and falsifying, and so must any official censorship.

Even the positive Lawrence cases illustrate this. The problematic aspects of the eroticism and of the social vision in *Lady Chatterley's Lover*—the sodomizing of the lady, the attacks on lesbianism, the phallic worship, the sexual-social subordination of the erotically converted female, the call for minority sexual-social religion, the apocalyptic view of modern commercial-industrial society—do not have much place in any of the trials. Nor, apparently, do many of the truer responses of the participants. Some of the American defenders seemed (on the basis of implications in other writings) to dislike what they were ostensibly praising (pointed out to me under anonymity by a prosecutor). After winning with the jury at the Old Bailey, the chief *Chatterley* defense barrister is quoted as having come out against "the words." He saw them not only as his main problem in presentation to the court and the public but as now in danger of being used by any "scribbler," not just a peculiar national literary icon such as Lawrence. He certainly had not learned much from his own defense, in spite of all his labors and arguments and notables, about the role of certain kinds of

143

writing. But we should expect such obtuseness in a publicly successful legal mind.

The editor of the published version of the British trial transcript concludes with related points: "It was the words that caused all the trouble, putting her Ladyship as an adulteress where a more conventionally spoken gamekeeper might have lent her the immunity of Emma Bovary and Anna Karenina."[19] Pathetically, the learned editorial defender of literary freedom is not only intolerably reductive of the issues but does not seem aware that even without "the words" Flaubert's *Madame Bovary* was prosecuted in Paris in 1856 (and proscribed numerous times in later and lesser places), and that Tolstoy's *Anna Karenina* was not proscribed because it was vehemently antisexual and self-censored (as evident, for example in the incoherent chapter 12, where Anna takes a negative view of her own sexuality, and as mocked for moralistic distortion by Lawrence in "The Novel" and implicitly countered in his fiction). As previously discussed, Mellors's vocabulary is not all that unconventional (but more social snobbery here?), and much of the trial was not really about "the words," nor are much of the response and issue.

For reasons that would seem to be beyond the ken of these establishment gentlemen, and their still many similars in both societies (including a good many contemporary scholar-critics who still disapprove of the "obscenity"), real freedoms must apply to obscene "scribblers" and to ladies and their out-class lovers as well as to literary icons. The legal and more general public licensing of *Lady Chatterley's Lover* appears to have so applied in the past generation. The dispute may have enlarged freedom of expression (curiously, in the mass media more in Britain than in America), and may have enlarged some broader erotic and social awareness. Lawrence, I suggest, was partly right, then, however sometimes pyrrhic some of the results, in engaging some of the issues of "obscenity" with which for two generations, and including elaborate legal proceedings in several countries, his role and influence have been significantly yoked.

One might want to employ a few obscenities (in a nonsexist way, of course, Ms. Greer) for the quality of mind and feeling often exposed in the obscenity-censorship disputes. Those tight ones need to be vigorously penetrated by such hard ideas as that critical and prophetic writings have, and should continue to have, tumescence against the juiceless and cold taboos and gentilities and proprieties which repeatedly prevail. That was part of what Lawrence was about, and it may remain a still warm and active part of his legated role.

Misogyny and Feminism

Lawrence has equally served as a focus of contention as an ideologist of male domination or, contrarily, as a feminine-sympathetic prophet of true passion. As I suggested earlier in introducing the censorship summary, the issues of censorship and male domination—obscene language ostensibly a male preserve and imposition—are not altogether separable. Certainly it now seems a bit odd that Lawrence's antifeminism, much less his peculiar gender politics and obsessive mythology of the destructive woman, was not publicly made more of and was discussed by only a very few commentators. It should be an embarrassment to ignore the obvious, as we scholar-critics often need to be reminded.

As summary reminders of points I have made in earlier chapters, recall that heroine Alvina in *The Lost Girl*, though a novel of a Midlands' spinster's liberation from a repressive ambience, views herself even in her own mind as her crude Italian peasant-husband's "sacred prostitute" and "slave," and as totally "submissive to his being." Even the supposedly New Woman, independent Ursula in *Women in Love* (and not just the masochistically slavish Pussum) must considerably accede to Birkin's demand that she be a "humble slave," submitting not only to his sodomizing her but abnegating her teaching career, her independence, her community, and, especially, her "will" until she makes "surrender of her spiritual being." In *Aaron's Rod*, in considerable part a fantasy and tract about homoerotic relations, the lesser role of women, when not largely destructive, is to achieve "deep unfathomable free submission." In *The Plumed Serpent*, the superior, middle-aged protagonist, Kate Leslie, must finally learn to make "submission absolute" to the male, including forgoing usual sexual orgasm (active, clitoral "beak-like friction"), and become subordinate partner to a military-sectarian thug and his utopian-reactionary ideology. Constance in *Lady Chatterley's Lover*, however involved in class and sexual liberation, must not only in the crucial love scene be a "passive, consenting thing, like a slave, a physical slave," but must mostly submit to Mellors's choices and views. Granted, there is a paradoxical twist in the stories of liberating women in that they (Constance, Kate, Ursula, Alvina, and others) will only achieve liberation into full desire and personhood by slavish submission, at least temporarily, *and* by some enduring submission to male purpose and dominant role. But paradoxes and qualifications do not change the basic, male-dominated reality that Lawrence repeatedly insists upon. The case could be elaborated through the other novels, including *The White Peacock* (the misogyny of the gamekeeper), *The Trespasser* (several male-destroying ladies), *Sons and Lovers* (the treatment of Gertrude and Miriam as well as the put-down of Clara's feminism, and finally her person), and so on through most of Lawrence's fiction, and nonfiction, too (such as the mockery of the "Queen Bee" mate throughout *Sea and Sardinia*, among others).

Any summary of Lawrence's antifeminism should also be elaborated with his shorter, and often more cogently done fictions. There appears a veritable legion of "destructive women" (as I analyzed them a generation ago), men-defying witches.[20] Some women he tendentiously drives to renouncing careers for patriarchal submission (*The Captain's Doll*, "Mother and Daughter"), or to emotional or actual suicide for not submitting to males ("The Princess," "None of That"), or even to embracing ritual assassination by males ("The Woman Who Rode Away"). And so on, into a mythic world of absolutized gender conflict unto death.

To the possible objection that these are, after all, fictions, the obvious reminder is that tendentious Lawrence is rarely the detached and clinical tale teller—anything but. Granted, he sometimes shows considerable complexity, and there are the satiric extensions that go with his often underrated sardonic sense of humor, but the direction of his antifeminism is intentional. Similar demands run through the nonfictional prose (ignored by so many commentators, who then torture the fictions to make the point). For example, from the middle period: "Teach a woman to act from an idea and you destroy her womanhood forever. Make a woman self-conscious, and her soul is barren as a sandbag." Instead of thinking, a woman must submit by her very nature: "When a woman is thoroughly herself, she is being what her type of man wants her to be" (Lawrence, *Studies*, 102–3). The main problem Lawrence often saw for woman was to find the right male template to responsively submit to. But didn't this moderate with his final long romance of positive coupling? Not substantially. Many of the last stories are sardonic put-downs of women. That was also the insistently recurrent subject of many of the late, little, often rather trite, periodical essays, whose titles sufficiently indicate the direction—"Give Her a Pattern," "Is England

Lawrence as Dissident Culture Hero

Still a Man's Country?" "Master in His Own House," "Cocksure Women and Hensure Men," and the other pathetic and sarcastic ruminations around his insisted upon extreme gender polarity.[21]

In another late-1920s essay, "The Real Thing," Lawrence rather ambiguously yokes his gender yowls with his fundamental call "to be renewed, reborn, revivified," by returning to the "life-flame," the beyond-ego primordial "*living* centre of the cosmos." The failure to do so in our "counterfeit" order has resulted in the loss of the true feminine, the "flower-like repose of a happy woman." For, with a sad irony, the woman's movement to emancipation, "the greatest revolution of modern times," has achieved too much "freedom" (after all, "freedom is a man's word") and has become a "tyranny of woman" with the male "subservient" and "submissive," and it has terribly broken the "unconscious sympathetic connexions" between the eternally opposite sexes.[22] Bluntly but accurately enough put: from literary beginning (as in his well-done early story of vehement domestic battle with the woman finally quite submissive to the male, "The White Stocking") to end (as in *The Man Who Died* with the submissively misled priestess servicing the man, who then abandons her in her pregnancy), Lawrence was essentially a "male chauvinist," obsessively emphasizing the destructive nature of women, insisting not only on their limited roles but on their submission and subservience to the male, often (as I detailed earlier) sexually dissatisfied. Undeniably, the Lawrencean is misogynistic.

There is, of course, much more, obsessively so. The over-mothered son and lover was trapped in female sensibility and ambivalent homoeroticism, and endless retaliation against the Christianity, social-class order, and manipulative culture he, with some practical reason, linked to the female. Lawrence's hypostatized ancient marriage code (dominated by supposed "male purpose," though he often has difficulty in finding it), his desperate replays of romantic passion (exalting female "passivity" as part of the conversion-transfiguration), the woman-caused and woman-cursed inadequacy of so many of his fictional males (awkwardly narcissistic autobiography), even his cosmology with the feminine moon only reflective of the potent male sun (and a dying sun worshipper's longing for potency), repeatedly dominate any more complex Lawrencean sexual dialectics.

But what excuses have the followers and so many of the commentators had for the complicity in misogyny? One can only conclude that it was widely accepted within the empathetic Lawrencean concern for women, especially by women. Much of his readership, always reported as heavily

147

female, seems to have been poignantly masochistic. Diana Trilling, moderate indeed in feminism, nonetheless suggests that for the early decades of literary influence "Lawrence's harshness to women, instead of alienating his female readers, would seem to have fed their well-stimulated appetite for blame" for not being properly happy in submission to males.[23] I think also that Lawrence's perceived role as a liberating sexual prophet obscured a sense of what kind of sexual relations he was, and wasn't, announcing. And *heroic* submissions have their own persuasiveness, as we know so well from politics and other institutions.

However, early on there were comments on Lawrence's harsh ideology of women by those who knew him, and a large case against Lawrence on women was made shortly after his death by his onetime close friend (and wife's sometime lover), John Middleton Murry, in the first of his three books on Lawrence, *Son of Woman*.[24] With some vindictive reductiveness, Murry held that the masculine weakness of Oedipal-victim Lawrence led him to grossly compensatory demands for female submission. Lawrence had, in effect, counterattacked Murry in advance in his satiric story "Jimmy and the Desperate Woman" in which an unmanly literary critic involves himself with a manly miner's vinegarish wife in a mixture of effete submission and exploitation for a consubstantial eroticism with the more manly husband. Probably both Lawrence and Murry were considerably right in their perceptions of each other, but as with much of the inverted hagiography by Lawrence's former women friends after his death, the personal motives may have obscured the reading of the works and the significance of the Lawrenceanism.[25]

For the "woman issue" was already pro and con. In contrast to Murry's denigrating expose of Lawrence's relation to the feminine was Anaïs Nin's enthusiastic notes collected into a little book, *D. H. Lawrence* (1932). There, for example, she not only accepted Lawrence's "intuitive" view of the female role (except for her self-exemption as "builder-artist")—"*the core of the woman is her relation to man*"—but emphasized his "androgynous writing": "Very often he wrote *as a woman would write*." In spite of Lawrence's frequent harshness towards women, he had a sympathetically feminine sensibility, womanish intuition, even the bodily diffuse ("all over") emotional sensitivity (her model here apparently the usual erotic physiology of woman as more diffusely than genitally aroused), and was unique as a man who "so wholly and completely expressed women accurately."[26] Here, and by a woman, are some of the basic lineaments of the

Lawrence as Dissident Culture Hero

later defense of Lawrence as a peculiarly feminine sensibility (Daleski, Mailer, Balbert, and others). Nin also (as previously discussed in chapter 4) strongly and rather incongruously influenced the Lawrenceanism of Henry Miller, and probably others later. The perception of she-man Lawrence certainly complicates the obvious misogyny.

The first intellectually sophisticated countering of Lawrence's misogynistic views of women—at least that received much public attention—was Simone de Beauvoir's short chapter in *The Second Sex* (1949), "D. H. Lawrence, or Phallic Pride." Earlier in the book she had incidentally commented on what was to become a nexus of feminist reaction, Lawrence's attack on female orgasm in *The Plumed Serpent*, which she sensibly condemned as "dreadful nonsense."[27] For the rest, within the confines she set herself of considering only a few of Lawrence's novelistic and expository statements on the subordination of women to phallic male power, she makes a reasonable case, though a limited one in that she does not note Lawrence's obsessive portrayals of "willful women," nor the complexities of his sexual dialectics of conversion and self-discovery. She also submerges Lawrence in an unjustifiably romantic view of nature. He most often more emphatically put nature, as in his "Snake" and "Fish" poems and New Mexico descriptions, as indifferent and excitingly alien to the human, what is now usually called the "biocentric"—carrying out the principle announced in *Women in Love* that "man is not the criterion." With Sartrean ontology, which has more than a little irony as a feminist methodology, Beauvoir summarizes Lawrence's insistence on the differentness of women and their required submissiveness to purposive males, including his exaltation of woman who "unreservedly accepts being defined as the Other."[28] Her context, of course—not applied much to Lawrence but emphasized elsewhere in *The Second Sex*—concerned not just the casting of the "feminine" role but the radical social issues of women's consequent lack of autonomy, social-economic engagements, and full personhood in male-ordered society.

Beauvoir's sort of feminist issue was largely ignored in the flood of Lawrence commentary with his literary revival in the 1950s and 1960s, perhaps partly because of the socially conservative bias (and often Christian prejudices, sometimes secularized in Leavisite moralisms) of most of the New Criticism dominant at the time in Anglo-American literary discussions. There were some philosophical commentators—Kathleen Nott and Philip Rieff are examples—who took note of Lawrence's antifeminism, and a very few literary commentators who did discuss in print some of his

149

misogyny in his fiction (as I did in the 1950s).[29] The *Zeitgeist* for the angry feminist responses was not yet evident.

At the end of the 1960s, the strong public renewal of militant feminism— the American women's liberation movement that partly developed out of the minority protest, antiwar, and counterculture movements—prepared the way to see Lawrence as a central sexist-reactionary literary representative. Apparently the most influential writing here was that of a celebrity-mongering feminist, Kate Millet. Her *Sexual Politics* included historical chapters around feminist ideology and chapters on exemplary antifeminists in twentieth-century literature. The one on Lawrence (leading to chapters on Henry Miller and Norman Mailer, whom I have discussed elsewhere and will not repeat here) was by far the longest. Her detailed case, though apparently ignorant of the history I have been summarizing, was an angrily denunciatory polemic. It mostly uses the novels and moves from Lawrence's mistreatment of women characters to his "doctrinaire male-supremacist ethic," concluding with the story, "The Woman Who Rode Away."[30] That is solely viewed as a "sadistic" exaltation of "the penis as deity," a "pornographic dream" and "demented fantasy" perverting sex into "slaughter" in the form of a ritual "death fuck."

Though she is unoriginal on that novella, except for some vehemence of language and perhaps some metaphoric discovery of penises, much of the rest of her anti-Lawrence case comes out quite forced. For example, she distorts both class and sexual issues in *Sons and Lovers*, and especially the tone of the novel, to conclude that Lawrence's surrogate Paul ends "actually in brilliant condition . . ., having extracted every conceivable service from his women, now neatly disposed of. . . ." While there have been critical disagreements about the final pattern (I long ago argued that the ending was quite negative; others have found it somewhat hopeful by merging Paul with the up-and-coming Lawrence or by Freudian-therapeutic logic), there is a plausible consensus that Paul has been considerably defeated by the frigid, puritanical Miriam and his mother's domination (and, I suggested in chapter 1, by her petty bourgeois Protestant ethos aspirations). Millet will have none of this simply because they are women.

Millet also views *The Rainbow* as an attack on the feminism of the time (most see it as more sympathetic to the New Woman), and ignores its other themes (and its muddles). *Women in Love* is taken mostly as an exercise in further punishment of independent women, on the way to the homosexual misogyny and lust for male power of *Aaron's Rod* and *Kangaroo*. Oddly,

Lawrence as Dissident Culture Hero

The Plumed Serpent, where Millet's charges of Lawrence's male narcissistic and "fascistic" tendencies might make her best case, is only lightly touched upon. Many of Lawrence's other writings, including such "liberationist" works as *St. Mawr* and his shorter fictions and their often cutting portrayal of women, are pretty much ignored (because the satire is pertinent?), as are what goes with Lawrence's misogyny, including his social negations, which would hardly allow him to make much positive of women's success in the despised commercial-industrial order, a "mechanical" debasement that he repeatedly attacks in his late fictions and essays. In sum, Millet's feminist polemic against Lawrence is relatively uninformed, and it does a dubious job of reading what works she does take up (as Mailer and Balbert, among others, have demonstrated), though not worse than a number of stock male accounts which pretty much ignored the misogyny. Millet's discussion mostly had its utility confined, as feminists in that period liked to announce, to a "consciousness-raising" device. But, I would suggest, Millet's attack may also have been of good service in sharpening later and better readings on the gender issues. Such are the uses of abuses.

With such attacks, and the counterattacks of Mailer (discussed in the preceding chapter) and others, Lawrence had become a focal totem for both feminists and misogynists to conjure with for the next two decades. Without attempting a full history of the dispute, I wish to note a few lines of battle. However, I want to again qualify that the use of Lawrenceanism may have been even more widespread than the polemical and critical literature indicates. For one of many examples: a best-selling lively novel of the 1970s, a feminist picaresque-confession, Erica Jong's *Fear of Flying*, takes its two final chapter epigraphs (and, I suspect, part of its sexual descriptions, including the primal response of the "zipless fuck") from Lawrence, who had become a brooding presence over gender conflicts.[31]

Where Norman Mailer had been more than broody in his Lawrencean exaltation of erotic desire as ultimate value, "meaning," in otherwise nihilistic modern life (and acute in savaging Kate Millet for dubious readings), other male defenses of Lawrence on women were more moderate. For example, American critic Charles Rossman, in a monograph-length essay, tried to wend his compromising way between Millet and Mailer by granting the near-sadism of "The Woman Who Rode Away", but emphasizing the overarching importance of man/woman relationships in Lawrence as the ultimate value.[32]

In contrast, a British scholar, Anne Smith, made a substantial case for

Defiant Desire

Lawrence's sexual ambivalence, homosexual-narcissistic demands, and egotistical treatment of women.[33] Another, Faith Pullin, argued, in the line of Millet, that in *Sons and Lovers* Lawrence revealed himself as a "ruthless user of women," confirming his inability to treat them as full human beings.[34] Mark Spilka, forever redoing his American positive thinking on the Lawrencean love ethic, attempted to considerably dissolve Lawrence's misogyny about willful women in a "Chatterley solution," and counter Millet, with an affirmative emphasis on Lawrence's more positive heroines, and on males, such as Mellors, therapeutically learning emotional tenderness.[35] Devout Lawrence biographer Harry T. Moore concluded again that Lawrence didn't really hate women because he finally regarded them "in a way that can only be called religious."[36] That, with an unintentional irony (also of course in Mailer), rather confirms an essential feminist critique that Lawrence did not treat women as fully human.

Such considered male defenses of Lawrence on women as those of decently concerned Rossman, Spilka, Moore, and others, perhaps better testify to a sincere way of responding to Lawrence and a desire for gender decency than to the issue. But then some of the feminist responses were more to Millet than to Lawrence. For an apparently influential example, Carolyn G. Heilbrun uncritically accepted Millet's case for Lawrence's "demeaning of the female" and then supported it with a thin and cursory mythic reading of *The Rainbow* in which we are to see Ursula as a "new Eve."[37] As with most loose metaphors, that is easily reversible as a feminist/ misogynist trope. While one might want to sympathize, as I do, with the broad direction of Heilbrun's argument, towards a more androgynous sense of the human, the specific case is not very persuasive. As for the reversibility, Carol Dix, a British journalist, wrote a not very perceptive burbling little book around the issue, *D. H. Lawrence and Women*, in which she confesses that as a Midlands schoolgirl she identified with the Ursula of *The Rainbow* as part of "a quest for the coming out of feminine consciousness."[38] When she read Millet on Lawrence in college in the 1970s, she reports, she reacted negatively—to Millet. Amidst potted summaries of Millet and Mailer, and some of Lawrence's fictions, her main argument (if it can be so called) is that Lawrence shows "better than any female novelist ever had, the strength and power of a woman's feelings," including "that she enjoys fucking." This is a testament to the loose *effect* of Lawrence that has its point for the more than ambiguous prophet of female sexual liberation, though mostly against strange old conventions of female incapacity.

Lawrence as Dissident Culture Hero

A more competent and scholarly account from a feminist point of view, Hilary Simpson's *D. H. Lawrence and Feminism*, draws together some of Lawrence's use of "suffragist" ideas and women in early writings (for example, Alice Dax for the character of Clara in *Sons and Lovers*, a figure whose feminist ideas are clearly denigrated by Paul, and apparently by Lawrence, in the novel). Simpson shows that while Lawrence's writings somewhat variously used the New Woman materials of the time, he had little sympathy with suffragists in his "rejection of reform in favor of individual [sexual] liberation and development."[39] That rings true. With increasing exacerbation, Lawrence's wartime fictions reveal an "insistent emphasis on submission and passivity for women," and a "growing anti-feminism," including a rejection of "the tradition of liberal sex-psychology" which feminism and his earlier work had in common. In the postwar antiwoman fictions, Lawrence asserted threatened masculine power, then developed his more qualified final view which held up "phallic conscious-ness" in somewhat uncertain glorification of predominant maleness. Simp-son's discussion often seems to me dubious in its readings. For examples: she erroneously assumes positive treatment of the Mrs. Witt in *St. Mawr* whom Lawrence savages for always "knocking everything in the head," and who ends up a self-defeated character; against the text, she claims that Clara is not allowed sexual satisfaction in *Sons and Lovers*; and she seems to selectively use texts to exaggerate the changes rather than consistencies in Lawrence's views. But she does place some of the gender issues in historical context.

Testimony to the considerable persuasiveness of the broad feminist case may be found in the ingenuity of the later masculinist, male-defending, arguments. For representative instance, Lawrence Lerner uncritically accepts the basic directions of the feminist polemics (especially Millet, but also Faith Pullin and others) but then pulls out some passages in the novels which show a more subtle or contrary (polarity) treatment of women.[40] Of Lawrence he admits to attempting to "rescue his fiction from its didactic purposes," the teller of the tales often being antifeminist but the tales showing us something else. Clearly, I suggest, Lawrence is sufficiently protean to show us a good many things, but the artistic/didactic polarity is too clever and far from complete in that in some of Lawrence's most achieved passages, as in the stories, we get harsh misogyny. Prejudice here gets partly disguised by methodology; while I, too, have deployed (as in chapter 3) Lawrence's shrewd distinction in *Studies in Classic American*

Defiant Desire

Literature about trusting the "tale" rather than the "artist," it was, of course, properly aimed at the duplicity of repressed American literature and can be easily overextended. Lawrence's tales, with such basic fables as that woman cannot come to self-realization in desire except by submission to a man, not just the intrusive author, give us misogyny.

A variation is Declan Kiberd's section on Lawrence in *Men and Feminism in Modern Literature* in which he goes after the "wrong-headed current feminist" responses to Lawrence by partly adopting their very argument and holding that Lawrence transcends his negative views of women by the process of androgynous mating. His primary text, following prevailing convention, is *Women in Love*, about which he is thoughtful enough to grant certain difficulties, such as Lawrence's "absolute differentiation into pure male and female."[41] But that is transcended by seeing it as a demand for ultimate individual being necessary for true marriage. Admittedly, there is the further perplexity that at "root Birkin suffers from the modern flaw of seeking in sex a consummation offered by religion." Such, as I have insisted throughout, is Lawrence's continuing and ultimate affirmation of desire. But marriage, and not least in *Women in Love*, where, as I, among others, emphasized before, Ursula and Birkin have given up jobs, homes, families, possessions, community, social roles, etc., for extremely alienated and narcissistic flight funded by a private income and no obligations, is patently no real resolution in the world.

There are a number of others (some of whom I cited in earlier contexts), but let me conclude the survey with a recent argument at hand, Peter Balbert's *D. H. Lawrence and the Phallic Imagination*. It is a continuation of Mailer's, of whom Balbert is an acknowledged epigone, plus the marriage case (which Mailer, married many times, certainly did not make). After a loose indignant polemic against feminist critics of Lawrence such as Millet and others (more exactingly discussed above), he provides counterreadings of a few of the fictions. He takes as earnestly proper Lawrence's attack by way of Paul on feminist Clara's lack of "organic" female role in *Sons and Lovers*, and emphasizes the positive rather than considerably defeated role of the protagonist. Even more lopsided is Balbert's emphasis on the "normative marriage" theme in *The Rainbow*, ignoring the negations (and muddles). A stronger case is made with the endless gender conflict in *Women in Love*, where the counterresponses and claims of Ursula in the middle of the novel, but certainly not in the final pattern, partly qualify Lawrence's male bias (and endless internal conflict?). Still, this is undercut with *Lady Chatterley's Lover* by accepting as literal Lawrence's magical metaphor that the "womb" feelings of Connie are of her female essence and that submissively "she must break the self-involved habits of clitoral stimulation if she is to achieve the isolate singleness of being that Birkin outlined to Ursula."[42] (The very rhetoric there seems fundamentally contradictory.) One of the more extreme dramatizations of Lawrence's misogyny (and Millet's centerpiece), "The Woman Who Rode Away", is gotten around by treating it as aesthetically autonomous from Lawrence's own feelings and views.[43] We should emphasize the clinical novelist rather than tendentious prophet. But, as Balbert concludes his study, Lawrence's dominant insistence on organic desire, and all the human passion and redemptive quality that goes with it, as against the ravages of the "industrial system," is at the heart (or perhaps we better say at the phallus and "arse") of most of what Lawrence was crucially doing. But doesn't that very radical opposition further the demand for woman's submission to the defiant prophet? Though admirable in its sense of appropriate impassioned response to Lawrence's writings and issues, this conventionally male-bigoted essay hardly makes a persuasive case on the antiwoman charges.

But is there a case to be made? Not, I suggest, by merely refining (often justifiably) the readings of the works and thus emphasizing Lawrence's feminine empathy, which certainly seems to be one of the current effects of the feminist attacks, or by dismissing Lawrence's obvious, and frequently extreme, male prejudices and rancors. The candidly knowledgeable can hardly deny Lawrence's misogynistic cast and his demand for the submission of women to men. Lawrence's misogyny is, comparatively, not as unilaterally dimensioned as that of such chronologically and ideologically overlapping figures as, say, Friedrich Nietzsche, August Strindberg, Ernst Juenger, and Henri Montherlant (though sometimes as irascible and vehement), or as uncomprehendingly exploitative of women as Ernest Hemingway, Henry Miller, Norman Mailer, and Edward Abbey (a more crassly womanizing but also sentimental and insecure he-man American tradition). After all, Lawrence had, unlike the above, an empathetic concern with women, dramatizing their erotic and identity conversions, if not their full social equalities and freedoms, and had a cast of sensibility long characterized as feminine, plausibly identified with in his own lifetime and by many responsive women readers since. There is no reason in reality (in contrast to stock dogma) that both understanding empathy for women and submission-demanding denigration of them in relation to men cannot coexist in the same, though perhaps a bit peculiar, sensibility. It might be fair to summarize the Lawrencean as significantly woman-liberationist, though often simultaneously woman-suppressionist.

Paradoxicality, of course, is not justification, though we might want to grant it a special (and non-normative) awareness. It gives us the rather heroic Louisa, Ursula, Alvina, Lou, Yvette, and Constance, among others. On the misogynistic side—for that is a not only ancient but sometimes perceptive tradition, however deplorable in some of its effects—Lawrence dramatizes and otherwise displays considerable insight into dominating, destructive and self-destructive, "willful women" (as with Dolly in "The Princess," Pauline in "The Lovely Lady," and so many others). He is also fictionally perceptive and powerful on the demands, not least the masochistic, of a good many actual women (he certainly suffered from, and mistreated, a number of them), continuing types. However one wants to explain it—by nature, by nurture, or by denaturing—there are a good many castrating, dominating, and otherwise vicious women around. This is not to deny—indeed, Lawrence insists—that men helped make them dominating and destructive (Dolly's overprotective father, Pauline's wimpy son, etc.), though Lawrence tends to see gender differences as absolute, or at least often wants them to be seen that way. Certainly the Lawrencean is bigoted male sexist, no less—the complexities and qualifications that the Lawrencean apologists come up with, sometimes (as I noted) merely ingeniously, do not change that—but his very extremity and peculiarity provided him with provocative dramatic power on the issues and considerable insights. And truths about gender realities.

But not sufficient truths. His obsessive demands for female submissions are not only bigoted and ugly and perverse but often dramatically incoherent. To find women incompatible or inadequate has no necessary result in domination or punishment. I doubt that one needs to be as radically egalitarian as I am to find the submissions of Ursula, Alvina, Kate, the Queen Bee, Frieda, Connie, and the others, unpersuasive. Apparently they even were to Lawrence, whose demands as well as fictional endings were so often pyrrhic. His feminine empathies and perceptions as well as oppositional cast did not allow him to be altogether self-persuasive on the inferiority of women and their acceptance of male dominance. That is not so much a conflict between the "artist" and the "tale" but a conflict apparently inherent in Lawrenceanism, and perhaps in much of the tradition of misogynistic dark prophecy.

Lawrence as Dissident Culture Hero

Lawrence has certainly been "usable" in the feminist/masculinist disputes of the past generation. I have emphasized such utility in dissidence, of course, because it partly confirms my larger view that a major role of literature is ideological dispute and provocation. That is a considerable part of its motive and purpose, function, and response. Criticism that does not somehow reckon with this is rather formalist flatulence in a historical windstorm. But the point here is also a re-revisionist view of Lawrence. The arguments and counterarguments, readings and revisions, around the feminist issue should pretty much set aside the blandly meliorist view of Lawrence as one who sought "creative balance between man and woman." How nice! And how dubiously relevant to that peculiar sensibility that provocatively unto perversity found an extremely, and perhaps permanently, conflictful sense of man/woman relations.

From his perceptive dissatisfaction with contemporary Western society, Lawrence often drew dubious social politics ("aristocracy," hierarchy, authoritarianism); so with his feminine empathy and androgynous sensibility, and his concern with women, he often drew dubious sexual politics (gender polarization, female submission, phallic power worship). Given the insistently extreme masculine/feminine divisions within Lawrenceanism (including many of the contenders about it), one may, indeed probably must, suppose that there can be no adequate resolution without far more radical changes. And the changes are not sufficiently encompassed, as a Lawrencean should be aware, by most current feminism, which is often trapped in the dilemmas of claiming both social equality and a superior feminine nature. Lawrence claimed the nurturing to deny the equality. I incline to radically egalitarian and androgynous and polymorphous possibilities—a new person beyond gender—but certainly Lawrence did not directly, and his very testimony might make one pause over the possibility that there is no gender resolution, rather a fundamental incompatibility, feminism and masculism, revenge and misogyny, forevermore. Possibly there is a more broad, and never quite resolvable, truth to that undercutting statement I quoted earlier from *The Rainbow* that representative Tom's life shows "the old brutal story of desire and offerings and deep, deep-hidden rage of unsatisfied men against women." As long as desire remains so perplexed, Lawrence provocatively suggests, the gender negations will continue. After all, we frail men learn from experience that women are . . .

Defiant Desire

Erotic Legacies

Probably Lawrence's largest effects, rather more than the specifically literary, are not blasphemous obscenity and the censoring conflicts, or misogyny and the feminist/masculinist controversies, but a heightened and enlarged eroticism. That passional prophecy, of course, should not be entirely separated from the more overt contentions, for they are specific applications (and misapplications sometimes) of the larger insistence on heightened sexual consciousness—a demand for what he perceived to be a radically different sensibility.

This prophetic, I have been variously arguing, can never fully be separated out from Lawrence's literary works, such as the fictions, except in an absurdly denaturing pedantry which defeats its own piety of understanding, because the works depend on the same passional perceptions and blasphemous purposes. While it might seem conveniently nice to discriminate between Lawrence as the propounder of a sexual metapsychology and Lawrence as a poet of the heightened moments of desire, or between Lawrence as an exacerbated social polemicist and Lawrence as a brilliantly sardonic storyteller (where, my old argument went, he achieved some of his finest art), it never quite works because the poetry and tale telling are about something else and driven by something other than themselves. Lawrence is not an art idolater. Otherwise put: Lawrence's passion for changes in how one feels and lives pulses through the works and becomes the dominating effect.

The discriminating critic might feel more comfortable if, say, "The Christening," "The Rocking-Horse Winner," "The Man Who Loved Islands," or the best poems, or the vivid descriptive writing (in, say, *Memoir of Maurice Magnus*, *St. Mawr*, some of the travel sketches, and various novel episodes), or the sometimes brilliantly provocative cultural interpretations (as in the extremely influential, I argued, *Studies in Classic American Literature*) were *the* dominant Lawrence that the culture spread and the society utilized. But historical consciousness does not so neatly, tastefully, confine itself, and it may be partly right sometimes in overriding mere intellectual discriminations by recognizing a larger prophetic reach. Probably those broader purposes come back to haunt, if not considerably determine, our mere literary distinctions. Surely Lawrence is perceived differently, even by the learned, in the postcensoring, postsexual revolution, post–feminist-polemicizing time. Part of that may be that our cultural

ambience has partially "Lawrenceanified." Quite diverse people and subjects are given markers of being in "the tradition of Lawrence" (as I had
occasion to note recently in such diverse materials as a discussion of
Schlegel and in a commentary on Native American rituals). Or a critic can
point to something as in "the heightened manner of D. H. Lawrence." Or
many will sense something of what is involved when someone says of a
heterosexual love affair, "Oh that's so Lawrencean!"—usually meaning a
conflictful and socially defiant heightened eroticism.

Here I want to briefly consider both serious and caricatural views of that
larger role and significance. Lawrence's lifelong claim that he stood for the
exaltation of deep "desire," and put it most often in a sexual nexus within
social negations, and insisted that it would culminate in a new state of
being, including ways of being in the tangible world, has had considerable
effects. For examples: An influential post–World War II left-Freudian social
critic, who became famous as a dissident libertarian in the American 1960s,
Paul Goodman, held for years as the fundamental principle of his views,
"Follow your deepest impulse!" (Compare Lawrence's statements on desire—a richer term?—quoted earlier.) One may suspect that some of the
impetus came from the Lawrence he said he admired, though of course
Goodman's adaption was in a quite different matrix, including a Jewish-
American communal heritage, a New York intellectual ambience, and a
militant bisexuality (so at odds with Lawrence's British post-Christian
Protestant individualism).[44] A related neo-Freudian, Reichean cultural theorist, Arthur Efron, has recently argued that Lawrence is a true proponent of
the significance of the sexual body as the reality of a totalistic consciousness
developing against millennia of false Western dualism. Lawrence's crucial
art is that which presents "the passional secret places of life" as confirmation
that the sexual is "the basis for human vitality."[45] Lawrence is thus a positive
liberating advocate of a new sexual consciousness, individual and social.

But can these avowed libertarians be right about the Lawrence who so
vehemently displayed authoritarian fantasies and made desperately tyrannical declarations? They take them, apparently, as just that, claiming as most
fundamental Lawrence's demands for a radical change in consciousness
and a metaethic of outgoing sexual liberation. I detect numerous others in
the recent past in this line of inheritance. But a more simple summary may
have been given by a student who wrote that "Lawrence said that you have
to find out what's your real feelings, then do it." In spite of the illiteracy,
not a bad student of Lawrenceanism.

Defiant Desire

Perhaps more intriguing are the rather antithetical judgments of what is taken as Lawrenceanism. A generation ago, a noted conservative meta-Freudean cultural theorist, Philip Rieff, propounded Lawrence's similar role as a "revolutionary imagination" and sexual "seer." In *The Triumph of the Therapeutic*, he also made a Durkheimean insistence that Lawrence's revolutionary view was finally "incoherent" because "heavily on the side of the remissions," that is, a deeply religious rebellion against an only vestigial structure of belief, which could no more shape its antagonist than itself into a community of meaning.[46] In this view, contemporary Western culture provides no ordered shape for a revolutionary such as Lawrence.

Rieff draws mostly on Lawrence's "psychological" polemics of the early 1920s, *Psychoanalysis and the Unconscious* and *Fantasia of the Unconscious*, and only touches on a few fictions (such as *The Plumed Serpent*, but never the better ones—no litterateur but a professional social scientist, the bad writing of the polemical works does not concern him). He takes seriously Lawrence's "religion of Sex," especially when seen as a "post-Christian" effort towards the "integration of the inner and outer man." Essentially this is the same prophetic Lawrence as that of the libertarians, but countered. Pagan Lawrence "staked his case on a revival of the erotic mode, as a therapeutic release from inwardness"—that is, from guilt and other defeating religious involution and withdrawal from worldly experience. Lawrence, in effect, did so in order to achieve "a new therapy of commitment" for a sense of now shattered "community." He was a major prophet of renewal.

Rieff reasonably noted that Lawrence's efforts were often negative, and thus he saw them as dangerous. Because of "its deliberate avoidance of restraining intellectualism, Lawrence's erotic doctrine permits a violence of expression in which anger and hatred represent more powerfully encouraged motives than that of love." A more positive Lawrencean might reply—as did Lawrence in denunciatory passages in *Aaron's Rod* and *Kangaroo* (quoted in chapter 2)—that the "love-disease" has brought on more destruction than any mere anger or hatred ever could. But the case is not simply passional release versus fearful moral restraint. Even Rieff's Lawrence was responding to a genuine need as "the most talented believer in the irrational yet to protest the manipulative Reason born of the wedlock of power with profit" that dominates Western culture. Lawrence's erotic therapy for this rationalistic-commercial denuding of full life, however, aimed at larger positive purposes, though in fact he little had them (no politics, really, no community, and little sense of any plausible socioeconomic ordering). So we get, says the sociological dialectician, "a spurious therapy of commitment to nothing in particular," which thus results in an impassioned cultural "nihilism."

Rieff's view of Lawrence, as far as it goes (he ignores the utopianism, and much of the function of the dissident), seems to me considerably accurate not only for the figure but for much of his influence (some of which seems to be the unstated focus of his argument). It is also part of a larger argument for a Freud-like stoicism and conservative meliorism which Lawrence, it is clear, profoundly, however inadequately and dangerously, rejected. Lawrence demanded a cultural revolution, for which he not surprisingly lacked a politics but also hopelessly lacked a sense of institutions, order, and community. Conservative moralists such as Rieff are not prepared to acknowledge a subversive semicommunity of dissidence. Not incidentally, Lawrence's last fiction, *The Man Who Died*, had a Messiah who deconverted from social salvation and erotically reconverted to intense individual being, positing a permanent condition of passion-defiance-and-return. Granted, in this given world, Lawrence's passional desire and social negation encourages an individual redemption with no assurance of a larger social salvation beyond an open-ended rebellious awareness, and its heightening of experience.

Another step, beyond Rieff, would be to recognize the ironic reversal of the Lawrencean when it has become such a significant part of the culture. In older dialectics, this is neutralization by co-option, which may well have partly happened to the Lawrencean. An argument of this sort seems to have been suggested in recent years by the late historian of culture Michel Foucault. ("Seems," I note, because Foucault's arguments are frequently elliptical to a condition of willful obscurantism.) In the first volume of his never completed *History of Sexuality*, he twice uses Lawrence in crucial places in his final chapter, which suggests this largest perspective.

The first is in his intermittent context of the relation of sex to political power. "It is sex," said Kate in *The Plumed Serpent*. "How wonderful sex can be, when men keep it powerful and sacred, and it fills the world" (436). Foucault does not directly explicate the passage, but soon comments: "We must not think that by saying yes to sex, one says no to power; on the contrary, one tracks along the course laid out by the general deployment of sexuality." In that myth-fiction's rather nasty effort to emphatically fuse male sex and power, this is an odd comment, but Foucault is not concerned with the literary context, only his paradigm. However, it may be read as a restatement of Foucault's earlier argument that in Western culture there was an apparent change in the "deployment of sexuality" from obsessive nineteenth-century "generalized repression" to claimed processes "that make it possible to free oneself both of repression and of domination and exploitation." (Here, as with the libertarians cited earlier, it is linked with the would-be sexual revolutionary doctrines of the early Wilhelm Reich.) But Foucault had concluded that it was not a real change since it has not substantially transformed political domination. Instead, we have had the "deployment of sexuality by power" as just a more subtle form of the modern "management of life."[47] Lawrence, such dialectics appear to posit, thought a new vision of sex could change the world; like some other radical modernists, he was misled into affirming the adequacy of such revolt against the fantastic earlier modes of repression because of their very absurdity. But, one can hardly avoid concluding, in *The Plumed Serpent* Lawrence's use of sex as power repeats the sexual distortion, and indeed repressively not only for woman (Kate) but more generally in the very sanctification of it.

However, Lawrence, as is widely recognized (though Foucault never acknowledges the steps of the argument), drastically modified this for the more individualistic, antipower, eroticism of his last works, which had been part of his view all along. Thus appropriately, however elliptically, Foucault's other quotation from Lawrence is from the justification of *Lady Chatterley's Lover* (the "A Propos . . ." essay): "There has been so much action in the past," said D. H. Lawrence, "especially sexual action, a wearying repetition over and over, without a corresponding thought, a corresponding realization. Now our business is to realize sex. Today the full conscious realization of sex is even more important than the act itself." Agreed that Lawrence, though with some irony given his attacks on self-conscious sex ("sex in the head; no real desire"—the primal manipulatively corrupted), is arguing for a changed awareness. But, Foucault holds, this ostensible move towards fuller liberation turns out to be the submission of sex to "the power mechanisms of sexuality." For Foucault has posited emphatic distinctions between "sexuality," which is a mode of discourse, and "sex" as the thing in itself. When such sexuality as Lawrence's becomes "normative" (I think the argument goes), it ironically defeats the reality by subordinating it to the prevailing modes. In exalting sex, then, Lawrence created a response—an ideology and its idioms of sexuality—which served new tactics of domination. The old, simpler repressions at least had the virtue of giving meaning to sexual defiance.

In effect, Lawrence developed a politics of sex (for that is what normative discourse finally is)—or, as I have argued, falsely domesticated it in part (literally)—which just ended up as more politics, more repression. The "sexual revolution" claimed for recent times took place alright, under the aegis of such as Lawrence, but like so many modern revolutions it ended changing very little. Put in more American terms, the sexual revolution has turned out to be another ornate scam, an advertising and entertainment justificatory shuck, diversions for the fractured beings whose actual desires are to carry out the pervasive tyrannies of our technocracies. And *that* is why Lawrence has been so broadly accepted, enshrined, co-opted.

The counterarguments might be that liberating sexual realization, and what it implies in a more free society and new modes of unrepressive being, is still ongoing. But that does seem, if not a bit counterfactual, at least perplexed. Or one might argue that the liberation was subverted, not only by institutionalization but by the bland ideologizing. (No doubt most collections of Lawrence studies, or scholars, could be used in confirmation). But that smacks of the semiotic paranoia that seems to go with Foucaultism. Or one might hold that it was a false revolution, and we await the true one. But that leans to the pathetic and fanatic, contra-AIDS.

Foucault's suggestiveness with the issue seems to be substantial. The broad diffusion of Lawrenceanism (not just literary popularity) has often resulted in more parody and anomaly than new reality. His blasphemous obscenity was less realized than given patronizing exemption. His sexual heightening by extremity of masculine/feminine was rather more polemically exhausted than polymorphously and androgynously resolved. His sacral eroticism became just another exhibit in the Sunday marketplace. His demands for passional being mostly produces rococo therapies in the pseudo-indulgent culture of a relentlessly insane and self-destructive technocratic ordering. Yet Lawrence, it should be clear from the discussion of the later works, was envisioning radical changes in sensibility and society much larger than sexual discourse.

On the Other Hand . . .

Yes, but. I want to complicate as well as concretize a bit the perspective on Lawrence's role. With the indulgence of the scholarly reader, I wish to draw a bit more on some anecdotal, documentary, and speculative, as well as more traditional scholarly-critical, sources for considering further the peculiar legacies of Lawrence. I am still discussing, and arguing with, the Lawrencean dialectics of desire and negation, but with a sense of reverberations not always taken into account. Granted, I have no simple single line of argument, not least because I find the legacies, like the figure, often peculiar and puzzling. For example, I am still uncertain, after four decades, with quite how to take an enthusiastic witticism Saul Bellow made to me in a seminar in countering my commonsensical criticisms of Lawrence's often "stormy and damp" literary manners: "Of course, but with Lawrence, you can see the sky through the umbrella."

For later instance, from the pages of a personal journal of a generation ago: "Met a puzzling Lawrence devotee." In summary, I fell into chance conversation with an American male in his early twenties in the plaza of a mountain town in central Mexico. Costumed in a Lawrence-like reddish full beard (then uncommon), work boots, jeans, backpack, and rather un-Lawrencean stutteringly earnest manner, I recognize him now as a precursor of what was soon to become a counterculture type. A college dropout of middle-class, midwestern, origins, he explained that he was in the Mexican hinterlands searching, "ya know," for a "real experience." With a reverential gesture, he took a dog-eared paperback book from his pack, *The Plumed Serpent*, with the explanation that this, "ya know," was a "real book." Had I read it? When I nodded assent, he rather shimmeringly nodded back in an almost conspiratorial way, "I really dig it, ya know."

But I didn't (and still don't) know quite why Lawrence's authoritarian erotic-religious fantasy, with its primitivistic-cum-Methodist salvational rhetoric around a middle-aged British woman, appealed to him. Wouldn't Malcolm Lowry's *Under the Volcano* have been a more appropriately inappropriate bible in its lush occultism? Perhaps my incomprehension was partly my own fault, my impatient pedagogical questioning, since I have always viewed it as Lawrence's worst novel, and undoubtedly in part a product of physical-psychological as well as ideological illness. What could this exceedingly healthy innocent of a quite different generation find in the synthetic Quetzacoatl worship? I was not to further know. After being joined by a modern witch—a young woman in black tights, black turtleneck, densely patterned Indian skirt, and long, straight blonde hair, whose manner seemed an odd fusion of the submissive and the dominating as she stroked his arm and disdained our conversation—the young man left the brilliantly sunny plaza for the further obscurities of what I took to be a *Wanderjahr*, with Lawrence apparently as exotic cicerone for sexual experimentation and mystical yearning.[48]

I start my addendum of some of the social-cultural roles of D. H. Lawrence in the past half-century or so with this slight anecdote because it appropriately remains with me as a vivid but intellectually uncertain reminder of some of Lawrence's special effects. As various writings also seem to confirm, Lawrence has long had some peculiar functions in Anglo-American culture. His equally famous, and probably almost as much written on, British contemporary writers, such as James Joyce and Virginia Woolf, have not had that kind of role or influence. My example is only one of many times that I have come across what we academic critics are inclined to treat, with a perhaps too-facile defensive disdain, as an "extraliterary" use of Lawrence, though it seems integral with his didactic and prophetic role. It may also identify in its own right. "Oh yes," said a newly met traditional European scholar, "an American student of D. H. Lawrence— perhaps a specialist in heterodoxies?"

Indeed. But it also applies in more commonplace ways (though heresies, too, are more common than often granted even by the heretical). A no longer young academic colleague informed me a few years ago, in a tone of superior bravery, that his current domestic arrangements were "a true Lawrencean marriage." While I don't know if he baked bread and smashed dishes, I must suppose he referred to intense sex (and intense fights?) with his plump mate (escapee from a dull earlier marriage) in a cabin in the mountains, a style that also combined quasi-primitive partial alienation from mainstream customs with dubiously merited academic tenure. (He specialized in older women students writing on Lawrence and Buddhism and the like.) More ironically reporting on an earlier generation, well-known traditionalist Anglo-American poet Donald Davie has written that "some of us . . . tried to conduct our marriages on Lawrentian principles, with touching and comical consequences."[49] Behind such recurrent identification with an earlier couple lies, I must suppose, the biographical romance of Lawrence/Frieda "coming through," as Lawrence insisted in his poem-sequence as well as in semi-undisguised fictions. Perhaps, however, the publication in the mid-1980s of the second half of *Mr. Noon*, with its Frieda figure (Johanna) casually promiscuous and its Lawrence figure (Noon) sexually inadequate and timorously jealous, will contribute, along with changed sexual mores, to undercutting the never very coherent Lawrence romance-marriage mythology. Still, the sacralization of man/woman mating, however dependent on the now-recognized ambivalent sexuality and erotic transference of Protestant conversion experience ("baptism of fire"), may well continue as a watershed for passional desire in negating an old repressive ordering.

The Lawrencean, of course, has served as but a piece of a larger, shifting, mythology of personal therapy, renewal, and transcendence. In the mid-1970s, a late-thirtyish, upper-middle class divorcée, understandably retreading herself after the restrictiveness of a life as a corporate top-executive wife, wanted me to confirm for her that Lawrencean rhetoric (which she fashionably claimed to have been led to by Doris Lessing), new sexual openness, Joseph Campbell mythomaniaizing, enthusiastic stays in New Mexico, tasteful post–pop art-consumerism, and feminist countergambits to elite quasi-patriarchy were all one authenticity of "self-actualization." My mockeries, it seems evident, less deflated her self-indulgent manipulations than deflected them into aggrandizing ways. She soon distanced herself from the Lawrencean demands for personal transformation and erotic commitment and went in for sex displaced into power and Southern practical politics—no doubt more decent as well as useful than Lawrence's political fantasies—and rather successfully. That, of course, is but a variation on the "willful woman" and her erotic perversion that the sardonic side of Lawrence, as in so many of his later tales, delighted in satirizing. For several generations, then, Lawrenceanism may have ambiguously attracted certain types of manipulative ladies by seemingly sanctioning self-enlarging amoral aggrandizements with an aura of passional transcendence.

No doubt Lawrence does not deserve blame for this (though he did play encouraging sycophant-guru to a few), anymore than for his later journalistic exploiters, such as best-selling author Gay Talese, who in *Thy Neighbor's Wife* credits Lawrence, with no qualifications, as one of the heroic forerunners of the 1970s American sexual revolution.[50] Lawrence plausibly stood for the break with conventional sexual repressions, though hardly for the suburban sex games that Talese trumpeted. But one practice Talese does not report from the 1970s is that recorded by a specialist in the clinical treatment of "sexually dysfunctional males."[51] This employed (along with pornographic movies and a Japanese auditory tape of sexual climaxes) the required reading of *Lady Chatterley's Lover*. It is claimed that the treatment was often successful. And, in spite of the fiction's sexual peculiarity, why not? It is only theoreticians repressed into abstractions of "aesthetic distancing" who fail to recognize that literature exists in the mixed realities of the ongoing world.

To take a more immediate example. Delores La Chapelle, current (1989) radical-ecological propagandist of the Earth First! movement and mystic ritualist, caps an essay on countering technocratic society by quoting the passage of the Paul-Clara sexual consummation in a night field from *Sons and Lovers* (discussed in chapter 1). She fervently concludes of it that we all should "go a-Maying—sleep out together in nature on Mayday eve" and experience the "blossoming" of "human nature within all nature that D. H. Lawrence writes of" so persuasively, and so against the grain of our ecologically destructive ordering.[52]

This continuing umbrella role, and power, of Lawrence for the dissident is not inappropriate. Lawrenceanism has a long history of such use, including a series of periodicals dedicated to what has been perceived as his doctrines. These include a couple edited by John Middleton Murry with Lawrence's cooperation in the Great War period, Spud Johnson's *Laughing Horse* in New Mexico in the 1920s, Dexter Martin's *Lawrence News* in the 1950s, Arthur Efron's *Paunch* in the 1960s (and later), Gerald Butler and friends' *Continuing Literature* in the 1980s (not to mention such ostensibly, and genteelly, anti-ideological academic journals as the *D. H. Lawrence Review*), and some variety of more ephemeral "newsletters." Some years ago the editor of an obscure journal dedicated to Lawrence wrote asking me to turn my supposed erudition to a "serious purpose" and spell out the lineaments of "true orgasm" for women which Lawrence had discovered. When I submitted a little piece with several qualifications of Lawrence's treatment of the subject—certainly problematic (as feminist discussions noted above indicate)—and cited several clinical points drawn from the writings of psychoanalyst Alexander Lowen (a post-Reichean specialist in "true orgasmic response"), the editor fired back a denunciation of me as "not a real Laurentian," and informed me that he had destroyed my "disgusting manuscript."

One could probably write more than a chapter in the history of contemporary sexual ideologies around disputes using Lawrence (including responses to the sexual research publications of Kinsey, then of Masters and Johnson, then of the Hite reports, etc.) as a sort of modern semi-Tantric instructor. Even with the highly sophisticated, the view seems to currently prevail that Lawrence is *the* twentieth-century prophet of "a brave new sexual world."[53]

Defiant Desire

As a careful and skeptical scholar of the Romantics, the late E. E. Bostetter (my dissertation advisor), warned me long ago, "No matter how you make your interpretations of Lawrence, you should reckon with the historical situation that Lawrence is taken as a combination of Enlightenment liberator and romantic myth-maker."

No doubt Lawrence would have reacted with rage at some of the abuses of his sacral eroticism. But the use and misuse of Lawrence, be it in cultish expositions, titillating popular journalism, clinical sexual therapies, willful woman aggrandizements, ecological rituals, ideologies costumed as scholarship, or widespread personal erotic codes, as my examples suggest, does seem to brigade into a large legacy of Lawrenceanism. That such may sometimes have only a tangential relation to the originating figure and writings is not an unusual condition of cultural and social history, though it also may raise some intriguing issues of larger literary/cultural theory. Certainly writings of the Lawrencean sort should not be separated from the world in which they have played a significant role, with him as sexual prophet.

One can also hardly ignore Lawrence's considerable role as an "antiindustrial" social critic. This appears not only in the antimechanical, ecological living styles that the man and his writings suggest, and in his many apocalyptic pronouncements against the "mechanical" and the worship of the "Mammon" resulting in "industrial ugliness and greed," with the "disintegration of all positive living," but in the most basic sensibility. His insistence on organic responsiveness and passional desire must run antithetical to the very fiber and feelings enshrined in the technocratic.

A generation ago, Lawrence was one of the totemic references in the "two cultures" debate of C. P. Snow and F. R. Leavis, a pro- and antitechnocracy argument that attracted considerable attention but must now seem quaint and irrelevant because of the lack on both sides—though not on Lawrence's—of a sense of the deep ecological ravages of the overpopulated market-technocratic ordering which is literally destroying the world. In a looser but perhaps more immediately tangible sense, Lawrenceanism has long been a trope identifying the antimechanical (as I noted when neo-Marxist Herbert Marcuse mocked my lack of up-to-date kitchen appliances—my then wife was lamenting their absence to him—as an effect of my reading too much D. H. Lawrence). More recently, I listened warily to a paper by Canadian Lawrence scholar Paul Delaney in which, with a stock left-ideological prejudice not all that much different from reigning

Lawrence as Dissident Culture Hero

Thatcherism, he partly blamed the past British generation's devotion to Lawrence (he cited sociological studies indicating that *The Rainbow* was the favorite serious novel of British students in the 1970s) for the decline of Great Britain to industrially inefficient and economically depressed contemporary little England. A fancy version of blaming the messenger? Certainly the anti-industrial English tradition is far longer and larger than the Lawrenceanism which also announced its failure. That Lawrence, with several kinds of good reasons and responses, was anti-industrial, antitechnological, there can be no doubt—an early greening radical—even if that be judged by the conventionally inclined as the "politics of cultural despair."[54]

Unfortunately or not, the actual world does not always operate with ideological consistency, as I was reminded by fortuitously meeting a neighbor during a hike, a state-of-the-art Silicon Valley computer specialist, who was living with her surly lover and a menagerie of animals in a primitive cabin in the mountain redwoods above Santa Cruz. In the forest dialogue, I admitted to spending much of my time writing literary commentaries on such people as D. H. Lawrence (actually, an earlier version of this one). She beamingly announced that "Lawrence is one of my favorite writers." I couldn't resist the countering dig that he might not have thought altogether well of a female computer specialist. "Oh, Lawrence is wonderful, the way he understands women, but on some things he can use a little reprogramming." Such may often happen to legacies.

Lawrence also appears as an oddly favored anomaly in the views of some of the social commentators. In Dan Jacobson's "D. H. Lawrence and Modern Society," we have him as on the one hand a traditional English anti-industrialist (in the conglomerate nineteenth-century compound of Coleridge, Dickens, Carlyle, Ruskin, Morris—several, no doubt, provided early influences) who, however, succumbed to "hysterical patterns of reaction."[55] This largely means the vitriolic attacks on social love ethics in the "leadership novels" (as I previously discussed). But finally, for Jacobson, Lawrence really belongs on the left in his search for a fuller human and humane "balance," which makes him really "a thoroughgoing revolutionary and radical" in the modern sociopolitical sense. Given Lawrence's longterm raging against so many kinds of egalitarianism (and isn't social-political equality the crux of genuine leftism?), the earnest commentator's rhetoric seems a bit incoherent. Was Lawrence's?

Certainly it has had some quite varying interpreters. In a rather arch summary by intellectual journalist Diana Trilling at the end of the 1960s,

Defiant Desire

"Lawrence and the Movements of Modern Culture," we have a touchingly old-fashioned and passé Lawrence. The commentator's image of him must be so characterized as well, for she condescendingly claims that Lawrence's novelistic heroes were, like the author, limited to the "working class."[56] That is simply wrong for most of the novels—*The White Peacock, The Trespasser, The Rainbow, The Lost Girl, Women in Love, Kangaroo, The Plumed Serpent*, and does not really apply to ex–working-class Aaron, of the ambivalent rod, or Mellors of the last novel (as I elaborated in chapter 3). But Trilling may be right that Lawrence's major influence, whatever the mythicized social origins of his passion, in the 1930s and beyond was towards "the release of sexuality" from harsh societal restraints. However, she holds, in the 1950s Lawrence's emphasis on puritanical purpose and marriage as the outcome of eroticism became irrelevant to the cultural changes taking place. This became even more emphatic in the 1960s search for erotic "sensation" and "casual sex."[57] While the "make love, not war," attitude of the youthful protest movement certainly had things in common with Lawrence, she glibly pronounces, after all, he exalted in profound "mating" rather than mere "coupling." For what Lawrence was really about was "ideology-bound sexual ardor" based in a view "heavily charged with superego." That has not been the direction of modern American social and cultural changes. Apparently, then, the modern uses of Lawrence are not really Lawrencean, however sometimes colored in his name, and his American role is only vestigial. However tritely defined, there may be some truth to the claim, though a number of partisans have yet to discover it.

For a more British emphasis, we have, nearly a decade later, a survey of Lawrence's social-cultural acceptance by Keith Sagar, English Lawrence biographer, who describes his subject's views as "essentially utopian" (which utopianism not specified since it is used as a curse term), and also now irrelevant.[58] The description (per my earlier analysis) seems rather more pertinent than the judgment (especially when that is linked to the fashionable proposal of replacement prophet for a later generation of Ted Hughes, who hardly has analogous roles).

Sagar divides Lawrence's now terminal broad influence into four sketchy generations. "For his own generation Lawrence was a prophet, obscure but erratic, but felt to be in touch. . . with the sources of vitality and hence able to see more clearly than anyone else the sickness of his society." Though vague in relation to crucial class, sexual, and cosmic issues, that may have some appropriateness. For the 1930s and 1940s, Sagar simply

170

Lawrence as Dissident Culture Hero

dismisses any significant Lawrencean role, even literary (one must suppose
he does not know of Miller, Nin, Durrell, Auden, Williams, Olson, Sillitoe,
Lessing, et al., as well as more ordinary followers).[59] With the literary
revival in the 1950s, at least in England Lawrence represented "life-enhanc-
ing" values in overcoming sexual hypocrisy. But in the next decade that
quite succeeded, in evidence of which Sagar quotes Philip Larkin's "Annus
Mirabalis" that direct sex began in 1963 "Between the end of the Chatterley
ban / And the Beatles first LP."[60] Without disputing Larkin's wry wit about
the erotic watershed (at least for the British map), and granting that he
rightly saw it (in the poem) as dependent on the earlier fording of drying-
up traditional Christianity, I have noted other streams, some still turbulent,
and not in historical or ideological fact to be reduced, as Sagar would
have it, to a now merely old-trail antihypocrisy about sex and a dried-out
utopianism.

My anecdotal and documentary examples may suggest, but certainly do
not delimit, some of what Lawrence's dissident culture hero legacy has
served. A more thorough consideration might well take up, for example,
what I am not aware of anyone having done: examining, in relation both
to the literature and to the responses, the feature-length films made around
Lawrence's life and fictions.[61] A preliminary conclusion might emphasize
not only the diversity of the legacy but, my more general theme here, the
unity in the sense of dissidence. No doubt this memorializing, as it were,
creates its own traditions, which also becomes Lawrenceanism and its roles
of cultural dissidence (as I suggested in discussing Miller, Mailer, and the
Melvilleans as well as the Nietzschean). This even seems evident, though
perhaps insufficiently emphasized, in two recent academic collections of
essays on Lawrence's more specifically, and strikingly broad, literary influences.[62] However, isn't all this past cultural history? Surely, and to
project it into the future would indeed be problematic. I recall a once
notable critic, Lawrence scholar, and writer with considerable presumption
to a sense of the American cultural scene, Mark Schorer, insistently explaining that Lawrence's "sexual philosophy" had "run its course," and, at
least for America, no longer had much pertinence, though his art, at its
formally ragged best, might still be relevant.[63] That was more than three
decades ago, but evidently Lawrence's dissident ideological role—as suggested by the trials and multimillion sales of *Lady Chatterley*, the sometimes
Lawrence-costumed 1960s "sexual revolution," the 1970s (and continuing)
feminist/masculinist controversies, the many movie versions, the critical-

171

scholarly output previously cited, and the variety of my anecdotes and citations—shows it continued a bit longer. Fair warning.

Still, by and large, and the thrust of my collective examples, however varying the Lawrence legacy has been to the assertively sexual, the dissident and forbidden, the ways of marginal living, the extreme doctrines, and the like, it is widely embedded. Not accidentally, it is those of conservative (or trimmer, with Schorer and Spilka) temper who keep finding ideological Lawrence no longer relevant. And hoping that they are right?

I am suggesting—and that is all that I can properly do in this loose area—that Lawrence's radical dialectical cast has been much of his cultural influence. This is as it should be, though that is not the dominant bent of the learned commentators. Lawrenceanism, my varied examples suggest, has for more than a generation obviously shown considerable cultural phenomena—literary, cinematic, ideological, personal, even cultish. That, I propose, is not just a matter for cultural sociology. It is, with whatever skepticism and tough-mindedness one brings qualifyingly to bear, proper context for considering the writings and the role. For Lawrence, patently, was a didactic writer, both very good and very bad, and a driven man. He often demanded that his readers, as well as his characters (and erstwhile friends, as we see in the letters) do nothing less than drastically change their lives. The way the lessons have been mongered provides the ambience (however disguised in academic literary scientism) in which—really, by way of which—the responses exist.

I am not suggesting the fatuities and intellectual irresponsibility of "reader response" literary methodologies. But the engagement with Lawrence is considerably inseparable from his cultural roles and the responses they have engendered. What of, in several senses, "wrong" responses? Certainly the works can be badly read, and have been (as I have repeatedly tried to note), but the broad direction of dissidence and peculiarity is clear enough, however much it ignores the considerable skepticism and ambiguities in those writings. And the defiant stance—whether against the "censor morons," or for sexual conversion and "profound mating," or for a radically conservative gender mythology (which in effect demands something else) or as an apocalyptic prophet—is informingly around however dubiously it sometimes fits the mixed realities. Lawrence, I conclude, remains important above and below his mixed literary artistry for raising so many dissident issues, not just on literature and social class and sexuality and gender and revulsive prophecy but on much of the relation of imaginative culture to dominant society. We should now well see him as a major opponent of prevailing "humanism," the arrogant assumption of our aggrandizing omnipotence.[64] Thus the cast of Lawrence, including the inhumanism of his biocentric emphasis on nature and his antitechnocracy, is pertinent to a radical ecological vision. Yet another example from this matrix: Western he-man American writer, and anarchist-environmentalist, Edward Abbey, drew on Lawrencean values, and finally commented, "There is much to admire in the work of D. H. Lawrence—excepting his queer, soft, gooey, and epicene prose."[65] Lawrence is important, then, in spite of himself (I suspect that Abbey had been reading the usually most praised novels.) But perhaps a more widespread double response to Lawrence (as I illustrated in earlier discussion) has been to take him up as a liberationist, sexually and socially defiant, and then put him down as not enough so.[66] An appropriately endless dialectic.

Lawrence is exemplary, though often, as I have also tried to demonstrate, in some negative senses. Some of them are quite peculiar and dubious, as are some of their uses by others. There may be a good bit to learn from, and around, Lawrence, more than a little of it provoking. That may be the most important condition of his success. But as he put it in a fine defiant aphorism: "Anything that *triumphs*, perishes."[67] If he has not fully perished, it is because he has not fully triumphed. But how could he really, with that endless oppositional insistence, which even breaks through so much of our characteristic bland processing? Probably his proper heritage would be to go beyond his very partial triumph, including not a little ugliness and viciousness, though not beyond eroticized consciousness of desire and radical social negation, to a new and countering mode of passional being. And to a world to go with it. That is what we may dialectically learn from Lawrenceanism.

173

Notes

Works Cited

Index

Notes

1. Defiant Desire: Introduction, Examples, Adumbrations

1. While a number of my essays from the mid-1950s eventually became
   The Art of Perversity: D. H. Lawrence's Shorter Fictions (Seattle:
   University of Washington Press, 1962), my first study of Lawrence
   was prior to the revival (in a context of comparative counterromanti-
   cism), and perhaps therefore edgily suspicious of the normative revi-
   sionists. My references to the stories and novellas, which are only
   discussed incidentally here, frequently assume my earlier discussions.
   The edition of the novellas for both is D. H. Lawrence, *The Complete
   Short Novels*, 2 vols. (London: William Heinemann, 1956); of the
   stories for both is the incomplete *Complete Short Stories*, 3 vols.
   (London: William Heinemann, 1955).
2. D. H. Lawrence, "The Reality of Peace," in *Phoenix*, ed. Edward D.
   McDonald (London: William Heinemann, 1936), p. 680. The dehy-
   phenating in a later reprinting seems to weaken Lawrence's point.
   Reflections on the Death of a Porcupine and Other Essays, ed. Michael
   Herbert (Cambridge: Cambridge University Press, 1988), p. 27. (This,
   incidentally, is not quite a reprinting of the titled volume, as often in
   the somewhat misleading Cambridge edition.)
3. D. H. Lawrence, "The Crown," in *Reflections on the Death of a
   Porcupine* (London: Martin Secker, 1934), p. 6. I take it as no disservice to the perspective to select out quotes from this frequently bombas-
   tic and generally murky piece. I return to this collection in some detail
   later in the chapter.
4. "The Crown," in *Reflections* (1934), p. 18.
5. See the charming little essay, "Insouciance," in Lawrence's *Assorted*

Articles, reprinted in *Phoenix II*, ed. Warren Roberts and Harry T. Moore (New York: Viking, 1970), pp. 352–55.

6. See Dennis Jackson and Fleda Brown Jackson, Introduction to *Critical Essays on D. H. Lawrence*, ed. Jackson and Jackson (Boston: G. K. Hall, 1988).

7. "The Crown," p. 60.

8. See, for example, my *Edges of Extremity: Some Problems of Literary Modernism* (Tulsa, OK: University of Tulsa Monographs, 1980).

9. For my criticisms of neo-Marxists, see, for examples, "The Sociology of Literature?" *Studies in the Novel* 11 (1979): 99–105; and *Counterings: Utopian Dialectics in Contemporary Contexts* (Ann Arbor, MI: UMI Research, 1988), especially chap. 5.

10. D. H. Lawrence, "A Propos of *Lady Chatterley's Lover*," in Lawrence, *Sex, Literature, and Censorship*, ed. Harry T. Moore (New York: Twayne, 1953), p. 105.

11. It was first cited with early shock by Jessie Chambers; it also appears in Lawrence, "The Reality of Peace," in *Phoenix*, p. 680.

12. "A curse on idealism!" D. H. Lawrence, "Education of the People," in *Phoenix*, p. 631. "If we want to find the real enemy today, here it is: idealism." Lawrence, "Democracy," in *Phoenix*, p. 711. There are many others, including negative dramatizations in the fictions, frequently linked to Platonism or other monistic views (see the later discussion of Lawrence's Nietzscheanism).

13. Lawrence, "Democracy," in *Phoenix*, p. 713.

14. D. H. Lawrence, "Love," *Phoenix*, p. 156. The language here seems indebted to such evolutionists as Herbert Spencer, discussed later in this chapter.

15. D. H. Lawrence, "Prologue to *Women in Love*," in *Phoenix II*, p. 103.

16. In surveying the small number of commentaries in the last thirty years on *The Virgin and the Gipsy*, I do find one that is apt and useful: John Turner, "Purity and Danger in D. H. Lawrence's *The Virgin and the Gipsy*," in *D. H. Lawrence: Centenary Essays*, ed. Mara Kalnins (Bristol, U. K.: Bristol Classic Press, 1986), pp. 139–71. Though he does not quote the "desire" declaration I give here, he does appropriately note: "The word 'desire' itself is won out of all the mystificatory froth . . . and it retains the purity of its subversive force. . . . It is the word around which the possibilities of change, newness and energy cohere," p. 155.

17. D. H. Lawrence, *Fantasia of the Unconscious* (New York: Seltzer, 1922), p. 128. The following quote is from Lawrence's *Psychoanalysis and the Unconscious* (New York: Seltzer, 1921), p. 23.
18. D. H. Lawrence, *The White Peacock* (1911; reprint, Hammondsworth, U. K.: Penguin, 1950), p. 292. The following Annable quotations are found on pp. 198 and 196. For a more positive but not very insightful discussion of the early novels, see Michael Black, *D. H. Lawrence: The Early Fiction* (London: Macmillan, 1986).
19. D. H. Lawrence, *The Trespasser* (1912; reprint, London: William Heinemann, 1950), p. 57. For a discussion of the Helen Corke material, see my "Profiling an Erotic Prophet," *Studies in the Novel*, 7 (Summer 1976): 234–45.
20. D. H. Lawrence, *Sons and Lovers* (1913; reprint, New York: New American Library, 1953). Quotations are from pp. 343, 308, and 343, respectively. A useful selection of contrasting views is *Twentieth Century Interpretations of Sons and Lovers*, ed. Judith Farr (Englewood Cliffs, N.J.: Prentice-Hall, 1970). See also the citations in chap. 5, note 34. For a detailed case on Lawrence's early social "marginality" see Colin Holmes, "Lawrence's Social Origins," in *D. H. Lawrence, New Studies*, ed. Christopher Heywood (London: Macmillan, 1987), pp. 1–14. "Lawrence was born into a working class home, in terms of his father's occupation, but it was one full of aspirations" of a middle-class sort, thus encouraging a self-conscious and conflicted sense of class, resulting in a marginal view of role," p. 10. A full case for *Sons and Lovers* might require a detailed analysis of the novel's patterns of taste and sensibility, which certainly are not primarily of the working class, then or now. The first two novels, of course, are quite emphatically not working-class in materials and perspective. In Jeffrey Meyers, *D. H. Lawrence* (New York: Knopf, 1990), an acute biography from which I have several times profited in final revisions, emphasis is put on the working-class conditions but properly balanced by insistence on the mother as "narrow, genteel, respectable, rigid, repressed, puritanical, sanctimonious and self-righteous," p. 19. She obviously had the larger part in determining the ambience and character. Another way of coming at the working-class issue is the argument that Lawrence's critical political views "drove him to adopt a narrative perspective on his class origin which was external to that class," not least in *Sons and Lovers*. More generally, Lawrence was "culturally antagonis-

tic" to the working class. Jeremy Hawthorne, "Lawrence and Working-class Fiction," in *Rethinking Lawrence*, ed. Keith Brown (Milton Keynes, U. K.: Open University Press, 1990), p. 75.

21. Lawrence, "The Reality of Peace," *Phoenix*, p. 672.
22. Lawrence, "Prologue to *Women in Love*," in *Phoenix II*, p. 103.
23. See D. H. Lawrence, "Introduction to *Memoirs of the Foreign Legion*," in its reprinting in *Phoenix II* (1970), pp. 303–61, and more recently as a textually corrected separate volume, *Memoir of Maurice Magnus*, ed. Keith Cushman, rev. ed. (Santa Rosa, Calif.: Black Sparrow, 1987). A critical argument for it as one of Lawrence's best pieces of writing was recently made by Howard Mills in David Ellis and Howard Mills, *D. H. Lawrence's Non-Fiction* (Cambridge: Cambridge University Press, 1988), chap. 5. Unfortunately, this is not only poorly informed (as unaware of earlier reprintings by Alexander Woolcott [1937] and Saul Bellow [1960], and of earlier literary analysis [Widmer 1962]), it also seems unable to understand the significance of the work, both thematically and for what it tells us about Lawrence as a writer.
24. D. H. Lawrence, *The Rainbow* (1915; reprint, London: William Heinemann, 1950), with citations parenthetical in text. For a provocative survey of the criticism of the novel (including an attack on my earlier version of this commentary as too formalist and sexually repressed), see Gerald J. Butler, *This Is Carbon: A Defense of D. H. Lawrence's "The Rainbow" Against His Admirers* (Seattle: Genitron, 1986). I am also responding to some unpublished criticism of my view by Professor Warren Tallman of the University of British Columbia. Other aspects of *The Rainbow* are also discussed later.
25. "Sexual fulfillment is really all that seems to matter in this novel." Butler, p. 63. In his rather literal-minded taking of Lawrence's apparent intention for the literary reality, and in a partial-Freudian explication, Butler unproblematically treats it as simple-minded defense of conventional heterosexuality against a repressive society.

Lawrence's insistence on the state most often described as "wonder" parallels with Rudolf Otto's *The Idea of the Holy: An Inquiry into the Non-rational Factor in the Idea of the Divine and Its Relation to the Rational*, trans. John W. Harvey (New York: Oxford University Press, 1950). It also has strong similarities with the phenomenologist's emphasis on "being filled with wonder" at the world, which also continues the earlier romantics who "counsel wonder" as the vital relation to the world. For some examples (though not Lawrence), see Neil Evernden, *The Natural Alien* (Toronto: University of Toronto Press, 1985), pp. 137–39. I also find similar usage and experience in some radical nature writers (cited later).

26. See Hilary Simpson, *D. H. Lawrence and Feminism* (DeKalb: Northern Illinois University Press, 1982).

27. *Women in Love* (1920; reprint, New York: Viking, 1960), with citations parenthetical in text. Lavish information on Lawrence's many revisions of the text may be found in the editors' introduction to the Cambridge edition, *Women in Love*, ed. David Farmer, Lindeth Vasey and John Worthen (Cambridge: Cambridge University Press, 1987). I find more pertinent than the earlier critical interpretations some of the recent more tough-minded commentaries. For example, Joyce Carol Oates emphasizes the drastic extremities of Lawrence's views, including "the total absence of a concern for community," and an obsessive nightmare of "apocalypse without resurrection," or any adequate human meaning. "Lawrence's Götterdammerung: The Apocalyptic Vision of *Women in Love*," in *Critical Essays on D. H. Lawrence*, pp. 47, 107. Cornelia Nixon, in an often rigorous analysis, emphasizes the antifeminism, including that the oppositional eroticism is pretty much "subsumed" in male dominance and in a "fulfillment . . . asexual, anti-fertile, undemocratic and deeply misanthropic." See *Lawrence's Leadership Politics and the Turn Against Women* (Berkeley: University of California Press, 1986), pp. 213, 32, respectively. However, I think she overemphasizes Lawrence's "break," a "change in his thinking" in 1915, supposedly caused by his revolt against "powerful women" and to "express the homoeroticism he found unacceptable in himself." Both motifs are clearly evident earlier, and the continuity seems rather more important. Peter Balbert, who gave an exaggerated emphasis on the "normative marriage" theme in *The Rainbow*, better grants unresolved conflict in *Women in Love* (though he obviously exaggerates the equality given to Ursula), *D. H. Lawrence and the Phallic Imagination* (New York: St. Martin's, 1989), pp. 85–100. In a milder antifeminist countering, Declan Kiberd also exaggerates the marriage resolution but, more interestingly, insists on the androgynous implications in spite of Lawrence's gender polarization in his religiousized eroticism. *Men and Feminism in Modern Literature* (London: Macmillan, 1985), pp. 145, 149. Other recent commentaries seem weaker, as with that

of Margery Sabin, who simply emphasizes the "precarious" shape of the male/female verbal battles and (especially confirmed in *Sea and Sardina*) Lawrence's evident confusions. *The Dialect of the Tribe* (New York: Oxford University Press, 1987), pp. 106–38, 140–62. As with earlier symbolistical readings, more recent semiotic readings of *Women in Love* are ingeniously off the human issues, as with Michael Ragnissis, *The Subterfuge of Art* (Baltimore: Johns Hopkins University Press, 1978), pp. 172–225, who uses language games to confirm the inadequacy of language, especially Lawrence's, but fails to resolve at all the significance of the forced language. I find that one of the few others to insist on the necessary utopianism is Peter New (his lengthy neo-Leavisite commentary on *Women in Love* is placed within a utopian history): *Fiction and Purpose in Utopia, Rasseles, The Mill on the Floss and Women in Love* (London: Macmillan, 1985), pp. 231–303. But he emphasizes that Lawrence's utopianism is self-defeating and undisciplined fantasy based in "negation," which ends as mostly an intensified negative "model" of life purpose.

28. Lawrence, "Prologue to *Women in Love*," *Phoenix II*, pp. 92–108.

29. Lawrence, "Education of the People," *Phoenix*, p. 647.

30. "The secret, shameful things are most terribly beautiful." *The Rainbow*, p. 235. It is the same rhetoric as in the other anal-erotic passages.

31. D. H. Lawrence, *The Lost Girl* (1920; reprint, London: William Heinemann, 1950), citations parenthetical in text. A brief survey of the usually too-dismissive critical treatment of this novel is provided by Peter Balbert, "Ten Men and a Sacred Prostitute: The Psychology of Sex in the Cambridge Edition of *The Lost Girl*," *Twentieth Century Literature* 36 (Winter 1990): 381–402. Balbert reasonably emphasizes that much of "Lawrence's actual aim is to dramatize from 'afar' the destructive effects of . . . British notions of propriety on the passion and love-life of his generation." He also grants part of the failure of the work in "Lawrence's ambivalent relation to his fictional material." But, it seems to me, by overriding the externals of a prostitute metaphor, Balbert misses the deeper conflict of Lawrence's social awareness against his insistence on a primordial, salvational sexual passion.

32. D. H. Lawrence, *Mr. Noon*, ed. Lindeth Vasey (Cambridge: Cambridge University Press, 1984), with citations parenthetical in text. The conversion experience here has at least been noted, in an otherwise weak discussion of the novel: "Rebirth is a religious concept; and

Lawrence . . . is taking it back from orthodox religion for his own use." Michael Black, "Gilbert Noon, D. H. Lawrence and the Gentle Reader," *D. H. Lawrence Review*, 20 (Summer 1988): 23–45. This is too vague, both as to source tradition and as to use. Quite possibly, though I cannot specifically confirm it, Lawrence was also strongly influenced by William James, *Varieties of Religious Experience* (1902; reprint, Cambridge: Harvard University Press, 1985), which he probably read in his teacher-college period, and which is still an appropriate delineation of part of the "twice-born" experience. Jeffrey Meyers aptly points out that the fervently practicing Congregationalist mother had been raised a Methodist, which was also a popular sect in the Eastwood community. Meyers, *Lawrence*, pp. 23 ff. I suggest this may have added a subjective emotionalism to the more general Nonconformist individualism. That Noon's multiple-quick sexual peculiarity was also the author's is further confirmed by the description of Lawrence's relationship with Alice Dax, as cited by Meyers, p. 46.

33. F. R. Leavis, *Thought, Words and Creativity: Art and Thought in Lawrence* (New York: Oxford University Press, 1976). A well-known collection of "moral formalist" readings in this vein is Mark Spilka, *The Love Ethic of D. H. Lawrence* (Bloomington: Indiana University Press, 1955). But in fairness I should note that Spilka has acknowledged "radical modifications" in his approach in his later writings on Lawrence. Introduction to "D. H. Lawrence in Changing Times: A Normative Progress" (from the manuscript of a book in process). (Professor Spilka kindly made available to me the manuscript of his book, whose more sophisticated biographical and neo-Freudian–therapeutic character analyses I refer to later, though our views remain far apart.)

34. D. H. Lawrence, ". . . Love Was Once a Little Boy," *Reflections* (1934), pp. 161–92.

35. Harry T. Moore suggests a bit earlier, *The Priest of Love*, rev. ed. (New York: Farrar, Straus, and Giroux, 1974), p. 82; Emile Delavenay suggests the college period, *D. H. Lawrence, the Man and His Work: The Formative Years, 1885–1919* (London: William Heinemann, 1972), p. 48. Perhaps because of his later anti-evolutionary remarks, the persisting effects of highly popular social Darwinism on him do not seem to have been given due emphasis. However, I recently find a partly corrective study by Roger Ebbatson, "A Spark Beneath the

Wheel: Lawrence and Evolutionary Thought," in *D. H. Lawrence, New Studies*, ed. Christopher Heywood, pp. 90–113, who properly emphasizes that "Spencer's evolution is part of Lawrence's imaginative being," and that Spencer (and related thought, such as in the also popular writings of T. H. Huxley and Ernst Haeckel) is crucial to understanding much of Lawrence. But Ebbatson doesn't seem to recognize Lawrence's drastic economic twisting and social negation of social Darwinism's glorification of capitalistic competition. It is not clear to me whether Lawrence is drawing on Spencer's *First Principles* (1862), or *Principles of Biology* (1865)—this would tie in with the Ursula lab scene in *The Rainbow*—or later ethical essays. For analysis of Spencer, I am drawing on David Wiltshire, *The Social and Political Thought of Herbert Spencer* (Oxford: Oxford University Press, 1978), pp. 192ff. Since social Darwinism was so widespread in Lawrence's youth, other sources are certainly possible (though not all other sources—certainly, and unfortunately, I would say, there is nothing of Kropotkin's *Mutual Aid*). "Study of Thomas Hardy" was first published posthumously, *Phoenix*, pp. 398–516.

36. D. H. Lawrence, "Reflections on the Death of a Porcupine," in *Reflections* (1934), pp. 193–222. For the following *St. Mawr* passage, see *The Complete Short Novels*, 2: 141–42. References to other novellas and stories are also to this edition.

37. D. H. Lawrence, "Aristocracy," in *Reflections* (1934), pp. 223–40.

38. D. H. Lawrence, "Blessed Are the Powerful," in *Reflections* (1934), pp. 145–60. The interpolated quote is from "Red Trousers," *Assorted Articles* (New York: Knopf, 1930), p. 103.

39. D. H. Lawrence, "Him with His Tail in His Mouth," in *Reflections* (1934), pp. 127–44.

40. Lawrence, "Democracy," in *Phoenix*, pp. 699–718. The essay was apparently written in 1919—see Herbert's Introduction to *Reflections* (1988), p. xxviii. Birkin's attacks on equality are essentially continuous with the essay; see, for example, *Women in Love*, pp. 96ff.

41. Michael Bentley, "Lawrence's Political Thought: Some English Contexts, 1906–19," *D. H. Lawrence*, ed. Heywood, p. 64. The context is an admixture of early socialism, revulsion to bourgeois democracy and its Great War, authoritarian fantasies, and an extreme individualism which I find more continuous than Bentley seems to suggest, and more indebted to dissenting religion, social Darwinism, and Nietz-

scheanism. Another recent commentator rightly notes that Lawrence's extreme individualism is antimarket, that the bent of some of his reflections on democracy is less towards authoritarianism than a "kind of anarchistic syndicalism," and that the last works are dominantly antiauthoritarian. Rick Rylance, "Lawrence's Politics," in *Rethinking Lawrence*, ed. Keith Brown (Milton Keynes, U. K.: Open University Press, 1990), pp. 167, 168, 178.

2. Dark Prophecy of Negative Desire: Lawrence's Nietzschean Matrix

1. Most emphatically, of course, with F. R. Leavis, *D. H. Lawrence: Novelist* (London: Chatto and Windus, 1955), and *Thought, Words and Creativity* (New York: Oxford University Press, 1976).
2. A particularly but by no means uniquely egregious example is Richard Swigg, *Lawrence, Hardy, and American Literature* (New York: Oxford University Press, 1972).
3. For example, Emile Delavenay, *D. H. Lawrence and Edward Carpenter: A Study in Edwardian Transition* (London: William Heinemann, 1971), a rather forced conjoining. For some of the intellectual relations with Carlyle, see several of the studies cited later, and the interesting discussion of the tradition of English "imagination" in John Brian, *Supreme Fictions* (Montreal: University of Toronto Press, 1974).
4. Among many sentimental examples, see the otherwise useful Harry T. Moore, *The Priest of Love, A Life of D. H. Lawrence*, rev. ed. (New York: Farrar, Straus, and Giroux, 1974); and Phillip Callow, *Son and Lover: The Young D. H. Lawrence* (New York: Viking, 1975).
5. For Whitman, see D. H. Lawrence, chap. 12, *Studies in Classic American Literature* (1923; reprint, New York: Doubleday, 1953); for a negative comment on Blake, p. 82 of the same work; for a more mixed comment on Blake, see Lawrence, *Phoenix*, ed. Edward McDonald (London: William Heinemann, 1936), p. 560. There are others. I cited an example of Lawrence's mockery of Wordsworth previously, in chap. 1. Further citations from Lawrence's *Studies* will appear parenthetically in text.
6. See Martin Green, *The von Richthofen Sisters* (New York: Basic, 1974). While I think much of Green's argument as to the influence of Frieda on Lawrence's *Lebensphilosophie* is patently wrong (and some

of the contrary evidence is indicated in this chapter), his more general emphasis on the ideological cast and subterranean traditions of sensibility (rather than just "sources" and "influences") is importantly appropriate.

7. See the following section of this chapter, and the citations in note 23, following.

8. Ford Madox Ford, *Return to Yesterday* (London: Methuen, 1931), p. 392. A sensible comment on the passage is provided by James Boulton, Introduction to D. H. Lawrence,*The Letters*, ed. James Boulton, vol. 1, *1901–1913* (Cambridge: Cambridge University Press, 1979), p. 9. I have elsewhere discussed Ford in some detail, both as memoir writer and counterculturist, as in "From Great War to Little Garden: Ford's Ford," *Antaeus* no. 56 (Spring 1986): 179–90.

9. Jessie Chambers, *D. H. Lawrence: A Personal Record*, 2d ed. (London: Barnes and Noble, 1965), p. 120. The passage had been previously discussed by Bentley and Steinhauer. Patrick Bridgewater in *Nietzsche in Anglosaxony* (Leicester, U. K.: University of Leicester Press, 1972), p. 104, suggests that Lawrence read the Zimmerman translation of *Beyond Good and Evil* in 1908 (I would guess 1909, since he is unlikey to have read it immediately on publication), and other works shortly after, which were locally available in translation. While Lawrence read German, and was, at least later, relatively fluent—see Armin Arnold, *D. H. Lawrence and German Literature* (Montreal: University of Toronto Press, 1963)—it seems likely that most of his Nietzsche was in English, with later German tags picked up from Frieda, though possibly he reread some in German. In annotating Lawrence allusions in some of his essays, a recent editor reasonably enough cites *Beyond Good and Evil*, *Thus Spoke Zarathustra*, and the pieces collected as *The Will to Power*. See Lawrence, *Study of Thomas Hardy and Other Essays*, ed. Bruce Steele (Cambridge, U. K.: Cambridge University Press, 1985). While the translations he used were most likely those collected in the Levi edition (London, 1908–13), my few quotations below are taken from later translations since my main issues are not source texts but intellectual parallels, ideological similarities, and sensibilities.

10. In "A Modern Lover," D. H. Lawrence, *Complete Short Stories*, 3 vols. (London: William Heinemann, 1955), 1:6–22. There are various other Nietzsche references in Lawrence, such as the innocuous one in

his *Collected Letters*, ed. Harry T. Moore (New York: Viking, 1962), 1:204. More importantly, Lawrence indicates in a letter in early 1915 that he thought of calling his first "philosophical" essays "*Le Gai Savaire*" (24 Feb. to Bertrand Russell), apparently after Nietzsche's *Die Frohliche Wissenschaft* (usually translated as "The Gay Science"), which certainly suggests the important role of the Nietzschean for him at that relatively early date. It also employs the twisting by way of the French to distinguish himself from the German (but still be foreign?), which I have noted elsewhere. *The Letters of D. H. Lawrence*, ed. George J. Zytaruk and James T. Boulton, *1913–1916* (Cambridge: Cambridge University Press, 1981), 2:295. There is also one of many negative references to *Wille zur Macht* in a letter of December of that year, p. 489, and a reference the following year to *Zarathustra*, p. 546. Throughout many works, some not discussed here, Lawrence negatively uses Will to Power, even as late as *Etruscan Places*, one of his very last works (published posthumously).

11. D. H. Lawrence, *The Trespasser* (1912; reprint, London: William Heinemann, 1955), p. 57. The protagonist brings a Nietzsche book (unspecified) to a love tryst.

12. "Georgian Poetry: 1911–12," in Lawrence, *Phoenix*, p. 304. One notes that Lawrence rings Nietzsche into all sorts of unlikely subjects in this period.

13. Lawrence, "Study of Thomas Hardy," in *Phoenix*, pp. 490–92. Elsewhere in his meandering ruminations around Hardy, Lawrence shrewdly rejects Nietzsche's late doctrine of Eternal Recurrence by insisting that "each cycle is different. There is no real recurrence." "Study," p. 461. This may be taken as a moral as well as logical objection to the doctrine, as usually interpreted. One can, however, interpret Nietzsche as pointing towards something else—"eternal recurrence is not a theory of the world but a view of the self." Alexander Nehamas, *Nietzsche, Life as Literature* (Cambridge: Harvard University Press, 1985), p. 157. Apparently that means accepting, contrary to afterlife doctrines, becoming what one is as a culmination of what one has been.

14. D. H. Lawrence, "Education of the People" (first published 1920), *Phoenix*, p. 640.

15. Egbert, the Georgian aesthete protagonist of this awkward story, seems admirable but lacks an "acrid courage, and a certain will-to-power."

He ends by revealing his (and the English genteel cultural tradition's) longing for self-destruction. Lawrence, "England, My England," *Complete Short Stories*, 2:303–33. For the biographical dimensions (which may muddle the literary coherence of the story), see Jeffrey Meyers, *D. H. Lawrence, A Biography* (New York: Knopf, 1990), pp. 174–77.

16. See the similar attack in the later essays, as discussed in chapter 1. These are not the only probable Nietzscheanisms in the novel. For example, at one point Ursula identifies with the dark (as against the lighted town—a negative image for Lawrence, as with the conclusion to *Sons and Lovers*), and scornfully says to herself, "What are you, you pale Citizens?"— perhaps adaption of Nietzsche's conquering "pale Galilean"; she then somewhat improbably concludes in Nietzschean scorn of the middle-class conventionalized male, "You subdued beast in sheep's clothing, you primal darkness falsified to a social mechanism" (*Rainbow*, p. 448.) The pretty obvious Nietzscheanism in *The Rainbow* raises doubts about a number of commentators who would find a crucial ideological turning point (for reasons of personal problems or response to the war) *after* that novel. For example, Cornelia Nixon (as is crucial for her argument of a psychological watershed to authoritarian misogyny) holds that the Nietzschean influence only comes in later years. *Lawrence's Leadership Politics and the Turn Against Women* (Berkeley: University of California Press, 1986), p. 229, etc. The strong evidence suggests that is not true.

17. Lawrence, "Prologue to *Women in Love*," in *Phoenix II*, ed. Warren Roberts and Harry T. Moore (New York: Viking, 1970), p. 94.

18. "Prologue," *Phoenix II*, p. 103.

19. Nietzche, "On Self Conquest," *Thus Spoke Zarathustra*, part 2 in *The Portable Nietzche*, trans. and ed. Walter Kaufmann (New York: Viking, 1968).

20. In context, this applies to the people in the early twentieth-century mining town but also fits the "slavish" submission of Alvina to the dark mastery of her lover (a more commonsense as well as almost comical version of the demon-lover).

21. D. H. Lawrence, "None of That," *Complete Short Stories*, 3:701–21.

22. D. H. Lawrence, *Reflections on the Death of a Porcupine and Other Essays* (London: Martin Secker, 1934), p. 145. In a later edition of some of these essays (and others), the editor does note the influence of Nietzsche, pp. xxi and 405, but does not note it in this passage,

though it seems confirmed in the passage shortly following that "the Germans again [following Judeo-Christian religion] made the mistake of deifying the egoistic Will of Man: the will-to-power." *Reflections on the Death of a Porcupine and Other Essays*, ed. Michael Herbert (Cambridge: Cambridge University Press, 1988).

23. "The final aim is not *to know*, but *to be*." D. H. Lawrence, *Fantasia of the Unconscious* (New York: Seltzer, 1922), p. 60. The point is variously repeated elsewhere—central valuation in Lawrence. And, I think, in Nietzsche, though neither writer's terms and ontology seem altogether consistent.

24. Eric Bentley, *A Century of Hero-Worship, A Study of the Idea of Heroism in Carlyle and Nietzsche* (New York: Duell-Sloan, 1944), pp. 221–53. (I should probably acknowledge here that I was a student of Bentley's in 1948.) The following references: H. Steinhauer, "Eros and Psyche: A Nietzschean Motif in Anglo-American Literature," *Modern Language Notes* 64 (1949): 217–28; Kingsley Widmer, *The Art of Perversity: D. H. Lawrence's Shorter Fictions* (Seattle: University of Washington Press, 1962), pp. 241–42, and implicitly throughout; Eugene Goodheart, *The Utopian Vision of D. H. Lawrence* (Chicago: University of Chicago Press, 1963), throughout; Ronald Gray, *The German Tradition in Literature, 1871–1945* (Cambridge: Cambridge University Press, 1965), pp. 326–54; David S. Thatcher, *Nietzsche in England, 1890–1914* (Toronto: University of Toronto Press, 1970); Patrick Bridgewater, *Nietzsche in Anglosaxony*, pp. 104–9; Emile Delavenay, *D. H. Lawrence, the Man and His Work: The Formative Years,1885–1919* (London: William Heinemann, 1972), throughout; John B. Humma, "D. H. Lawrence as Frederich Nietzsche," *Philological Quarterly* 53 (1974): 110–20; Eleanor Green, "Blueprints for Utopia: The Political Ideas of Nietzsche and D. H. Lawrence," *Renaissance and Modern Studies* 18 (1974): 141–61; Jennifer Michaels-Tonks, *D. H. Lawrence* (Bonn, Germany: Bouvier, 1976); John Burt Foster, Jr., *Heirs to Dionysus: A Nietzschean Current in Literary Modernism* (Princeton: Princeton University Press, 1981), pp. 180–255; Colin Milton, *Lawrence and Nietzsche* (Aberdeen, U.K.: Aberdeen University Press, 1987), pp. 202, 232; Keith M. May, *Nietzsche and Modern Literature* (New York: St. Martin's, 1988), pp. 4, 111–43. H. M. Robinson, "Nietzsche, Lawrence, and the Somatic Conception of the Good Life, *New Comparison* 5 (1988): 40–56.

While not complete, the chronological sampling seems reasonably representative.

25. The Nietzscheanism also seems important to emphasize not least because this one can be documented where other radical or peculiar influences (outside the British mainstream) cannot be (see the problems of the previously cited Delavenay and Green), though many thoughtful readers note strangely un–Anglo-American notions and emphases in Lawrence which are not to be explained by conventional lineages.

26. The quote is found in "On the Despizers of the Body," *Zarathustra*, part 1.

27. This quote is from D. H. Lawrence, *Memoir of Maurice Magnus*, ed. Keith Cushman, rev. ed. (Santa Rosa, Calif.: Black Sparrow, 1987), p. 95. In context, this seems to contrast with the decadent (to Lawrence) Catholicism-homosexuality of Magnus. Lawrence's "The Border Line," can be found in *Complete Short Stories*, 3. See p. 589 for the specific reference to Nietzsche. Moore summarized the biographical background, *Priest of Love*, pp. 381, 386–87.

28. Other examples of the Lawrence projection into military-aristocrat heroes includes Captain Hepburn of the novella *The Captain's Doll* and Count Dionys of the novella *The Lady Bird*, both tales of *Übermensch* romantic adultery and dominance. The contrasting effete intellectual Phillip of "The Border Line" is not only of a piece with the similar character in "Smile" and "The Last Laugh" (both trivial *romans à clef*) but with the recurrent figure of the inadequate cerebral man in the better-known tales, such as the intellectual clergyman Massey in "The Daughters of the Vicar" and the intellectual lawyer Bertie in "The Blind Man."

29. In *Reflections*, ed. Herbert, p. 311.

30. D. H. Lawrence, *Aaron's Rod* (1922; reprint, London: William Heinemann, 1950), with citations parenthetical in text. But consider also an issue in this novel where Lawrence seems to diverge from Nietzsche, such as, "Homage . . . is just a convention and social trick," p. 164. And he repeatedly demonstrates it in the fictions. Nietzsche, good middle-European, repeatedly praises social obeisance, and he would happily enforce it as an expression of the *"instinct for rank." Beyond Good and Evil*, trans. Walter Kaufmann (New York: Random House, 1966), p. 212. See, also, the comments in part 9, "What Is Noble." Yet Lawrence's intermittent emphasis on what he called the "aristocratic

principle" ends up with a similar prejudice, made especially crass around Ramon in *The Plumed Serpent*, in spite of the author's often out-class cynical wisdom, and this is especially strong in his most bigoted works. It has plausibly been noted that often in *Aaron's Rod* Lawrence "seems to be distorting Nietzsche to disguise his espousal of him." William Larrett, "Lawrence and Germany: A Reluctant Guest in the Land of 'Pure Ideas,'" in *Rethinking Lawrence*, ed. Keith Brown (Milton Keynes, U. K.: Open University Press, 1990), p. 90. Many discussions of this novel manage to ignore most of its problems, such as the Nietzschean ideology, the authoritarian politics and the homoeroticism. See, for example, John B. Humma, *Metaphor and Meaning in D. H. Lawrence's Later Novels* (Columbia: University of Missouri Press, 1990), pp. 7–15. Since Humma elsewhere discusses *The Plumed Serpent*'s indebtedness to Nietzsche, the forced critical ignorance may be the result of the vestigial New Critical emphasis on secondary metaphors.

31. There is also, though most commentators ignore it, some racist ranting, pp. 103ff.
32. The quotes are from "Aristocracy," *Reflections* (1934), p. 224.
33. See also Lawrence's preface to Dostoyevsky's "The Grand Inquisitor," reprinted *Phoenix*, pp. 283–91, for other praise of authoritarianism. For Nietzsche on socialism as an extension of the moral sickness of Christianity, see *The Will to Power*, trans. Walter Kaufmann and R. J. Hollingdale (New York: Random House, 1968), pp. 77–78, and many similar remarks elsewhere. Lawrence's attack in the novel on idealism undoubtedly intends it in a specific sense—Platonism. Nietzsche, of course, mounted it in *The Birth of Tragedy*, especially against the figure of Plato's Socrates in the later sections, and repeated it elsewhere. For Lawrence, idealism connected with Plato marks false authority and impotence, not just denaturing rationality—effete aristocrat-Platonist husband Boris in *The Lady Bird*, and impotent aristocrat-husband Clifford in *Lady Chatterley's Lover*, are representative. Given the exalted status of Plato in late-Victorian thought, Lawrence's villainizing of him would almost certainly have to derive from Nietzsche.
34. Robert C. Solomon, "Nietzsche, Nihilism, and Morality," in *Nietzsche*, ed. Solomon (South Bend, Ind.: University of Notre Dame Press, 1980), p. 203.

35. No attempt is made here to cover all the fictions, much less all the writings, only representative examples, usually in chronological order.
36. See Moore, *Priest of Love*, pp. 293–352.
37. D. H. Lawrence, *Kangaroo* (1923; reprint, London: William Heinemann, 1950), with citations parenthetical in text.
38. See my discussion of the various versions of *Lady Chatterley's Lover* in the following chapter.
39. Nietzsche uses the same dubious examples of historical heroes in *The Will to Power*, though the larger context of both suggests rather more vitalistic-cultural heroes.
40. For Nietzsche on *ressentiment* as the envious "morality" of the weak, see *On the Genealogy of Morals*, trans. Walter Kaufmann and R. J. Hollingdale (New York: Random House, 1969), pp. 36ff. As indicated in the biographical discussion that follows, there were some similar motives for similar vices in the two writers.
41. For discussions of Nietzsche's Will to Power, see Walter Kaufmann, *Nietzsche: Philosopher, Psychologist, Antichrist*, 4th ed. (Princeton: Princeton University Press, 1974), pp. 178ff.; and for qualifications, J. P. Stern, *Nietzsche* (Hassocks, Sussex, U. K.: Harvester, 1978), pp. 76ff. I am particularly indebted to the commensensical discussion of Arthur C. Danto, *Nietzsche as Philosopher* (New York: Macmillan, 1965), pp. 214ff, in spite of doubts about his oversystematizing the essentially fragmented writer-thinker. Still, the other extreme, such as the demystification by reduction to mysterious fragments, as with Jacques Derrida, *Spurs/Eperons* (Chicago: University of Chicago Press, 1979), is hardly helpful, except as a remystifying witticism (though he does at least note Nietzsche's "venomous anti-feminism," p. 57). Some other perspectives on Nietzsche also seem to confirm my emphasis on Will to Power as an ontological metaphor, as with Martin Heidegger, *Nietzsche*, trans. D. T. Krell, vol. 1 (New York: Harper and Row, 1979).
42. Something similar to the doctrine, a kind of vitalist evolutionism, also appears in the description of the New Mexico scene in the final section of *St. Mawr*, Lawrence, *The Complete Short Novels* (London: William Heinemann, 1956), 2:138ff. The importance of this more generally in understanding Lawrence seems to me to have been undervalued.
43. D. H. Lawrence, *The Plumed Serpent* (1926; reprint, New York:

Knopf, 1951), with citations parenthetical in text. *Zarathustra* in *The Portable Nietzsche*.

44. The most usable detailed discussion remains L. D. Clark, *The Dark Night of the Body: D. H. Lawrence's "The Plumed Serpent"* (Austin: University of Texas Press, 1964). He puts some emphasis on the forced, and inconsistent, pattern of Lawrence's mythicizing. This at least corrects the many silly studies of this novel, following the 1950s revival, which overrode the arbitrariness and incoherence. For examples of that, see the Introduction by William York Tindall (1951, the edition cited here); and Jascha Kessler, "Descent into Darkness: The Myth of *The Plumed Serpent*", in *A D. H. Lawrence Miscellany*, ed. Harry T. Moore (Carbondale: Southern Illinois University Press, 1959), pp. 239–60. For a moderate discussion of Lawrence's attitude towards his tangible materials, see Charles Rossman, "D. H. Lawrence and Mexico," in *D. H. Lawrence, A Centenary Celebration*, ed. by Peter Balbert and Phillip L. Marcus (Ithaca, N. Y.: Cornell University Press, 1985), pp. 180–209.

The "morning star" metaphor also appears in *Zarathustra*, and many other parallels could also be suggested, including the synthetic rhetorics (neither at his best), the lack of plausible character development— unusual in Lawrence but not in Nietzsche (see Stern, *Nietzsche*, pp. 102ff.). Unlike the previous novels, *The Plumed Serpent* does not turn away from its own mythicizing to extreme individualism. And that for both may be the most pertinent tradition. I suspect that John Carroll may be right to hold (in contrast to commentators such as Kaufmann) that Max Stirner lies significantly behind Nietzsche (see Carroll's *The Break-Out from the Crystal Palace* [London: Routledge and Kegan Paul, 1974], and his annotations to Stirner's *The Ego and His Own*, trans. Steven Byington [1844; reprint, London, 1971], pp. 24–25. Carroll is not interested in Lawrence, whose sexual emphasis he elsewhere crassly attacks.) Behind Stirner, who also savaged sexual renunciation, among other conventions, one might point to certain Enlightenment libertarian sexual psychologies, such as that of Charles Fourier. Steinhauer (see note 24) also related Nietzschean-Lawrencean views to the French Enlightenment, by way of Heinrich Heine. While it is usual to see Schopenhauer (also read by Lawrence) behind Nietzsche's doctrine of will—and it is libidinal: Nietzsche wrote, "My body and my will are one" (discussed by Ronald Hayman, *Nietzsche: A Critical*

Life [New York: Oxford University Press, 1980], p. 72). Still, there may be other heritages to these essential tropes, such as, speculatively, Fourier, Stirner, Nietzsche, and Lawrence, including not least Enlightenment reactions, recurrent paganizing, and radical Protestantism.

45. I may have borrowed the epithet from Kenneth Rexroth.

46. See my discussion in the following chapter on *Lady Chatterley's Lover.* Norman Mailer, as discussed in chapter 4, took up the issue—and may be partly viewed as continuing some of the peculiar tradition, though apparently sans Nietzsche.

47. While the phrases supposedly apply to "bad" murderers, the sadism in describing their execution—"the clutching throb of gratification as the knife strikes in and blood spurts out!" (*Pumed Serpent*, p. 133)—confirms that the nastiness is merely ritualized in the "good" viciousness of Cipriano and Ramon. Mark Spilka attempts to round the unpleasant ideology by reducing it to the biographical and interpreting the novel as a desperate demand for wife Frieda, off in Europe, to submit, which may not be wrong but is not responsive at other levels of concern. "D. H. Lawrence in Changing Times: A Normative Progress" (manuscript). Even in emphasizing the personal motives, Meyers properly notes the "deification of personal terror and sexual slavery," in *D. H. Lawrence*, p. 322. For further summary of Lawrence's racism, see my chap. 3, note 10.

48. For other explorations of late values, see Donald Gutierrez, *Lapsing Out: Embodiments of Death and Rebirth in the Last Writings of D. H. Lawrence* (Cranbury, N. J.: Associated University Presses, 1980).

49. "Education of the People," *Phoenix*, pp. 621, 632, 631. The point of comparison was apparently first passingly made by Eric Bentley, *A Century of Hero-Worship*, p. 233. I have extended the argument, drawing on the previously cited biographies of Lawrence and Nietzsche.

50. Nietzsche, *Zarathustra*, in *The Portable Niertzsche*, p. 124; Lawrence, "On Being Religious," in *Phoenix*, p. 726. There are many similar statements.

51. Lawrence, "Democracy," in *Phoenix*, p. 702.

52. Hayman, p. 64.

53. See the previously cited Nietzsche commentators, especially Stern.

54. See, for example, Nietzsche's vitriolic attacks on feminism, *Beyond Good and Evil*, pp. 162–70, and the juvenile epigrams on women

scattered through part 4 of the same book. Lawrence had a somewhat more complex sense and view of women, discussed in my chap. 5.

55. Lawrence, *Collected Letters*, 1:234 (1913, long before his more exacerbated illnesses).

56. For one of many examples with Lawrence, see the inaccurate and confused study of Frank Kermode, *D. H. Lawrence* (New York: Viking, 1973). The Nazi twisted adaption of Nietzsche is notorious and discussed by many commentators.

57. In a conversation a generation ago, Eric Bentley granted that Kenneth Burke may have been right in suggesting that Bentley should have understood Zarathustra's "When thou goest to woman, take thy whip" as sexual rather than punitive, but it still looks like impotent sadism to me. The Lawrence demand that children be whipped appears in "Education of the People" (in spite of the earlier revulsion he showed via Ursula in the school scene in *The Rainbow*, though she ends up feeling that she has to beat the child). The convict reference is to an irritated outburst on killing the "evil" early in *The Sea and Sardinia* (New York: Robert McBride, 1931), p. 27.

58. For example, in "Books," *Reflections* (1988), p. 197. The editor, Herbert, cites some of the many repetitions of the statement in an explanatory note.

59. I am conjoining, of course, with a certain perspective on Nietzsche: "Nihilism is the central concept in his philosophy," further defined as the "idea that there is no order or structure objectively present in the world antecedent to the form we ourselves give it." Danto, pp. 22, 195. Lawrence's partial variation is that the possible limited meaning of the world in terms of "desire" was in an "inhuman" mystery. The ramification in moral nihilism is the especially important one (for the nontechnical philosopher).

60. The quote from Nietzsche is found in *Beyond Good and Evil*, aphorism 23; the agricultural reference is from Lawrence, "On Human Destiny," *Phoenix II*, p. 629.

3. *Problems of Desire in* Lady Chatterley's Lover

1. For convenience, a readily available reprint of the Florence edition is cited, *Lady Chatterley's Lover* (New York: New American Library, 1962), with some of the references to chapters. Citations will appear

parenthetically in text. A representative selection of Lawrence studies will be confined to the notes, without mostly repeating those cited in my previous articles and reviews.

2. Ernest Hemingway, *A Farewell to Arms* (New York: Scribner's, 1929), p. 191. Finally another commentator has noted the obvious parallelism: Peter Balbert, *D. H. Lawrence and the Phallic Imagination* (New York: St. Martin's, 1989), pp. 149–50. But since my emphasis is somewhat different, I leave it in.

3. Lawrence, "A Propos of *Lady Chatterley's Lover*," in *Sex, Literature, and Censorship*, ed. Harry T. Moore (New York: Twayne, 1953), p. 20. I also repeatedly emphasize his term for the dominant culture as "counterfeit" from this essay, and several other broad points.

4. But there are some exceptions in the authorities; for a brief annotation of the word as either positive or negative, see Wentworth and Flexner's *The Dictionary of American Slang* (1975). While I have also consulted with several sociolinguists on the taboo words, there would not seem to be any applicable definitive statement on usage and connotation, especially for that time and place. The closest I am able to come is Allen Walker Read, *Classic American Graffiti* (1935; reprint, Waukesha, Wis.: Maledicta Press, 1977). This is near Lawrence in time, recording 1928 usage in the western U. S. Read notes, from his later researches in Britain, that "the vocabulary is practically the same" (except for British *arse*, which Lawrence uses, and *bugger* and *bloody*, which he does not), p. 24. Read records no instances of Lawrence's tender, intimate use of *cunt*, but the lack of that in public graffiti is hardly defining. I can find nowhere any usage in what I point to as Lawrence's ontological and transcendent *cunt*, which may be idiosyncratic. I grant that who is probably the world's leading authority on obscenity in several languages, Gershom Legman (*The Horn Book*), advised me that he had never found a modern obscenity which was uniquely used, but that could be his overriding theory. I am also indebted to some curious discussions, such as that of Berger. He suggests that in writing about "the central moment of sex" the "nouns denote the objects in such a way that they reject the meaning of the experience," for in coitus (at least of a Lawrencean sort) "nothing is left exterior to it, and thus becomes nameless." Partly, then, "sexual verbs . . . remain less foreign than the nouns." However, both are more successful when presented (as in the novel) in the form of charac-

ter dialogue "because they then refer to the speaker speaking and not directly to acts of sex." John Berger, *G.* (1972; reprint, New York: Pantheon, 1980), pp. 112–13. To cite another somewhat Lawrencean novelist who uses obscenity in a positive way: "Sure, there are people whose puritanical brainwashing makes them wince at the mere mention of such four-letter words—but at least these words represent the language of *feeling*, the language of powerful emotion, while the latinate words smell of disinfectant. . . . *fuck* and *cunt* can be virginified [as language] (or perhaps one should say 'gentrified') by an able writer, an able talker." Erica Jong, *Parachutes and Kisses* (New York: New American Library, 1984), p. 123. She is more largely expounding a rather Lawrencean theme—"cunt with heart." In his frequently useful book, Michael Squires's genteel argument is that the "obscene" words lack sufficient context and meaning and thus become "incongruous and disturbing." *The Creation of Lady Chatterley's Lover* (Baltimore: Johns Hopkins University Press, 1983), p. 182. Since he little analyzes how they are used, the point is unclear; just possibly, this could mean that the sexual polymorphousness, and taboo words, ought to have been increased, thus expanding the context, as I am holding. Typically, academically, Allen Ingram's *The Language of D. H. Lawrence* (London: Macmillan, 1990) has nothing to say about Lawrence's sexual language, much less his obscenity. I return to some of the issue in chap. 5, following.

5. Part of the issue seems to be something else. There is a large, and suspiciously obsessive, range of discussion of the "sodomy scene." Eliseo Vivas, for example, developed an obtusely self-righteous general application of it to Lawrencean sexuality in *D. H. Lawrence, The Triumph and the Failure of Art* (Evanston, Ill.: Northwestern University Press, 1960), pp. 130ff. Colin Welch viewed it as an immoral "black mass" in "Black Magic, White Lies," *Encounter* 16 (Feb. 1961): 75–79. A series of further arguments, mostly disapproving, and some crassly bigoted, followed in *Encounter*: 17 (Sept. 1961): 63–64; 18 (Feb. 1962): 35–43; 18 (Mar. 1962): 63–65, and 94–96; 18 (Apr. 1962): 93–95; 18 (May 1962): 91–94); 18 (June 1962): 83–88. G. Wilson Knight, with usual inflated metaphorical reading, continued the attack on Lawrence's "anal eroticism" in "Lawrence, Joyce and Powys," *Essays in Criticism* 11 (Oct. 1961): 403–17. There were attempted positive qualifications by John Peters, "The Bottom of the

Well," *Essays in Criticism* 12 (Apr. 1962), (Oct. 1962), and 13 (July 1963). Among later redoings of the anal eroticism issue was cutely quasi-Freudian Mark Spilka, "Lawrence Up-Tight, Or the Anal Phase Once Over," *Novel* 4 (Spring 1971): 257–67, with qualifying statements by George H. Ford, Frank Kermode, Colin Clarke, and Spilka again in "Critical Exchange on 'Lawrence Up-Tight': Four Tail Pieces," *Novel* 5 (Fall 1971): 54–70. Elaborate extensions of the issue of anal eroticism into theories of corruption and fixation include Colin Clarke, *River of Dissolution: D. H. Lawrence and English Romanticism* (New York: Barnes and Noble, 1969); and L. D. Clark, *The Dark Night of the Body* (Austin: University of Texas Press, 1964). Some of the issues are rehearsed, and commonsensically qualified, by Donald Gutierrez, " 'The Impossible Notation': The Sodomy Scene in *Lady Chatterley's Lover,*"in *The Maze in the Mind and the World* (Troy, N.Y.: Whitston, 1985), pp. 55–74. The fuss over a little sexual polymorphousness does seem peculiar in the commentators.

6. John Updike, *Rabbit Is Rich* (New York: Fawcett, 1981), pp. 390 ff. Updikean eroticism, of course, is mostly quite un-Lawrencean. For misogynist sodomizing of women see Norman Mailer's "The Time of Her Time" in *Advertisements for Myself* (New York: New American Library, 1959), pp. 427–51; and *An American Dream* (New York: New American Library, 1965).

7. The issue of Lawrence's homosexuality probably receives its most simple summary analysis in Jeffrey Meyers, *Homosexuality and Literature, 1890–1930* (Montreal: McGill-Queens University Press, 1977), pp. 131–61. He concludes that Lawrence's "triumphant expression of heterosexual love . . . depends on male dominance and is seriously qualified by an ambivalent longing for homosexuality." See also his recurrent discussion of the evidence in his biography, *D. H. Lawrence* (New York: Knopf, 1990). Whether or not Lawrence had a direct homosexual relationship in the Cornwall period (the most likely time) is taken up with some thoroughness by C. J. Stevens, *Lawrence at Tregerthen* (Troy, N.Y.: Whitston, 1988), but ends inconclusively.

8. Contrary to the evidence that I am suggesting, in and out of the novel, is a recent well-intentioned summary: "There is no substantial reason to believe that in recording Mellors' dogmatic opinions about women, Lawrence intends to promote them." Joan D. Peters, "The Living and the Dead: Lawrence's Theory of the Novel and the Structure of *Lady*

Chatterley's Lover," *D. H. Lawrence Review* 20 (Spring 1988): 12. She also insists there is no problem of point of view or style in the novel, which is equally uninformed. A more clever discussion insists on Lawrence's usual "fluid, flexible handling of 'point-of-view,'" and ornately links it to fashionable literary theorizing of the "dialogic" (a notion which thinly overlaps my concept of the "dialectical"). David Lodge, "Lawrence, Dostoyevsky, Bakhtin: Lawrence and Dialogic Fiction," in *Rethinking Lawrence*, ed. Keith Brown (Milton Keynes, U. K.: Open University Press, 1990), p. 99.

9. Besides drawing on cumulative Lawrence responses, see the biographies, especially Harry T. Moore, *The Priest of Love*, rev. ed. (New York: Farrar, Straus, and Giroux, 1974), and Meyers, *D. H. Lawrence*. I am also interpreting (from a previous article) Helen Corke's writings: *In Our Infancy: An Autobiography* (London: Cambridge University Press, 1975) and *D. H. Lawrence: The Croydon Years* (Austin: University of Texas Press, 1964), which reprints her earlier writings on Lawrence (and provides displaced justification of Mellors's attack on lesbianism), and which Lawrence turgidly anguished about in his novelization of her affair in *The Trespasser*. In an article kindly brought to my attention by James T. Cox, it is suggested that the Helena of Lawrence's second novel, *The Trespasser* (based, all agree, on Helen Corke's journal) provides the prototype experience for Mellors's history: see J. R. L. Reyner, "The Three Versions of *Lady Chatterley's Lover*," *Geste* (Univ. of Leeds), 7 (1961): 31. Incidentally, this article also holds, though on different grounds than mine, that "the third version is much more satisfactory."

10. Connie, for example, twice expresses conventional British class anti-Semitism, rather irrelevantly applied to Clifford: In ambition he is "as corrupt as any low-born Jew" (*Lady*, p. 67), and, to his face, "You only bully with your money, like any Jew or any Schieber!" (*Lady*, p. 181). Since Lawrence expresses similar bigotries in other works (in *Aaron's Rod* and *Kangaroo*, as I pointed to in the previous chapter), this is not, yet again, to be confined to the character. The prejudice also appears without fictional displacement in various essays. For example: As "the clue to the *bourgeois*" he refers to "the mean, Jewish competition in production, in money-making," which is unlike true and proper productivity of the English sort. "Education of the People," *Reflections on the Death of a Porcupine and Other Essays*, ed. Michael

Herbert (Cambridge: Cambridge University Press, 1988), p. 157. In a later essay reprinted in the same volume: "If an Arab or a negro or even a Jew sits down next to me on that train, I cannot proceed with my knowing. . . . A strange vibration comes from him . . . there is strong pressure. . . ." And, as so often, Lawrence suspiciously connects the racial disturbance with sexually arousing and hostile male/female disturbance. "On Being a Man," p. 215. There are others, but the racism should be sufficiently evident. Jeffrey Meyers rather cooly summarizes other evidence: "Lawrence had a pronounced and unpleasant strain of anti-Semitism, activitated by his provincial background and by the prejudice of his fashionable friends." *D. H. Lawrence*, p. 132. While I am inclined to agree, the morally loaded evolutionism (as discussed for *The Plumed Serpent* in the previous chapter), sometimes made it something rather nastier, an enlarging biological racism. Another student of the subject, Sam Hardin, argues with me that I should put more emphasis on Lawrence's anti-Semitism as a product of resented poverty, but that seems to me the less nasty side of it.

11. The crucial point, it seems to me, is finally becoming more widely recognized, though without the appropriate Protestant background, and without application to the later works. See my citations elsewhere, as with chap. 1, note 31.

12. See, for example, what is usually treated as the standard clinical work on such matters: William H. Masters, Virginia E. Johnson, and Robert C. Kolodny, *Masters and Johnson on Sex and Human Love* (Boston: Little, Brown, 1986). In a debunking reading, Robert Scholes, in his chapter "Uncoding Mama: The Female Body as Text," raises several interesting points about anticlitoral mythology, including *Lady Chatterley*. "Exactly as Freud does, so Lawrence, too, orders the clitoris to cease and desist, orders women to be more 'feminine,' to become the perfect binary opposites that men require. . . ." In *Semiotics and Interpretation* (New Haven: Yale University Press, 1982), p. 140. (Clitorectomy, among other female-controlling traditions, would also confirm the issue.) However, Scholes quite ignores the major point of male need, especially those relating to premature ejaculation (Michaelis specifically, Mellors apparently, and, given the example I cited from the autobiographical *Mr. Noon*, Lawrence probably). Degrees of impotence may also be relevant, as may possibly be fundamental male-female disparities. Scholes may be appropriate on Lawrence's attack

on female masculinity, by way of Mellors about Bertha: "A masculinity expressed in her desire to take charge, to be in control of the sexual scene . . . concentrated physically in her clitoral orientation." But Scholes most emphasized broad issue—the fearful male "feeling that women experience a deeper, more thorough gratification from sex than men do" (p. 131) is misused in implied application to Lawrence, whose woman-conversion sexuality requires such a feminine premise in crucial scenes. A more encompassing sexual experience than that represented by the clitoral is necessary for Connie's all-over transformation feelings. And, apparently, it is needed for the validation of the necessity of the male, and his phallic prowess (beyond the digital and oral lesbian). Scholes, incidentally, also seems to lack some "clit" wit on colloquial terms for the clitoris: Mellors, not uniquely, uses the term "beak"; Alice Walker uses the term "button" in *The Color Purple* (New York: Harcourt Brace Jovanovich, 1982). This suggests a genteel as well as feminist bias to Scholes's supposed decoding. Mark Spilka, in qualifying Scholes's interpretation, argues that Mellors is in the therapeutic process of maturing to a tenderly "secure male identity." See Spilka's "Epilogue: Lawrence and the Clitoris," "D. H. Lawrence in Changing Times: A Normative Progress" (manuscript, 1990). In early chapters, Spilka's argument also is that the "Chatterley solution" is for men to achieve "manly tenderness," which may be true but rather fudges, as usual, the problems and gender disparities.

13. The most lavish detailing of the circumstances in which the three versions were written is Derek Britton, *Lady Chatterley, The Making of the Novel* (London: Unwin Hyman, 1988). However, most of it consists of dubiously relevant possible sources, with little sense of developing purpose. And it is marked by a rage of distaste for the author, with his "impotence," and hence "sadistic anger that seeks to subjugate and depersonalize" women; his "physical degeneration," which resulted in "despairing revulsion for modern man and his works" and "the misanthropic dejection of a sick man"; his "paranoia" dominated by "the fear of failure" which is "the key to . . . his social malaise, his aggression, his nervous irritability, his pretense of conventional virility and perhaps his sexual problems"; in sum, much of the final version expresses Lawrence's "desire to avenge himself." See, especially, pp. 188, 251–52. This reductive confusion of motives with results is as unclear about what is going on and its possible meanings

as it is unsympathetic. Obviously I have no objection to tough-minded negative criticism, but this one-way negativity leads to an emphasis on obtuse trivia, such as what Lawrence might have remembered from his last walk in the Midlands or what he might have adapted from the Sitwells for the Chatterleys.

14. Lawrence, "Morality and the Novel," *D. H. Lawrence: Selected Literary Criticism*, ed. Anthony Beal (New York: Viking, 1966), p. 110. Britton, cited in note 13, gives the chronology of Lawrence's rewriting. Comments on the process can be seen in D. H. Lawrence, *Collected Letters*, ed. Harry T. Moore (New York: Viking, 1962), 2:948, 964, 970, 972–3, 983, 1026, 1030, 1038ff., and 1194. The final novel, of course, was not the first in which Lawrence had revised by replacement: there were at least two distinct versions of *Sons and Lovers* and apparently numerous versions of a novel variously entitled "The Sisters" and "The Wedding Ring," which finally resulted in *The Rainbow* and *Women in Love*. See the editors' Introduction to *Women in Love*, ed. David Farmer, Lindeth Vesey, and John Worthen (Cambridge: Cambridge University Press, 1987). For a discussion of Lawrence's earlier methods of revision, see Keith Cushman, *D. H. Lawrence at Work: The Emergence of "The Prussian Officer" Stories* (Chapel Hill: University of North Carolina Press, 1978).

15. Lawrence, of course, had used important elements of the story in his first novel, including gamekeeper loving a lady, woods and bird imagery, and misogyny and misanthropy, in *The White Peacock*. The social angers are also more rather than less continuous over many works.

16. There is a recurrent critical overly positive evaluation of one or another of the earlier versions of the novel. A few examples: Stephen Gill, "The Composite World: Two Versions of *Lady Chatterley's Lover*," *Essays in Criticism* 21 (Oct. 1971): 347–64, argues from a more or less Marxist aesthetic that the first, however rough and incomplete, must be the truer, proletarian, work. Keith Sagar also patronizingly finds the early, crude gamekeeper more acceptable in *The Art of D. H. Lawrence* (Cambridge: Cambridge University Press, 1966), p. 190. While less explicit, Derek Britton's attacks on the final version in his *Lady Chatterley* have the same effect. What I take to be the representative L. E. Sissman granted that while the final version was obviously

often "more polished, more persuasive," the lesser didacticism and other extremity of its predecessor made it the better book, but the crux seems to have been class: the gamekeeper of *John Thomas and Lady Jane* is more truly "lower-class, decidedly well cast to assume the inarticulate pride and hardship of his kind in that era." "The Second Lady Chatterley," *New Yorker*, 6 Jan. 1973, 73–75. It was partly such patronizing snobbery—"his kind"—which I see Lawrence struggling against in his rewriting because it was antithetical to his most profound sense of human relations and desirable society. Other defenses of the earlier versions are summarized by Michael Squires in *The Creation of Lady Chatterley's Lover* who, however, makes a qualified strong case for the final version as "one of Lawrence's best" novels. For other doctrinaire Marxist impositions on Lawrence, and especially his last novel, see Scott Sanders, *D. H. Lawrence: The World of the Five Major Novels* (New York: Viking, 1974); and Graham Holderness, *D. H. Lawrence: History, Ideology, and Fiction* (Dublin: Gill and Macmillan, 1984).

17. The other versions are used in their first American editions: *The First Lady Chatterley* (New York: Dial, 1944), and *John Thomas and Lady Jane* (New York: Viking, 1972). I am, of course, only pointing to a few representative differences which relate to a major line of interpretation. For simplification, I have identified the gamekeeper of the second version as Seivers, though he is also often Parkin, as in the first. Lawrence says that Seivers is his real name, Parkin that of his stepfather, a shift which points to Lawrence's changing—declassing—conception. Incidentally, Squires suggests that Seivers is a misprint for Leivers—the farm family name in *Sons and Lovers* (and therefore, I add, positive and nonproletarian). *Creation of Lady Chatterley's Lover*, p. 67.

18. The emphasis on the internal conflict of strident polemics and regenerative mythology in the final version now seems widely accepted. See John B. Humma, "The Interpenetrating Metaphor: Nature and Myth in *Lady Chatterley's Lover*," *PMLA* 98 (1983): 77–86.

19. "The land of Arcadia is really the landscape of an idea," comments an apparently representative summary by Peter V. Martinelli, *Pastoral* (London: Metheun, 1971), p. 37. Though this does not discuss class issues or Lawrence, it does suggest that the earlier traditions confirm

several of my points, such as that social "criticism is inherent in all pastoral," and that "pastoral retirement is not an end in itself," pp. 12, 14.

20. Julian Moynahan, rather vaguely defining pastoral as heroine in nature and values of "growth, wholesomeness and vitality, deep feeling and sexuality," sees *Lady Chatterley's Lover* as a "diminished and pathetic perspective" on the pastoral tradition because in crowded and industrialized England after World War I, the pastoral cannot amount to much. (Of course not, and that is why exasperated Lawrence wanted the English massively dead [as in the passage quoted from *Kangaroo* in chapter 2] or apocalyptic termination of the society [as in previously cited passages from *Women in Love* as well as in *Lady*]). Moynahan, "Pastoralism as Culture and Counter-Culture in English Fiction, 1800–1928," *Novel* 6 (Fall 1972): 35ff. In a more incisive discussion, Michael Squires argued that Lawrence "successfully updates the content, though not the form, of pastoral," but that he could not complete "the pastoral pattern of retreat-reorientation-return," apparently because he could not accept it as just an "interlude." Squires, "Pastoral Patterns and Pastoral Variants in *Lady Chatterley's Lover*" *ELH* 39 (1972): 129–46.

21. Nearly forty years ago, I did a paper (unpublished) which relentlessly applied motifs from Theocritus, Sidney, and others, to Lawrence's late fiction, which I will not repeat here. In also noting a generation ago that Lawrence was writing pastoral, I discussed such works largely as "religious romance," thus paying insufficient attention to social declassing. See my final chapter, "Parables of Regeneration," in *The Art of Perversity: D. H. Lawrence's Shorter Fictions* (Seattle: University of Washington Press, 1962).

22. Lawrence, *John Thomas*, p. 367.

23. "Proletarian literature usually has a suggestion of pastoral . . . but isn't," noted William Empson, *Some Versions of Pastoral* (Norfolk, Conn.: New Directions, [1952]), p. 6. He also cryptically comments that "D. H. Lawrence's refusal to write proletarian literature was an important choice," p. 7. I am attempting to suggest several reasons why. In a gross misreading of my earlier article, Evelyn J. Hinz and John J. Teunissen claim that my view is "oriented toward 'proletarian' fiction." "War, Love, and Industrialism: The Ares/Aphrodite/Hephaestus Complex in *Lady Chatterley's Lover*," *D. H. Lawrence's "Lady":*

A New Look at Lady Chatterley's Lover, ed. Michael Squires and Dennis Jackson (Athens: University of Georgia Press, 1985), p. 221. They then provide a portentously archetypal reading which many would find considerably irrelevant to most of the novel. This apparently follows up the earlier discussion which, with strange twists of terminology, weirdly judged the first version as "pornography," the second as "sociology," and the third as "cosmic" and "mythic." Evelyn J. Hinz, "Pornography, Novel, Mythic Narrative: The Three Versions of *Lady Chatterley's Lover*," *Modernist Studies: Literature and Culture, 1920–40*, 3 (1979): 35–47. A more balanced emphasis on the classical allusions, with the point being Lawrence's neo-paganism, is Dennis Jackson, "The Old Pagan Vision: Myth and Ritual in *Lady Chatterley's Lover*,"in *Critical Essays on D. H. Lawrence*, ed. Dennis Jackson and Fleda Brown Jackson (Boston: G. K. Hall, 1988), pp. 128–44.

While, as indicated in citations in previous notes, Marxianizers and conservatives like their alternate, patronizing, "proletarian" literature, in fairness one should note that some contemporary, sophisticated, neo-Marxists have been vociferously critical of it. See, for example, the condemnation of the "proletarian" as parochial, resentful, antirevolutionary, etc., by Herbert Marcuse, in chap. 3 of *Counter-Revolution and Revolt* (Boston: Beacon, 1972); see also the discussion of his view in chap. 5 of my *Counterings: Utopian Dialectics in Contemporary Contexts* (Ann Arbor: UMI Research, 1988).

24. Lawrence was already emphatically rejecting class in *John Thomas*, with such sardonic remarks as, "There was no longer any such thing as class. The world was one vast proletariat," p. 288. But no alternative seems meaningful. In a passage unique to the second version, he puts the lovers near the end in yet another woods, one "where Byron walked so often," but they are, with pathetic irony, interrupted in an embrace by another gamekeeper, pp. 368ff. This seems to be part of a suggestion that there should be an heroic alternative but it is not allowed, and so they are but babes in the woods, pastoral losers—a depressed ending Lawrence sought to go beyond in the final version.

25. Lawrence, *First Lady Chatterley*, p. 291.

26. I have further discussed Lawrence's utopianism elsewhere, as in my *Counterings*, chap. 1. It should be noted that the repeated red tights metaphor of the last novel was not peculiar to the late Lawrence. For example, he had positively referred to dressing up male legs in "scarlet

trunk-hose" some years earlier in "Education of the People." In *Reflections* (1988), p. 152. It also appears in the late essay "Red Trousers,"in *Assorted Articles* (New York: Knopf, 1930), pp. 101–7.

27. Gavriel Ben Ephraim argues that the ending is appropriate and positive, "the search for 'a small farm of their own' striking a compromise between natural escape and social necessity." "The Achievement of Balance in *Lady Chatterley's Lover*," *D. H. Lawrence's "Lady,"* p. 152. I see it as more problematic in several ways, not least because Lawrence so often used it. It also contradicts the implicit attack throughout on marriage, though that was perhaps most directly put in the second version where Connie rejects the idea of "a master of any sort." "She recognized, emotionally, that the idea of eternal love, of life-long love even, and the idea of marriage, had a disastrous effect upon the will. The idea of permanency stimulates the possessive instinct, the possessive instinct arouses the egoistic will to self-assertion, and there is a vicious circle . . . let there be no convention of permanency, especially in emotional or passional relationships." *John Thomas*, pp. 258, 149. Lawrence somewhat ambivalently backtracked in the final version, perhaps in a kind of defensiveness around what else he had done.

28. I am arguing, of course, that the usual academic-ameliorist interpretations of Lawrence are wrong. Typically, Northrop Frye writes, "The regressive myth in Lawrence has much the relation to the pastoral vision that the 'noble savage' myth has to Rousseau's conception of a natural society. That is, it is separable from his real social vision. . . ." *The Critical Path* (Bloomington: University of Indiana Press, 1971), p. 91. While perhaps fairly motivated as a warning not to be a literal-minded reader, it overextends the point to the refusal of much of Lawrence's central negation of modern society, without which, I am insisting, there can be no adequate understanding of him.

4. Lawrence's Desiring and Negating American Progeny: Henry Miller, Norman Mailer, and Some Melvilleans

1. Henry Miller, *The World of Lawrence, A Passionate Appreciation*, ed. with introduction by Evelyn J. Hinz and John J. Teunissen (Santa Barbara, Calif.: Capra, 1980). Further citations are parenthetical in text. Unfortunately, since the work was done for Miller, there is no

analytic or critical comment by the editors on the manuscript and the late changes.

2. Anaïs Nin, *D. H. Lawrence: An Unprofessional Study* (1932; reprint, Denver: Alan Swallow, 1964). Some of her view of Lawrence is discussed in chap. 5, following. See also the notes on her helping Miller in *The Diary of Anaïs Nin, 1930–34*, ed. Gunther Stuhlman (New York: Alan Swallow and Harcourt, Brace, 1966). And see generally Miller's *Letters to Anaïs Nin*, ed. Gunther Stuhlman (New York: G. P. Putnam's Sons, 1965). Miller's *Tropic of Cancer* (1934; reprint, New York: Grove, 1961) apparently underwent some revisions at this time but I do not detect, beyond the general sexual emphasis (though of a quite different cast) and social negation, much relation to Lawrence.

3. There is, however, little specific evidence of *Reflections* in the finally published version. See also my discussion of the Lawrence essays in other chapters here. Miller had little sense of the social-political issues that concerned Lawrence.

4. Henry Miller, *My Life and Times*, ed. Bradley Smith (Chicago: Playboy, 1972), p. 156. Since much of this material was elicited by the energetic flattery of Bradley Smith (as he acknowledged to me in a private conversation), and since (as I have documented elsewhere) Miller was quite unreliable on recall of crucial points in his life, perhaps such claims should not be taken literally.

5. Henry Miller, *Wisdom of the Heart* (Norfolk, Conn.: New Directions, 1941); Miller, *Sunday After the War* (Norfolk, Conn.: New Directions, 1944); Miller, *The Cosmological Eye* (Norfolk, Conn.: New Directions, 1939); Kingsley Widmer, *Henry Miller*, rev. ed. (New York: Twayne, 1990); Philip Rahv, "Henry Miller," *Image and Idea* (New York: New Directions, 1957), pp. 159–66.

6. Henry Miller, *Black Spring* (New York: Grove, 1963), p. 40.

7. Jeffrey Meyers, "Lawrence and Travel Writers," in *The Legacy of D. H. Lawrence*, ed. Meyers (London: Macmillan, 1987), pp. 81–108. Henry Miller, *The Colossus of Maroussi* (Norfolk, Conn.: New Directions, 1941).

8. Henry Miller, *The Books in My Life* (Norfolk, Conn.: New Directions, [1952]), in widely scattered comments, and repeatedly mentioned elsewhere. For Miller's self-discovery mythology in *The Rosy Crucifixion*, and elsewhere, see my *Henry Miller*, rev. ed.

9. J. D. Brown, *Henry Miller* (New York: Ungar, 1986), p. 107.

10. Henry Miller, *Tropic of Capricorn* (New York: Grove, 1962), with surrealistic sex running intermittently throughout much of the book, according to its self-description.
11. Henry Miller, *Genius and Lust: A Journey Through the Major Writings of Henry Miller*, ed. Norman Mailer (New York: Grove, 1976). Mailer repeatedly emphasizes he-man lusty sex in the series of exuberant introductions to the sections.
12. Donald Gutierrez, "D. H. Lawrence's 'Pornography and Obscenity,'" in *The Dark and Light Gods: Essays on the Self in Modern Literature* (Troy, N. Y.: Whitston, 1987), pp. 155–77.
13. Henry Miller, *Dear, Dear Brenda, The Love Letters of Henry Miller to Brenda Venus*, ed. Gerard Seth Sindell (New York: William Morrow, 1986), p. 44.
14. Henry Miller, *Big Sur and the Oranges of Hieronymous Bosch* (New York: New Directions, 1957). It was also printed separately as *The Devil in Paradise* (New York: New American Library, 1958).
15. The most readily available reprinting of Lawrence's novella-length piece around Magnus is in D. H. Lawrence, *Phoenix II*, ed. Warren Roberts and Harry T. Moore (New York: Viking, 1970), pp. 303–63. See also the citations for chap. 1 of the present work.
16. Miller, *The Books in My Life*, pp. 317–19.
17. Henry Miller, *The Henry Miller Reader*, ed. Lawrence Durrell (New York: New Directions, 1959), p. 204.
18. Miller is quoted from his and William A. Gordon's *Writer and Critic* [letters] (Baton Rouge: Louisiana State University Press, 1968), p. 68.
19. Henry Miller, *From Your Copernican Friend* [letters], ed. Irving Stettner (New York: New Directions, 1984), p. 100.
20. Bradley Smith in Miller's *My Life and Times*, p. 150.
21. Jeffrey Meyers, "Memoirs of D. H. Lawrence: A Genre of the Thirties," *D. H. Lawrence Review* 14 (1981): 1–32.
22. Miller, *Tropic of Cancer*, 69.
23. See John Middleton Murry, *Son of Woman* (London: Jonathan Cape, 1931), an early, and rather negative, example of the many lavish Oedipal interpretations.

     Miller's very thin jottings on *Aaron's Rod* are available in *Notes on "Aaron's Rod"*, ed. Seamus Cooney (Santa Barbara, Calif.: Capra, 1980). He is busy resisting the obvious homoeroticism. A rather burbly account of another, and apparently more enthusiastic, Miller manuscript partly on Lawrence ("Paris Notebook," Humanities Research Center, University of Texas at Austin) is by David Stephen Calonne, "Euphoria in Paris: Henry Miller Meets D. H. Lawrence," *Library Chronicle of the University of Texas at Austin*, 2d ser., no. 34 (1986): 89–98.

24. I am briefly restating several points developed in an earlier commentary on Mailer, through an *American Dream*, in my *Literary Rebel* (Carbondale: Southern Illinois University Press, 1965), pp. 175ff.

25. These notebooks are in the collection of the Humanities Research Center at the University of Texas at Austin, which Warren Roberts kindly allowed me to examine.

26. Norman Mailer, *Advertisements for Myself* (New York: New American Library, 1959), p. 246. Many other examples, often more crass than wry, can be found in other Mailer collections, such as *The Presidential Papers* (New York: New American Library, 1964).

27. Jeffrey Meyers, Introduction to *The Legacy of D. H. Lawrence*, ed. Meyers (London: Macmillan, 1987), p. 10.

28. Mailer, "The Time of Her Time, in *Advertisements*, 427–50.

29. Joseph Wenke, *Mailer's America* (Hanover, N. H.: University Press of New England, 1987), p. 185.

30. Mailer, "The White Negro," in *Advertisements*, pp. 294ff.

31. "The White Negro," *Advertisements*, p. 348.

32. See also the varied sexual politics discussed in Richard King, *The Party of Eros* (Chapel Hill: University of North Carolina Press, 1972); and the notes on Lawrencean sexual ideologists in chap. 5 of the present work.

33. Mailer, "The White Negro," *Advertisements*, p. 308.

34. Jean Radford, *Norman Mailer* (London: Macmillan, 1975), p. 145.

35. I will not repeat here my discussion of these two themes of *Armies of the Night*, which I gave in "The Post-Modernist Art of Protest: Kesey and Mailer," *Centennial Review*, 19 (Summer 1975): 121–35.

36. Norman Mailer, *The Prisoner of Sex* (New York: New American Library, 1971), with citations parenthetical in text. I have discussed Millet and Mailer on Miller in the revised edition of my *Henry Miller*. Some indication of Mailer's continuing influence on views of Lawrence is Peter Balbert, who quite uncritically uses Mailer as the guiding spirit of his indignant polemic against feminist interpretations, *D. H. Lawrence and the Phallic Imagination* (New York: St. Martin's, 1989).

37. Iris Murdoch, *A Severed Head* (1961; reprint, New York: Penguin, 1987). For further detailing in the context of her fictions, see my "Wages of Intellectuality . . . and the Fictional Wagers of Iris Murdoch," *Twentieth Century Women Novelists*, ed. Thomas F. Staley, (London: Macmillan, 1982), p. 16–38.
38. Martin Amis, *London Fields* (New York: Crown, 1989), p. 131.
39. D. H. Lawrence, *The Collected Letters*, ed. Harry T. Moore (New York: Viking, 1962), 1:424. I have discussed Lawrence and Melville in the context of a variety of modernist and later writers in "Melville and the Myths of Modernism," *A Companion to Melville Studies*, ed. John Bryant (Westport, Conn.: Greenwood, 1986), and have drawn here on parts of it (excluding discussions of Winters, Auden, Camus, Updike, etc., who do not draw strongly on Lawrence), though obviously depending on my earlier studies of Melville, such as *The Ways of Nihilism: Melville's Short Novels* (Los Angeles: Ward-Ritchie, 1970).
40. Armin Arnold, *D. H. Lawrence and America* (New York: Philosophical Library, 1959), pp. 28–29.
41. D. H. Lawrence, *The Symbolic Meaning: The Uncollected Versions of Studies in Classic American Literature*, ed. Armin Arnold (New York: Viking, 1964).
42. In Edmund Wilson, *The Shock of Recognition* (Garden City, N. Y.: Doubleday, 1943).
43. As recently, for example, by Robert K. Martin's positive emphasis on homosexuality, *Hero, Captain, and Stranger: Male Friendship, Social Critique, and Literary Form in the Sea Novels of Herman Melville* (Chapel Hill: University of North Carolina Press, 1986). He seems remarkably ignorant of most of the literary history I cite following though highly relevant to his homoerotic theme.
44. For Lawrence's attacks on Shakespeare, *Hamlet*, and modern consciousness, see *Twilight in Italy* (1916; reprint, London: William Heinemann, 1950), pp. 97ff.; and "When I Read Shakespeare," which dismisses the characters and themes and ambiguously praises the language ("like the dyes from gas-tar"), in *The Complete Poems*, ed. Vivian de Sola Pinto and F. Warren Roberts (New York: Viking, 1971), p. 494. While I have not checked everything of Lawrence's for Melville allusions, I note that even a poem such as "Whales Weep Not!" seems to have little Melvillean. *Complete Poems*, p. 694. A contrary emphasis, and rather forced one otherwise, that I know of is

by Andrew Peek on Lawrence's use of a whale analogy (and perhaps vaguely of Ahab) for the rather underdeveloped entitling character of *Kangaroo*: "The Sydney *Bulletin*, *Moby Dick*, and the Allusiveness of *Kangaroo*," in *D. H. Lawrence*, ed. Christopher Heywood (London: Macmillan, 1987), pp. 84–89. L. D. Clark has very loosely suggested an effect of *Moby Dick* on Lawrence's middle-period novels by way of "digressive structure," and similar vague organizational analogues. "Making the Classic Contemporary: Lawrence's Pilgrimage Novels and American Romance," in *D. H. Lawrence in the Modern World*, ed. Peter Preston and Peter Hoare (London: Macmillan, 1989), pp. 193–216. In this manner, all sorts of abstracted analogies with all sorts of sources would be equally valid.

45. See Crane's letters (cited in note 47), a matter first brought to my attention by the citation in R. W. Butterfield, *The Broken Arc: A Study of Hart Crane* (Edinburgh: Olivier, 1969), pp. 132ff. There are many admiring references to various prose works of Lawrence, early and late, by Crane.

46. Crane is quoted by John Unterecker, *Voyager: A Life of Hart Crane* (New York: Farrar, Straus, and Giroux, 1969), p. 739.

47. Hart Crane, *Complete Poems and Selected Letters and Prose*, ed. Brom Weber (New York: Liveright, 1966), p. 239. For explication, see my "Melville," p. 674. Crane's poetic style, of course, is little related to Lawrence.

48. The crucial title poem in Crane's final volume; see the explication in my *Literary Rebel*, pp. 111ff.

49. Charles Olson, "The Escaped Cock, Notes on Lawrence and the Real," *Human Universe and Other Essays* (New York: Grove, 1967), pp. 123ff.

50. Charles Olson, *Call Me Ishmael* (New York: Reynal and Hitchcock, 1947), pp. 13, 15, with further citations parenthetical in text. F. O. Matthiessen's *American Renaissance* (New York: Oxford University Press, 1941), a dominant academic study in the period, cited and drew on his student Olson's earlier work on Melville.

51. Paul Christenson, *Charles Olson, Call Him Ishmael* (Austin: University of Texas Press, 1979), p. 40.

52. See Charles Olson's mockery of the academicization in a polemical poem, *Letter to Melville* (Black Mountain, N. C.: n.p., 1951), and in the Melville essays in Olson, *Human Universe*, pp. 105–22.

53. *Human Universe*, p. 112.

54. Lawrence's preface to *Bottom Dogs*, reprinted in *Phoenix*, ed. Edward D. McDonald (London: William Heinemann, 1936), pp. 267–73.

55. See my discussion in "American Poetic-Naturalism: Edward Dahlberg," *Shenandoah* 16 (Autumn 1964): 69–74. For a different view, see Fred Moramarco, *Edward Dahlberg* (New York: Twayne, 1973).

56. Edward Dahlberg, *Can These Bones Live* (New York: New Directions, 1960), with citations parenthetical in text.

57. Edward Dahlberg, "*Moby-Dick*: An Hamatic Dream," in *The Edward Dahlberg Reader*, ed. Paul Carroll (New York: New Directions, 1967), pp. 170–201, with citations parenthetical in text. It was earlier published in *Alms for Oblivion* (1964).

58. This is from the "Preface to the First Edition," which I am quoting from the revised edition, Leslie Fiedler, *Love and Death in the American Novel*, rev. ed. (New York: Stein and Day, 1966), p. 15. Though Fiedler treated the "innocent homosexuality" as part of the heterosexual immaturity, disguised, of American culture, the previously cited defender of homosexuality in Melville, Robert Martin, writes, "Fiedler's book has had enormous importance over the almost twenty-five years since it was published . . .," *Hero, Captain and Stranger*, p. 9, but fails to recognize related responses. For a broader discussion of Fiedler's role, see chapter 11 of my *Literary Rebel*.

5. Desirable and Negative Legacy of Lawrence as Dissident Culture Hero

1. See, for example, "Pornography and Obscenity," in D. H. Lawrence, *Sex, Literature, and Censorship*, ed. Harry T. Moore (New York: Twayne, 1953), pp. 69–88. The fullest justificatory discussion of this is Donald Gutierrez, "D. H. Lawrence's Pornography and Obscenity," in *The Dark and Light Gods: Essays on the Self in Modern Literature* (Troy, N. Y.: Whitston, 1987), pp. 155–77.

2. Public conversation, Tulsa, Okla. (December 1980).

3. Germaine Greer, *The Female Eunuch* (New York: Bantam, 1972), p. 194; "Dark Age of the Steroid," *Literary Review* (London), 85 (1985): 12.

4. Some historical and legal material on this is in *Literary Censorship*, ed. Kingsley and Eleanor Widmer (Belmont, Calif.: Wadsworth, 1961).

5. For a feminist criticism of feminist censoring of obscenity, see, for

example, Marcia Pally, "X-rated Feminism," *Nation* 241 (29 July 1985): 784–93.

6. For examples of attempts to exclude Lawrence from the academic canon, see Peter Balbert, Introduction to *D. H. Lawrence and the Phallic Imagination* (London: St. Martin's, 1989).

7. The too-helpful Edward Garnett edited out some of the sexual references. See the discussion of the revisions of *Sons and Lovers* by Mark Spilka in chap. 1 of " D. H. Lawrence in Changing Times: A Normative Progress" (forthcoming).

8. Harry T. Moore, *The Priest of Love*, rev. ed. (New York: Farrar, Straus, and Giroux, 1974), pp. 242ff. Emile Delavenay, *D. H. Lawrence: The Man and His Work: The Formative Years, 1885–1919* (London: William Heinemann, 1972), pp. 237ff. Jeffrey Meyers, *D. H. Lawrence, A Biography* (New York: Knopf, 1990), pp. 178ff.

9. Moore, *Priest of Love*, p. 414.

10. A crass example may be found in Mary Doyle Springer, *Forms of the Modern Novella* (Chicago: University of Chicago Press, 1975). There are others as well.

11. Charles Rembar, *The End of Obscenity* (New York: Random House, 1968), pp. 59–160 (documents of the three hearings and trials are in the appendix; Rembar also kindly provided me with copies of some of the pertinent materials).

12. Part of the Cowley and Kazin testimony was reprinted, with other materials, in *Literary Censorship*, ed. Kingsley and Eleanor Widmer, pp. 92–138.

13. Rembar, p. 490.

14. Fuller argument is given in my "Beyond Censorship? The Restrictive Processing of American Culture," in *Freedom and Culture*, ed. Eleanor Widmer (Belmont, Calif.: Wadsworth, 1970), and the revised version, "The Real Censorship," in *The End of Culture* (San Diego: San Diego State University Press, 1975).

15. Rembar, p. 493.

16. The crown prosecutor is quoted in *The Trial of Lady Chatterley*, ed. C. H. Rolph (Baltimore: Penguin, 1961), p. 17. This volume includes the larger part of the trial transcript, plus some summary and brief commentary.

17. Rembar, pp. 152ff.

18. For example, Eliseo Vivas, *D. H. Lawrence, the Triumph and the*

Failure of Art (Evanston, Ill.: Northwestern University Press, 1960), pp. 137–47. He makes such hard-hitting arguments as that Lawrence's popularizing of obscenity will reduce the effectiveness of his own language when he hits his thumb with a hammer.

19. *Trial of Lady Chatterley*, p. 250.

20. Kingsley Widmer, "The Destructive Woman," chap. 3 in *The Art of Perversity: D. H. Lawrence's Shorter Fictions* (Seattle: University of Washington Press, 1962). All novellas and short stories, here and there, are cited from D. H. Lawrence, *The Complete Short Novels*, 2 vols. (London: William Heinemann, 1956); and D. H. Lawrence, *The Complete Short Stories*, 3 vols. (London: William Heinemann, 1955).

21. These are periodical pieces of the late 1920s, first collected in Lawrence, *Assorted Articles* (New York: Knopf, 1930), reprinted in Lawrence, *Phoenix II*, ed. Warren Roberts and Harry T. Moore (New York: Viking, 1970), pp. 529–623.

22. D. H. Lawrence, "The Real Thing," *Phoenix*, ed. Edward D. McDonald (London: William Heinemann, 1936), pp. 196–203.

23. Diana Trilling, "Lawrence and the Movements of Modern Culture," in *D. H. Lawrence: Novelist, Poet, Prophet*, ed. Stephen Spender (New York: Harper and Row, 1973), p. 3.

24. John Middleton Murry, *Son of Woman* (London: Jonathan Cape, 1931). In fairness to Murry, he did take a somewhat different view in later writing on Lawrence, as in *Love, Freedom, Society* (London: Jonathan Cape, 1957), part 1.

25. See Jeffrey Meyers, "Memoirs of D. H. Lawrence: A Genre of the Thirties," *D. H. Lawrence Review* 14 (1981): 1–32.

26. Anaïs Nin, *D. H. Lawrence: An Unprofessional Study* (1932; reprint, Denver: Alan Swallow, 1964), pp. 49, 59, 65–66.

27. Simone de Beauvoir, *The Second Sex* (New York: Knopf, 1971), p. 39.

28. Beauvoir, pp. 214–24.

29. For example, my "D. H. Lawrence and the Fall of Modern Woman," *Modern Fiction Studies* 5 (Spring 1959): 47–57. Philosopher Kathleen Nott discussed in 1960s articles Lawrence's male dominance obsessions, later reprinted in *A Soul in the Quad* (London: Routledge and Kegan Paul, 1969), pp. 297–319. Sociologist Rieff (1966; discussed later) intriguingly claims that Lawrence's "aggressions against women" were part of the paranoia of "religiously burdened men."

30. Kate Millet, *Sexual Politics* (New York: Doubleday, 1970), pp. 237–93.

31. Erica Jong, *Fear of Flying* (New York: Holt, Rinehart, and Winston, 1973), pp. 319 and 335. The second epigraph—about women being pushed to male theories about them—seems unintentional irony in coming from Lawrence. See also the citation to another Jong fiction in chap. 3 of the present work.

32. Charles Rossman, " 'You are the call and I am the answer': D. H. Lawrence and Women," *D. H. Lawrence Review* 8 (Fall 1973): 255–328. Further feminist-qualified surveys include Donald Gutierrez, "D. H. Lawrence and Sex," *Liberal and Fine Arts Review* 3 (Jan.–June 1983): 49–74.

33. Anne Smith, "A New Adam and a New Eve," in *Lawrence and Women*, ed. Anne Smith (New York: Barnes and Noble, 1978), pp. 9–48.

34. Faith Pullin, "Lawrence's Treatment of Women in *Sons and Lovers*," *Lawrence and Women*, pp. 49–74. An unprobing attempt at a meliorist view of the feminist/masculinist issue in the early novel proposes that Lawrence "foregrounds feminist issues, rather than simply ignoring them . . . he demonstrates a consciousness far ahead of its time—but not so far advanced as the consciousness of feminist critics . . . writing today." Ross C. Murfin, *Sons and Lovers, A Novel of Division and Desire* (Boston: Twayne, 1987), p. 115. See also my discussion and citations in chap. 1.

35. Mark Spilka, "On Lawrence's Hostility to Wilful Women: The Chatterley Solution,'" *Lawrence and Women*, pp. 180–211. More recently, he granted that Lawrence was a wife beater but sensitively progressing in exemplary self-therapy and male maturation, in "Postscript: Hemingway and Lawrence as Abusive Husbands," in his manuscript, "D. H. Lawrence in Changing Times."

36. Harry T. Moore, "Bert Lawrence and Lady Jane," in *Lawrence and Women*, pp. 178–88. (I am ignoring some of the more fatuous studies, in this collection and elsewhere.)

37. Carolyn G. Heilbrun, *Toward a Recognition of Androgyny* (New York: Knopf, 1973), pp. 101–12. The argument is undoubtedly weakened by loosely employing the already indiscriminately merging spiritualist metaphors of Carl Jung and Joseph Campbell. Perhaps better mythic/Jungian arguments for androgyny (though not applied to Lawrence) may be found in June Singer, *Androgyny* (Garden City, N. Y.: Double-

day, 1976). But more rigorously persuasive are the Freudian-cast arguments (again, not using Lawrence) of Dorothy Dinnerstein, *The Mermaid and the Minotaur: Sexual Arrangements and Human Malaise* (New York: Harper and Row, 1976); and Nancy Choderow, *The Reproduction of Mothering: Psychoanalysis and the Sociology of Gender* (Berkeley: University of California Press, 1978), among others. Another attempt to turn dubious mythological readings into feminist declarations concludes that Lawrence's myths show that woman "is not permitted the gratification of her own sexual desire and consciousness," and "must prostrate herself before . . . the superior male principle." Barbara A. Milliaras, *Pillar of Flame, The Mythological Foundations of D. H. Lawrence's Sexual Philosophy* (New York: Peter Lang, 1987), p. 288.

38. Carol Dix, *D. H. Lawrence and Women* (Totowa, N. J.: Rowman and Littlefield, 1980), p. 81.

39. Hilary Simpson, *D. H. Lawrence and Feminism* (Dekalb: Northern Illinois University Press, 1982), p. 81; later quotes, pp. 72, 122.

40. Lawrence Lerner, "Lawrence and the Feminists," in *D. H. Lawrence: Centenary Essays*, ed. Mara Kalnins (Bristol, U.K.: Bristol Classic Press, 1986), pp. 69–87. There are, of course, many other uses of Lawrence in gender disputes. A more recent one is Camille Paglia, *Sexual Personae* (New Haven: Yale University Press, 1990). She repeatedly uses typology from Lawrence, simplified, in her elaborate literary exposition of erotic male/female conflicts, around such assertions that "all love is combat," that there is "radical disjunction between the sexes," and that there is pervasively "the terrible duality of gender," such as the different freedom in urinating, and other rather quaint metaphoric extensions of biology. (Was it not Herodotus who first reported that there were other lands where men squatted while women stood?)

41. Declan Kiberd, *Men and Feminism in Modern Literature* (London: Macmillan, 1983), pp. 140, 146.

42. Peter Balbert, whose book is subtitled as an attack on feminism, p. 169.

43. Balbert, pp. 130–31. It might seem ungracious of me to criticize Balbert here since he positively acknowledges my distinctions (in earlier writings) about Lawrence's use of "primitivistic" materials in

his ritual-sacrifice, but Balbert has taken them out of their purpose and context which, as I emphasized, was clearly misogynistic.

44. The theme has been repeated, though in a somewhat defeating religious context, by Taylor Stoehr, "Paul Goodman and the New York Jews," *Salmagundi* 66 (Winter/Spring 1985): 50–103. Goodman told me in the early 1950s of his admiration for Lawrence, but I did not emphasize it in my *Paul Goodman* (Boston: Twayne, 1980).

45. Arthur Efron, "The Mind-Body Problem in Lawrence, Pepper, and Reich," *Journal of Mind and Behavior*, 1 (Autumn 1980): 247–70. Attempted massive empirical (and bibliographical) confirmation (including Lawrence) appears in his *Sexual Body: An Interdisciplinary Perspective* (double issue of *Journal of Mind and Behavior* 6 [1985]). After a more detailed application to Lawrence (primarily *Lady Chatterley*) in a paper (presented at the D. H. Lawrence Conference at Tufts University, 15 June 1985), part of a not yet completed book, Professor Efron suggested to me that my lack of knowledge of the empirical data might account for my too-skeptical view. While possibly applicable to the Reicheanism, its relevance to Lawrence seems doubtful. In " 'The Way Our Sympathy Flows and Recoils,': Lawrence's Last Theory of the Novel," Efron gives a one-sided discussion of the Constance reflections (which I discussed in chap. 3) and of a purified interpretation of Lawrencean sexuality, from which he rather fundamentalistically eliminates anality, male/female polarization, and other problems. "'The Way Our Sympathy Flows and Recoils,'" *The Passional Secret Places of Life*, ed. Efron, *Paunch* 63–64 (1990): 71–84. For a related, but simpler affirmative-libertarian, quasi-school of Lawrencean ideologists, see the writings of Wayne Burns, Jerry Zaslove, Gerald Butler, John Doheny, et. al.

46. Philip Rieff, *The Triumph of the Therapeutic* (New York: Harper and Row, 1966), pp. 189–231; other quotations are from pp. 191, 196, 230, 211, 217. An earlier version served as introduction to a combined reprinting of D. H. Lawrence, *Psychoanalysis and the Unconscious and Fantasia of the Unconscious* (New York: Viking, 1960). Some erotic theorists in this period viewed Lawrence as an unacceptable sexual "conservative," as did Norman O. Brown, *Life against Death* (New York: Knopf, 1959). Others, especially those emphasizing female assertion (such as Susan Sontag) treated Lawrence as "sexually

reactionary." Though used for negative purposes, Rieff's characterization seems more appropriate. For a later similar Rieff-conservative argument, Eugene Goodheart insists on the "cultural fact that the revolution of desire has in fact succeeded" but is enervated because it no longer meets sufficent "resistance," and thus has become the prevailing (dis)order. However, his view seems inconsistent in that the contemporary choice of desire does not fit an essential part of his description: "The profoundest students of desire (for example, Nietzsche and D. H. Lawrence) conceive of desire under the regime of necessity, not freedom." Obviously, the desire-vitalists insisted on *choosing* the conditions which maximize desire, which will otherwise necessarily turn to viciously self-defeating ways. (Nietzsche: "All instincts that cannot be released outward will turn inward.") Goodheart, "Desire and Its Discontents," *Partisan Review* 55 (1988), pp. 387–428.

47. Michel Foucault, *The History of Sexuality*, vol. 1 (New York: Pantheon, 1978); quotations are from pp. 157, 130–131, 155, and 158. The passage in Lawrence, *The Plumed Serpent*, in context, is Kate's intellectualized response to the lusting look of a peon, and is connected to a positive response to animal life. But she also quickly concludes, in her Western individualism, that she is not going to "submit" to it. A rather different use of Foucault applied to Lawrence, emphasizing the contradictions of discourse related to sexuality, is Lydia Blanchard, "Lawrence, Foucault, and the Language of Sexuality," *D. H. Lawrence's "Lady," A New Look at Lady Chatterley's Lover*, ed. Michael Squires and Dennis Jackson (Athens: University of Georgia Press, 1985), pp. 17–35.

48. My dozen or so selective anecdotes are, of course, not intended as criticism of any individuals, and identifying characteristics have been carefully excluded (even when the person is dead); my purpose is to illustrate certain reverberations of Lawrenceanism not so clearly evident in the usual published material.

49. Donald Davie, *Times Literary Supplement*, 1 October 1977, p. 1233.

50. Gay Talese, *Thy Neighbor's Wife* (New York: Random House, 1979).

51. Patricia Gillan, "Therapeutic Uses of Obscenity," in *Censorship and Obscenity*, ed. R. Dahavan (Totowa, N. J.: Rowman and Littlefield, 1978), p. 134.

52. Delores La Chapelle "Sacred Earth," *Earth First! Journal*, 1 May 1989, p. 28.
53. Quote is from a review of a Kinsey Institute report, *Sex and Morality in the U. S.* (1989), by Diane Johnson, who also characterizes the original Kinsey as having a "Lawrentian optimism" against "a Victorian legacy of repression and inhibition." Elsewhere she also links Lawrence with the "tradition of free-thinking post-Victorian sexologists like Havelock Ellis, or Edward Carpenter. . . ." "In Bed With Social Science," *New York Review of Books*, 12 October 1989, pp. 25, 27. (Others, such as Blanchard, have somewhat misleadingly linked Lawrence with the Marie Stopes he specifically attacks in his "A Propos *Lady Chatterley's Lover*.") While this is dubious for Lawrence's sacral eroticism, giving it a too liberal-rationalistic cast, it may, with such a sophisticated reviewer, nonetheless indicate considerable of Lawrence's legacy, the way he is often viewed (and he is now far better known than any of the others mentioned).
54. Paul Delaney, "Lawrence and the Decline of the Industrial Spirit" (Paper presented at the Centenary D. H. Lawrence Conference, Tufts University, 14 June 1985). The final phrase is quoted from the later revised published version in *The Challenge of D. H. Lawrence*, ed. Michael Squires and Keith Cushman (Madison: University of Wisconsin Press, 1990), pp. 77–88. Delaney does not very persuasively argue that Lawrence learned his horror of industrial-ugly England from the "Rural Myth" rather than personal experience, but weren't they reinforcing? The long-imbedded British anti-industrial tradition has been discussed from another Marxist perspective by Raymond Williams, *The Country and the City* (1973).
55. Dan Jacobson, "D. H. Lawrence and Modern Society,"in *D. H. Lawrence; A Collection of Criticism*, ed. Leo Hamalian (New York: McGraw Hill, 1975), pp. 133–43.
56. Diana Trilling, "Lawrence and the Movements of Modern Culture," pp. 1–7.
57. I bemusedly note that Mark Spilka adds a curious addendum to such a view by explaining that Widmer's "nihilistic" arguments received attention in the 1960s as a result of the nihilistic-rebellious temper of the times which they matched. I appreciate the compliment to my prescience in interpretations written in the mid-1950s.

58. Keith Sagar, "Beyond D. H. Lawrence," in *D. H. Lawrence: The Man Who Lived*, ed. Robert Partlow, Jr. and Harry T. Moore (Carbondale: Southern Illinois University Press, 1980), pp. 258–66.
59. Surprisingly, Joycean Anthony Burgess viewed Lawrence as one of "Britain's prophets" who used to, but no longer, "preached to a wilderness." Contrary to such as Sagar, Burgess emphasizes Lawrence's importance in his youth in the 1930s as a "way into the forbidden world" of eroticism, and as still a figure "bringing about sexual liberation." *New York Times Book Review*, 14 July 1985, pp. 3ff. See also his *Flame into Being: The Life and Work of D. H. Lawrence* (London: William Heinemann, 1985).
60. Philip Larkin, "Annus Mirabilis," in *High Windows* (London: Faber and Faber, 1974), p. 34.
61. I have viewed ten films made in the past generation: *Sons and Lovers* (two versions), *The Rocking-Horse Winner*, *Lady Chatterley's Lover*, *The Fox*, *The Widowing of Mrs. Holroyd*, *The Virgin and the Gipsy*, *Women in Love*, *The Rainbow*, and *The Priest of Love*. There may be others. Few modern authors have had such a plethora of cinematic adaptions, which ought to suggest several things, including the appeal as well as the diversity. There would also seem to be other matters to learn from them, such as (if memory serves) the movie version of *The Virgin and Gipsy* improved Lawrence's sense of historical-rebellious ambience for that interesting but heavily tendentious tale, or that Ken Russell's only partly "Lawrencean" (pace Pauline Kael) *Women in Love* was a somewhat more coherent melodrama than Lawrence's. While the various artifact forms are not equivalent, I do detect some common dissident threads, which is a purpose of my citations here.
62. Jeffrey Meyers, ed., *The Legacy of D. H. Lawrence* (London: Macmillan, 1987); and Cushman, Keith, and Dennis Jackson, eds., *The Literary Inheritance of D. H. Lawrence* (New York: St. Martin's, 1991). Since I contributed to both, I will not make further comment except to note that there is certainly room for others, especially those that go beyond a narrow literary concern.
63. In a twelve-page "Reader's Report" in 1958 (on my earlier book on Lawrence, *The Art of Perversity*), Schorer was quite emphatic on the issue.
64. I am referring to the ideological cluster in somewhat of the sense, increasingly widespread, of David Ehrenfeld, *The Arrogance of Hu-*

manism (New York: Oxford University Press, 1978), and Neil Evernden, *The Natural Alien: Humankind and Environment* (Toronto: University of Toronto Press, 1985), among other theorists of our humanistically biased "global genocide."

65. Edward Abbey, *A Voice Crying in the Wilderness (Vox Clamantis in Deserto)* (New York: St. Martin's, 1990), p. 66. He also drew on Lawrence, I think, in earlier writings emphasizing physical responsiveness, "touch," and antitechnology (such as "Down the River"). For further context, see some of my discussions, such as "Natural Anarchism: Edward Abbey, and Gang," *Social Anarchism* no. 15 (1990): 19–29.

66. An example I had recent fortuitous occasion to note might be Gore Vidal, who acknowledges early admiration of Lawrence as sexual writer (probably encouraged by his Lawrence-admiring close friends, such as Anaïs Nin and Tennessee Williams) and later revulsion to him as political writer, in scattered comments in Gore Vidal, *Matters of Fact and Fiction: Essays, 1952–1972* (New York: Random House, 1972). For further context, see my "Gore Vidal," *Contemporary Political Activists*, ed. David De Leon (New York: Greenwood, in press).

67. *Reflections on the Death of a Porcupine and Other Essays* (London: Martin Secker, 1934), p. 17.

Works Cited

Abbey, Edward. *A Voice Crying in the Wilderness (Vox Clamantis in Deserto)*. New York: St. Martin's, 1990.

Amis, Martin. *London Fields*. New York: Crown, 1989.

Arnold, Armin. *D. H. Lawrence and America*. New York: Philosophical Library, 1959.

———. *D. H. Lawrence and German Literature*. Montreal: University of Toronto Press, 1963.

Balbert, Peter. *D. H. Lawrence and the Phallic Imagination: Essays on Sexual Identity and Feminist Misreading*. New York: St. Martin's, 1989.

———. "Ten Men and a Sacred Prostitute: The Psychology of Sex in the Cambridge Edition of *The Lost Girl*." *Twentieth Century Literature* 36 (Winter 1990): 381–402.

Barron, Janet. "Equality Puzzle: Lawrence and Feminism." In *Rethinking Lawrence*, edited by Keith Brown, 12–22. Milton Keynes, U. K.: Open University Press, 1990.

Beauvoir, Simone de. *The Second Sex*. New York: Knopf, 1971.

Ben Ephraim, Gavriel. "The Achievement of Balance in *Lady Chatterley's Lover*." In *D. H. Lawrence's "Lady" : A New Look at Lady Chatterley's Lover*, edited by Michael Squires and Dennis Jackson, 136–53. Athens: University of Georgia Press, 1985.

Bentley, Eric. *A Century of Hero-Worship, A Study of the Idea of Heroism in Carlyle and Nietzsche, with Notes on Wagner, Spengler, Stefan George and D. H. Lawrence*. New York: Duell-Sloan, 1944.

Bentley, Michael. "Lawrence's Political Thought: Some English Contexts, 1906–19." In *D. H. Lawrence: New Studies*, edited by Christopher Heywood, 48–64. London: Macmillan, 1987.

Berger, John. *G*. 1972. Reprint. New York: Pantheon, 1980.

Works Cited

Black, Michael. *D. H. Lawrence: The Early Fiction*. London: Macmillan, 1986.

————. "Gilbert Noon, D. H. Lawrence and the Gentle Reader." *D. H. Lawrence Review* 20 (Summer 1988): 23–45.

Blanchard, Lydia. "Lawrence, Foucault, and the Language of Sexuality." *D. H. Lawrence's "Lady": A New Look at Lady Chatterley's Lover*, edited by Michael Squires and Dennis Jackson, 17–35. Athens: University of Georgia Press, 1985.

Bloom, Harold. *Anxiety of Influence*. New York: Oxford University Press, 1973.

Bostetter, Edward E. *The Romantic Ventriloquists*. Seattle: University of Washington Press, 1963.

Brian, John. *Supreme Fictions*. Montreal: University of Toronto Press, 1974.

Bridgewater, Patrick. *Nietzsche in Anglosaxony*. Leicester, U. K.: University of Leicester Press, 1972.

Britton, Derek. *Lady Chatterley, The Making of the Novel*. London: Unwin Hyman, 1988.

Brown, J. D. *Henry Miller*. New York: Ungar, 1986.

Brown, Norman O. *Life against Death*. New York: Knopf, 1959.

Burgess, Anthony. "D. H. Lawrence." *New York Times Book Review*, 14 July 1985, pp. 3ff.

————. *Flame into Being: The Life and Work of D. H. Lawrence*. London: William Heinemann, 1985.

Butler, Gerald. *This Is Carbon: A Defense of D. H. Lawrence's "The Rainbow" Against His Admirers*. Seattle: Genitron, 1986.

Butterfield, R. W. *The Broken Arc: A Study of Hart Crane*. Edinburgh: Olivier, 1969.

Callow, Phillip. *Son and Lover: The Young D. H. Lawrence*. New York: Viking, 1975.

Calonne, David Stephen. "Euphoria in Paris: Henry Miller Meets D. H. Lawrence." *Library Chronicle of the University of Texas at Austin*, 2d ser., no. 34 (1986): 89–98.

Carroll, John. *The Break-Out from the Crystal Palace*. London: Routledge and Kegan Paul, 1974.

Chambers, Jessie. [E. T., pseud.]. *D. H. Lawrence: A Personal Record*. 2d ed. New York: Barnes and Noble, 1965.

Chapelle, Delores La. "Sacred Earth." *Earth First! Journal*, 1 May 1989, p. 28.

Works Cited

Choderow, Nancy. *The Reproduction of Mothering: Psychoanalysis and the Sociology of Gender*. Berkeley: Unviersity of California Press, 1978.

Christenson, Paul. *Charles Olson, Call Him Ishmael*. Austin: University of Texas Press, 1979.

Clark, L. D. *The Dark Night of the Body: D. H. Lawrence's "The Plumed Serpent."*. Austin: University of Texas Press, 1964.

———. "Making the Classic Contemporary: Lawrence's Pilgrimage Novels and American Romance." In *D. H. Lawrence in the Modern World*, edited by Peter Preston and Peter Hoare, 193–216. London: Macmillan, 1989.

Clarke, Colin. *River of Dissolution: D. H. Lawrence and English Romanticism*. New York: Barnes and Noble, 1969.

Corke, Helen. *D. H. Lawrence: The Croyden Years*. Austin: University of Texas Press, 1964.

———. *In Our Infancy: An Autobiography*. London: Cambridge University Press, 1975.

Crane, Hart. *Complete Poems and Selected Letters and Prose*. Edited by Brom Weber. New York: Liveright, 1966.

Cushman, Keith. *D. H. Lawrence at Work: The Emergence of "The Prussian Officer" Stories*. Chapel Hill: University of North Carolina Press, 1975.

Cushman, Keith, and Dennis Jackson, eds. *The Inheritance of D. H. Lawrence*. New York: St. Martin's, 1991.

Dahlberg, Edward. *Can These Bones Live*. New York: New Directions, 1960.

———. *The Edward Dahlberg Reader*. Edited by Paul Carroll. New York: New Directions, 1967.

Daleski, H. M. *The Forked Flame: A Study of D. H. Lawrence*. London: Faber and Faber, 1965.

Danto, Arthur C. *Nietzsche as Philosopher*. New York: Macmillan, 1965.

Davie, Donald. *Times Literacy Supplement*, 1 Oct. 1977, p. 1233.

Delaney, Paul. "Lawrence and the Decline of the Industrial Spirit." In *The Challenge of D. H. Lawrence*, edited by Michael Squires and Keith Cushman, 77–88. Madison: University of Wisconsin Press, 1990.

Delavenay, Emile. *D. H. Lawrence and Edward Carpenter: A Study in Edwardian Transition*. London: William Heinemann, 1971.

———. *D. H. Lawrence, the Man and His Work: The Formative Years, 1885–1919*. London: William Heinemann, 1972.

Works Cited

Derrida, Jacques. *Spurs/Eperons*. Chicago: University of Chicago Press, 1979.

Dinnerstein, Dorothy. *The Mermaid and the Minotaur: Sexual Arrangements and Human Malaise*. New York: Harper and Row, 1976.

Dix, Carol. *D. H. Lawrence and Women*. Totowa, N. J.: Rowman and Littlefield, 1980.

Ebbatson, Roger. "A Spark Beneath the Wheel: Lawrence and Evolutionary Thought." In *D. H. Lawrence, New Studies*, edited by Christopher Heywood, 90–113. London: Macmillan, 1987.

Efron, Arthur. "The Mind-Body Problem in Lawrence, Pepper, and Reich." *Journal of Mind and Behavior* 1 (Autumun 1980): 247–70.

——. *The Sexual Body: An Interdisciplinary Perspective*. Double issue of *Journal of Mind and Behavior*, 6 (1985).

——. "'The Way Our Sympathy Flows and Recoils': Lawrence's Last Theory of the Novel." In *The Passional Secret* Places of Life edited by Efron. *Paunch* 63–64 (1990): 71–84.

Ehrenfeld, David. *The Arrogance of Humanism*. New York: Oxford University Press, 1978.

Ellis, David, and Howard Mills. *D. H. Lawrence's Non-Fiction*. Cambridge: Cambridge University Press, 1988.

Empson, William. *Some Versions of Pastoral*. Norfolk, Conn.: New Directions, [1952].

Evernden, Neil. *The Natural Alien: Humankind and Environment*. Toronto: University of Toronto Press, 1985.

Fiedler, Leslie. *Love and Death in the American Novel*. Rev. ed. New York: Stein and Day, 1966.

Ford, Ford Madox. *Return to Yesterday*. London: Metheun, 1931.

Foster, John Burt, Jr. *Heirs to Dionysus: A Nietzschean Current in Literary Modernism*. Princeton: Princeton University Press, 1981.

Foucault, Michel. *The History of Sexuality*. Vol. 1. New York: Pantheon, 1978.

Frye, Northrop. *The Critical Path*. Bloomington: University of Indiana Press, 1971.

Gertzman, Jay A. "Legitimizing *Lady Chatterley's Lover*: The Grove Press Strategy, 1959." In *The Passional Secret Places of Life*, edited by Arthur Efron. *Paunch* 63–64 (1990): 1–14.

Gill, Stephen. "The Composite World: Two Versions of *Lady Chatterley's Lover*." *Essays in Criticism* 21 (October 1971): 347–64.

225

Works Cited

Works Cited

Gillan, Patricia. "Therapeutic Uses of Obscenity." In *Censorship and Obscenity*, edited by R. Dahavan, 130–42. Totowa, N. J.: Rowman and Littlefield, 1978.

Goodheart, Eugene. "Desire and Its Discontents." *Partisan Review* 55 (1988): 387–428.

———. *The Utopian Vision of D. H. Lawrence*. Chicago: University of Chicago Press, 1963.

Gray, Ronald. *The German Tradition in Literature, 1871–1945*. Cambridge: Cambridge University Press, 1965.

Green, Eleanor. "Blueprints for Utopia: The Political Ideas of Nietzsche and D. H. Lawrence." *Renaissance and Modern Studies* 18 (1974): 141–61.

Green, Martin. *The von Richthofen Sisters: The Triumphant and the Tragic Modes of Love*. New York: Basic, 1974.

Greer, Germaine. "Dark Age of the Steroid." *Literary Review* (London), 85 (1985): 12–15.

———. *The Female Eunuch*. New York: Bantam, 1972.

Gutierrez, Donald. *The Dark and Light Gods: Essays on the Self in Modern Literature*. Troy, N. Y.: Whitston, 1987.

———. *Lapsing Out: Embodiments of Death and Rebirth in the Last Writings of D. H. Lawrence*. Cranbury, N. J.: Associated University Presses, 1980.

———. *The Maze in the Mind and the World: Labyrinths in Modern Literature*. Troy, N. Y.: Whitston, 1985.

Hawthorne, Jeremy. "Lawrence and Working-class Fiction." In *Rethinking Lawrence*, edited by Keith Brown, 67–78. Milton Keynes, U. K.: Open University Press, 1990.

Hayman, Ronald. *Nietzsche: A Critical Life*. New York: Oxford University Press, 1980.

Heidegger, Martin. *Nietzsche*. Translated by D. T. Krell, vol. 1. New York: Harper and Row, 1979.

Heilbrun, Carolyn G. *Toward a Recognition of Androgyny*. New York: Knopf, 1973.

Hemingway, Ernest. *A Farewell to Arms*. New York: Scribner's, 1929.

Hinz, Evelyn J. "Pornography, Novel, Mythic Narrative: The Three Versions of *Lady Chatterley's Lover*." *Modernist Studies: Literature and Culture 1920–40* 3 (1979): 35–47.

Hinz, Evelyn J., and John J. Teunissen. "War, Love, and Industrialism:

Works Cited

The Ares/Aphrodite/Hephacstus Complex in *Lady Chatterley's Lover*."
In *D. H. Lawrence's "Lady": A New Look at Lady Chatterley's Lover*,
edited by Michael Squires and Dennis Jackson, 186–217. Athens: University of Georgia Press, 1985.

Holderness, Graham. *D. H. Lawrence: History, Ideology, and Fiction*.
Dublin: Gill and Macmillan, 1984.

Holmes, Colin. "Lawrence's Social Origins." In *D. H. Lawrence, New
Studies*, edited by Christopher Heywood, 1–14. London: Macmillan,
1987.

Humma, John B. "D. H. Lawrence as Friedrich Nietzsche." *Philological
Quarterly* 53 (1974): 110–20.

———. "The Interpenetrating Metaphor: Nature and Myth in *Lady Chatterely's Lover*." *PMLA* 98 (1983): 77–86.

———. *Metaphor and Meaning in D. H. Lawrence's Later Novels*. Columbia: University of Missouri Press, 1990.

Ingram, Allen. *The Language of D. H. Lawrence*. London: Macmillan,
1990.

Jackson, Dennis. "The Old Pagan Vision: Myth and Ritual in *Lady Chatterley's Lover*." In *Critical Essays on D. H. Lawrence*, edited by Dennis
Jackson and Fleda Brown Jackson, 128–44. Boston: G. K. Hall, 1988.

Jackson, Dennis, and Fleda Brown Jackson. Introduction to *Critical Essays
on D. H. Lawrence*. Edited by Jackson and Jackson. Boston: G. K.
Hall, 1988.

Jacobson, Dan. "D. H. Lawrence and Modern Society." In *D. H. Lawrence:
A Collection of Criticism*, edited by Leo Hamalian, 133–43. New York:
McGraw Hill, 1975.

James, William. *The Varieties of Religious Experience*. 1902. Reprint.
Cambridge: Harvard University Press, 1985.

Johnson, Diane. "In Bed With Social Science." *New York Review of Books*,
12 Oct. 1982, 25–27.

Jong, Erica. *Fear of Flying*. New York: Holt, Rinehart, and Winston,
1973.

———. *Parachutes and Kisses*. New York: New American Library, 1984.

Kaufmann, Walter. *Nietzsche: Philosopher, Psychologist, Antichrist*. 4th
ed. Princeton: Princeton University Press, 1974.

Keller, Karl. *The Only Kangaroo among the Beauty*. Baltimore: Johns
Hopkins University Press, 1979.

Kermode, Frank. *D. H. Lawrence*. New York: Viking, 1973.

Works Cited

Kessler, Jascha. "Descent in Darkness: The Myth of *The Plumed Serpent*." In *A D. H. Lawrence Miscellany*, edited by Harry T. Moore, 239–60. Carbondale: Southern Illinois University Press, 1959.

Kiberd, Declan. *Men and Feminism in Modern Literature*. London: Macmillan, 1985.

King, Richard. *The Party of Eros*. Chapel Hill: University of North Carolina Press, 1972.

Knight, G. Wilson. "Lawrence, Joyce and Powys." *Essays in Criticism* 11 (Oct. 1961): 403–17.

Larkin, Philip. "Amus Mirabilis." In *High Winows*, p. 34. London: Faber and Faber, 1974.

Larrett, William. "Lawrence and Germany: A Reluctant Guest in the Land of 'Pure Ideas.'" In *Rethinking Lawrence*, edited by Keith Brown, 79–91. Milton Keynes, U. K.: Open University Press, 1990.

Lawrence, D. H. *Aaron's Rod*. 1922. Reprint. London: William Heinemann, 1950.

———. *Assorted Articles*. New York: Knopf, 1930.

———. *Collected Letters*. Edited by Harry T. Moore. 2 vols. New York: Viking, 1962.

———. *The Complete Poems*. Edited by Vivan de Sola Pinto and F. Warren Roberts. New York: Viking, 1971.

———. *The Complete Short Novels*. 2 vols. London: William Heinemann, 1956.

———. *The Complete Short Stories*. 3 vols. London: William Heinemann, 1955.

———. *D. H. Lawrence: Selected Literacy Criticism*. Edited by Anthony Beal. New York: Viking, 1966.

———. *Etruscan Places*. London: William Heinemann, 1950.

———. *Fantasia of the Unconscious*. New York: Seltzer, 1922.

———. *The First Lady Chatterley*. New York: Dial, 1944.

———. *John Thomas and Lady Jane*. New York: Viking, 1972.

———. *Kangaroo*. 1923. Reprint. London: William Heinemann, 1950.

———. *Lady Chatterley's Lover*. New York: New American Library, 1962.

———. *The Letters of D. H. Lawrence*. Edited by James Boulton. Vol. 1, *1901–1913*. Cambridge: Cambridge University Press, 1979.

———. *The Letters of D. H. Lawrence*. Edited by George J. Zytaruk

Works Cited

and James T. Boulton. Vol. 2, *1913–1916*. Cambridge: Cambridge University Press, 1981.

———. *The Lost Girl*. 1920. Reprint. London: William Heinemann, 1950.

———. *Memoirs of Maurice Magnus*. Edited by Keith Cushman. Rev. ed. Santa Rosa, Calif.: Black Sparrow, 1987.

———. *Mornings in Mexico*. London: William Heinemann, 1950.

———. *Mr. Noon*. Edited by Lindeth Vasey. Cambridge: Cambridge University Press, 1984.

———. *Phoenix*. Edited by Edward D. McDonald. London: William Heinemann, 1936.

———. *Phoenix II*. Edited by Warren Roberts and Harry T. Moore. New York: Viking, 1970.

———. *The Plumed Serpent*. 1926. Reprint. New York: Knopf, 1951.

———. *Psychoanalysis and the Unconscious*. New York: Seltzer, 1921.

———. *The Rainbow*. 1915. Reprint. London: William Heinemann, 1950.

———. *Reflections on the Death of a Porcupine and Other Essays*. London: Martin Secker, 1934.

———. *Reflections on the Death of a Porcupine and Other Essays*. Edited by Michael Herbert. Cambridge: Cambridge University Press, 1988.

———. *The Sea and Sardinia*. New York: Robert McBride, 1931.

———. *Sex, Literature, and Censorship*. Edited by Harry T. Moore. New York: Twayne, 1953.

———. *Sons and Lovers*. 1913. Reprint. New York: New American Library, 1953.

———. *Studies in Classic American Literature*. 1923. Reprint. New York: Doubleday, 1953.

———. *Study of Thomas Hardy and Other Essays*. Edited by Bruce Steele. Cambridge: Cambridge University Press, 1985.

———. *The Symbolic Meaning: The Uncollected Versions of Studies in Classic American Literature*. Edited by Armin Arnold. New York: Doubleday, 1953.

———. *The Trespasser*. 1912. Reprint. London: William Heinemann, 1950.

———. *Twilight in Italy*. 1916. Reprint. London: William Heinemann, 1950.

Works Cited

⸺. *The White Peacock*. 1911. Reprint. Hammondsworth, U.K.: Penguin, 1950.

⸺. *Women in Love*. 1920. Reprint. New York: Viking, 1960.

⸺. *Women in Love*. Edited by David Farmer, Lindeth Vasey, and John Worthen. Cambridge: Cambridge University Press, 1987.

Leavis, F. R. *D. H. Lawrence: Novelist*. London: Chatto and Windus, 1955.

⸺. *Thought, Words and Creativity: Art and Thought in Lawrence*. New York: Oxford University Press, 1976.

Legman, Gershom. *The Horn Book: Studies in Erotic Folklore and Bibliography*.New Hyde Park, N. Y.: University Books, 1964.

Lerner, Lawrence. "Lawrence and the Feminists." In *D. H. Lawrence: Centenary Essays*, edited by Mara Kalnins, 69–87. Bristol, U. K.: Bristol Classical Press, 1986.

Lodge, David. "Lawrence, Dostoyevsky, Bakhtin: Lawrence and Dialogic Fiction." In *Rethinking Lawrence*, edited Keith Brown, 92–108. Milton Keynes, U. K.: Open University Press, 1990.

Mailer, Norman. *Advertisements for Myself*. New York: New American Library, 1959.

⸺. *An American Dream*. New York: New American Library, 1965.

⸺. *Armies of the Night*. New York: New American Library, 1968.

⸺. *The Executioner's Song*. Boston: Little, Brown, 1979.

⸺. *The Presidential Papers*. New York: New American Library, 1964.

⸺. *The Prisoner of Sex*. New York: New American Library, 1971.

⸺. *Tough Guys Don't Dance*. New York: Ballantine, 1984.

⸺, ed. Introductions in *Genius and Lust: A Journey Through the Major Writings of Henry Miller*. New York: Grove, 1976.

Marcuse, Herbert. *Counter-Revolution and Revolt*. Boston: Beacon, 1972.

Martin, Robert K. *Hero, Captain, and Stranger: Male Friendship, Social Critique, and Literary Form in the Sea Novels of Herman Melville*. Chapel Hill: University of North Carolina Press, 1986.

Martinelli, Peter V. *Pastoral*. London: Metheun, 1970.

Masters, William H., Virginia E. Johnson, and Robert C. Kolodny. *Masters and Johnson on Sex and Human Love*. Boston: Little, Brown, 1986.

Matthiessen, F. O. *American Renaissance*. New York: Oxford University Press, 1941.

Works Cited

May, Keith M. *Nietzsche and Modern Literature*. New York: St. Martin's 1988.

Meyers, Jeffrey. *D. H. Lawrence, A Biography*. New York: Knopf, 1990.

——. *Homosexuality and Literature, 1890–1930*. Montreal: McGill-Queens University Press, 1977.

——. Introduction to *The Legacy of D. H. Lawrence*. Edited by Meyers. London: Macmillan, 1987.

——. "Lawrence and Travel Writers." In *The Legacy of D. H. Lawrence*, edited by Meyers, 81–108. London: Macmillan, 1987.

——. "Memoirs of D. H. Lawrence: A Genre of the Thirties." *D. H. Lawrence Review* 14 (1981): 1–32.

Michaels-Tonks, Jennifer. *D. H. Lawrence*. Bonn, Germany: Bouvier, 1976.

Miller, Henry. *Big Sur and the Oranges of Hieronymous Bosch*. New York: New Directions, 1957.

——. *Black Spring*. New York: Grove:, 1963.

——. *The Books in My Life*. Norfolk, Conn.: New Directions, [1952].

——. *The Colossus of Maroussi*. Norfolk, Conn.: New Directions, 1941.

——. *The Cosmological Eye*. Norfolk, Conn.: New Directions, 1939.

——. *Dear, Dear Brenda: The Love Letters of Henry Miller to Brenda Venus*. Edited by Gerard Seth Sindell. New York: William Morrow, 1986.

——. *From Your Copernican Friend*. Edited by Irving Stettner. New York: New Directions, 1984.

——. *Genius and Lust: A Journey Through the Major Writings of Henry Miller*. Edited by Norman Mailer. New York: Grove, 1976.

——. *The Henry Miller Reader*. Edited by Lawrence Durrell. New York: New Directions, 1959.

——. *Letters to Anais Nin*. Edited by Gunther Stuhlman. New York: G. P. Putnam's Sons, 1965.

——. *My Life and Times*. Edited by Bradley Smith. Chicago: Playboy 1972.

——. *Notes on "Aaron's Rod."* Edited by Seamus Cooney. Santa Barbara, Calif.: Capra, 1980.

——. "Paris Notebook." [n.d.] Humanities Research Center, University of Texas at Austin.

231

———. *Sunday After the War*. Norfolk, Conn.: New Directions, 1944.

———. *Tropic of Cancer*. 1934. Reprint. New York: Grove, 1961.

———. *Tropic of Capricorn*. New York: Grove, 1962.

———. *Wisdom of the Heart*. Norfolk, Conn.: New Directions, 1941.

———. *The World of Lawrence, A Passionate Appreciation*. Edited by, and introduction by, Evelyn J. Hinz and John J. Teunissen. Santa Barbara, Calif.: Capra, 1980.

Miller, Henry, and William A. Gordon. *Writer and Critic*. Baton Rouge: Louisiana State University Press, 1968.

Millet, Kate. *Sexual Politics*. New York: Doubleday, 1970.

Milliaras, Barbara A. *Pillar of Flame, The Mythological Foundations of D. H. Lawrence's Sexual Philosophy*. New York: Peter Lang, 1987.

Milton, Colin. *Lawrence and Nietzsche*. Aberdeen, U. K.: Aberdeen University Press, 1987.

Moore, Harry T. "Bert Lawrence and Lady Jane." In *Lawrence and Women*, edited by Anne Smith, 178–88. New York: Barnes and Noble, 1978.

———. *The Priest of Love, A Life of D. H. Lawrence*. Rev. ed. New York: Farrar, Straus, and Giroux, 1974.

Moramarco, Fred. *Edward Dahlberg*. New York: Twayne, 1973.

Moynahan, Julian. "Pastoralism as Culture and Counter-Culture in English Fiction, 1800–1928." *Novel* 6 (Fall 1972): 35–48.

Murdoch, Iris. *A Severed Head*. 1961. Reprint. New York: Penguin, 1987.

Murfin, Ross C. *Sons and Lovers, A Novel of Division and Desire*. Boston: Twayne, 1987.

Murphy, Robert F. *The Body Silent*. New York: Henry Holt, 1987.

Murry, John Middleton. *Love, Freedom, Society*. London: Jonathan Cape, 1957.

———. *Son of Woman*. London: Jonathan Cape, 1931.

Nehamas, Alexander. *Nietzsche, Life as Literature*. Cambridge: Harvard University Press, 1985.

New, Peter. *Fiction and Purpose in Utopia, Rasseles, The Mill on the Floss and Women in Love*. London: Macmillan, 1985.

Nietzsche, Friedrich. *Beyond Good and Evil*. Translated by Walter Kaufmann. New York: Random House, 1966.

———. *The Birth of Tragedy*. Translated by Francis Goffing. Garden City, N. Y.: Doubleday, 1956.

———. *Complete Works*. Edited by Oscar Levy. London: Allen and Unwin, 1909–1911.

Works Cited

———. *On the Genealogy of Morals*. Translated by Walter Kaufmann and R. J. Hollingdale. New York: Random House, 1969.

———. *The Portable Nietzsche*. Edited by Walter Kaufmann. New York: Viking, 1968.

———. *The Will to Power*. Translated by Walter Kaufmann and R. J. Hollingdale. New York: Random House, 1968.

Nin, Anaïs. *D. H. Lawrence: An Unprofessional Study*. 1932. Reprint. Denver: Alan Swallow, 1964.

———. *The Diary of Anaïs Nin, 1930–1934*. Edited by Gunther Stuhlman. New York: Alan Swallow and Harcourt Brace, 1966.

Nixon, Cornelia. *Lawrence's Leadership Politics and the Turn Against Woman*. Berkeley: University of California Press, 1986.

Nott, Kathleen. "Lawrence by Himself." In *A Soul in the Quad*, 297–319. London: Routledge and Kegan Paul, 1969.

Oates, Joyce Carol. "Lawrence's Götterdamerung: The Apocalyptic Vision of *Women in Love*." In *Critical Essays on D. H. Lawrence*, edited by Dennis Jackson and Fleda Brown Jackson 47–108. Boston: G. K. Hall, 1988.

Olson, Charles. *Call Me Ishmael*. New York: Reynal and Hitchcock, 1947.

———. *Human Universe and Other Essays*. New York: Grove, 1967.

———. *Letter to Melville*. Black Mountain, N.C.: N.p., 1951.

Otto, Rudolf. *The Idea of the Holy: An Inquiry into the Non-rational Factor in the Idea of the Divine and Its Relation to the Rational*. Translated by John W. Harvey. New York: Oxford University Press, 1950.

Paglia, Camille. *Sexual Personae: Art and Decadence from Nefertiti to Emily Dickinson*. New Haven: Yale University Press, 1990.

Pally, Marcia. "X-rated Feminism." *Nation* 241 (29 July 1985): 784–93.

Peek, Andrew. "The Sydney *Bulletin*, *Moby Dick*, and Allusiveness of *Kangaroo*." In *D. H. Lawrence: New Studies*, edited by Christopher Heywood, 84–89. London: Macmillan, 1987.

Peters, Joan D. "The Living and the Dead: Lawrence's Theory of the Novel and the Structure of *Lady Chatterley's Lover*." *D. H. Lawrence Review* 20 (Spring 1988): 3–21.

Peters, John. "The Bottom of the Well." *Essays in Criticism* 12 (Apr. 1962).

Pullin, Faith. "Lawrence's Treatment of Women in *Sons and Lovers*." In *Lawrence and Women*, edited by Anne Smith, 49–74. New York: Barnes and Noble, 1978.

Works Cited

Radford, Jean. *Norman Mailer*. London: Macmillan, 1975.

Ragnissis, Michael. *The Subterfuge of Art*. Baltimore: Johns Hopkins University Press, 1978.

Rahv, Philip. "Henry Miller." In *Image and Idea*, 159–66. New York: New Directions, 1957.

Read, Allen Walker. *Classic American Graffiti*. 1935, Reprint. Waukesha, Wis.: Maledicta, 1977.

Rembar, Charles. *The End of Obscenity*. New York: Random House, 1968.

Reyner, J. R. L. "The Three Versions of *Lady Chatterley's Lover*." *Geste* (Univ. of Leeds) 17 (1961): 2–31.

Rieff, Philip. *The Triumph of the Therapeutic*. New York: Harper and Row, 1966.

Robinson, H. M. "Nietzsche, Lawrence, and the Somatic Conception of the Good Life." *New Comparison* 5 (1988): 40–56.

Rossman, Charles. "D. H. Lawrence and Mexico." In *D. H. Lawrence, A Centenary Celebration*, edited by Peter Balbert and Phillip L. Marcus, 180–209. Ithaca, N. Y.: Cornell University Press, 1985.

———. "'You are the call and I am the answer': D. H. Lawrence and Women." *D. H. Lawrence Review* 8 (Fall 1973): 255–328.

Rylance, Rick. "Lawrence's Politics." In *Rethinking Lawrence*, edited by Keith Brown, 163–80. Milton Keynes, U. K.: Open University Press, 1990.

Sabin, Margery. *The Dialect of the Tribe*. New York: Oxford University Press, 1987.

Sagar, Keith. *The Art of D. H. Lawrence*. Cambridge: Cambridge University Press, 1966.

———. "Beyond D. H. Lawrence." In *D. H. Lawrence: The Man Who Lived*, edited by Robert Partlow and Harry T. Moore, pp. 258–66. Carbondale: Southern Illinois University Press, 1980.

Sanders, Scott. *D. H. Lawrence: The World of the Five Major Novels*. New York: Viking, 1974.

Scholes, Robert. *Semiotics and Interpretation*. New Haven: Yale University Press, 1982.

Simpson, Hilary. *D. H. Lawrence and Feminism*. DeKalb: Northern Illinois University Press, 1982.

Singer, June. *Androgyny*. Garden City, N.Y.: Doubleday, 1976.

Sissman, L. E. "The Second Lady Chatterley." *New Yorker*, 6 Jan. 1973, 73–75.

Works Cited

Smith, Anne. "A New Adam and a New Eve." In *Lawrence and Women*, edited by Anne Smith, 9–48. New York: Barnes and Noble, 1978.

Solomon, Robert C. "Nietzsche, Nihilism, and Morality." In *Nietzsche*, edited by Solomon, 180–205. South Bend, Ind.: University of Notre Dame Press, 1980.

Spencer, Herbert. *First Principles*. 1862. Reprint. New York: Collier, 1905.

———. *The Principles of Biology*. Rev. ed. 2 vols. New York: Appleton, 1900.

Spilka, Mark. "D. H. Lawrence in Changing Times: A Normative Progress" [manuscript, 1990].

———. "Lawrence Up-tight, Or the Anal Phase Once Over," *Novel* 4 (Spring 1971):257–67.

———. *The Love Ethic of D. H. Lawrence*. Bloomington: Indiana University Press, 1955.

———. "On Lawrence's Hostility to Wilful Women: The Chatterley Solution." In *Lawrence and Women*, edited by Anne Smith, 189–211. New York: Barnes and Noble, 1978.

Spilka, Mark, George H. Ford, Frank Kermode, and Colin Clarke. "Critical Exchange on 'Lawrence Up-Tight': Four Tail Pieces." *Novel* 5 (Fall 1971): 54–71.

Springer, Mary Doyle. *Forms of the Modern Novella*. Chicago: University of Chicago Press, 1975.

Squires, Michael. *The Creation of Lady Chatterley's Lover*. Baltimore: Johns Hopkins University Press, 1983.

———. "Pastoral Patterns and Pastoral Variants in *Lady Chatterley's Lover*." *ELH* 39 (1972): 129–46.

Steinhauer, H. "Eros and Psyche: A Nietzschean Motif in Anglo-American Literature." *Modern Language Notes* 64 (1949): 217–28.

Stern, J. P. *Nietzsche*. Hassocks, Sussex, U. K.: Harvester, 1978.

Stevens, C. J. *Lawrence at Tregerthen*. Troy, N. Y.: Whitston, 1988.

Stoehr, Taylor. "Paul Goodman and the New York Jews." *Salmagundi* 66 (Winter/Spring 1985): 50–103.

Swigg, Richard. *Lawrence, Hardy, and American Literature*. New York: Oxford University Press, 1972.

Talese, Gay. *Thy Neighbor's Wife*. New York: Random House, 1979.

Thatcher, David S. *Nietzsche in England, 1890–1914*. Toronto: University of Toronto Press, 1970.

Works Cited

The Trial of Lady Chatterley. Edited by C. H. Rolph. Baltimore: Penguin, 1961.

Trilling, Diana. "Lawrence and the Movements of Modern Culture." In *D. H. Lawrence: Novelist, Poet, Prophet*, edited by Stephen Spender, 1–7. New York: Harper and Row, 1973.

Turner, John. "Purity and Danger in D. H. Lawrence's *The Virgin and the Gipsy*." In *D. H. Lawrence: Centenary Essays*, edited by Mara Kalnins, 139–71. Bristol, U. K.: Bristol Classic Press, 1986.

Twentieth Century Interpretations of Sons and Lovers. Edited by Judith Farr. Englewood Cliffs, N. J.: Prentice-Hall, 1970.

Unterecker, John. *Voyager: A Life of Hart Crane*. New York: Farrar, Straus, and Giroux, 1969.

Updike, John. *Rabbit Is Rich*. New York: Fawcett, 1981.

Vidal, Gore. *Matters of Fact and Fiction: Essays, 1952–1972*. New York: Random House, 1972.

Vivas, Eliseo. *D. H. Lawrence, the Triumph and the Failure of Art*. Evanston, Ill.: Northwestern University Press, 1960.

Walker, Alice. *The Color Purple*. New York: Harcourt Brace Jovanovich, 1982.

Welch, Colin. "Black Magic, White Lies." *Encounter* 16 (Feb. 1961): 75–79.

Wenke, Joseph. *Mailer's America*. Hanover, N. H.: University Press of New England, 1987.

Widmer, Kingsley. "American Poetic-Naturalism: Edward Dahlberg." Shenandoah 16 (Autumn 1964): 69–74.

———. *The Art of Perversity: D. H. Lawrence's Shorter Fictions*. Seattle: University of Washington Press, 1962.

———. "Beyond Censorship? The Restrictive Processing of American Culture." In *Freedom and Culture*, edited by Eleanor Widmer, 200–210. Belmont, Calif.: Wadsworth, 1970.

———. *Counterings: Utopian Dialectics in Contemporary Contexts*. Ann Arbor, Mich.: UMI Research Press, 1988.

———. "Desire and Denial, Dialectics of Passion in Lawrence." *D. H. Lawrence Review* 18 (1985–86): 139–150.

———. "Desire and Negation: the Dialectics of Passion in D. H. Lawrence." In *The Spirit of D. H. Lawrence*, edited by Gamini Salgado and G. K. Das, 125–43. London: Macmillan, 1988.

Works Cited

———. "D. H. Lawrence and Critical Mannerism." *Journal of Modern Literature* 3 (Winter 1974): 1043–50.

———. "D. H. Lawrence and the Fall of Modern Woman." *Modern Fiction Studies* 5 (Spring 1959): 47–57.

———. *Edges of Extremity: Some Problems of Literary Modernism.* Tulsa, Okla.: University of Tulsa Monographs, 1980.

———. *The End of Culture: Essays on Sensibility in Contemporary Society* San Diego: San Diego State University Press, 1975.

———. "From Great War to Little Garden: Ford's Ford." *Antaeus* no. 56 (Spring 1986): 179–90.

———. "Gore Vidal." In *Contemporary Political Activists*, edited by David De Leon. New York: Greenwood, in press.

———. *Henry Miller.* Rev. ed. Boston: Twayne, 1990.

———. "Lawrence and the Nietzschean Matrix." In *D. H. Lawrence and Tradition*, edited by Jeffrey Meyers, 115–131. London: Athlone, 1985.

———. "Lawrence's Cultural Impact." In *The Legacy of D. H. Lawrence*, edited by Jeffrey Meyers, 156–174. London: Macmillan, 1987.

———. "Lawrentian Manias: A Survey of D. H. Lawrence Scholarship." *Studies in the Novel* 6 (Spring 1974): 547–58.

———. "The Literary Institutionalization of D. H. Lawrence: An Anti-review of the Current State of Lawrence Studies." *Paunch* no. 26 (April 1966): 5–13.

———. *The Literary Rebel.* Carbondale: Southern Illinois University Press, 1965.

———. "Melville and the Myths of Modernism." *A Companion to Melville Studies.* Edited by John Bryant Westport, Conn.: Greenwood, 1986.

———. "Natural Anarchism: Edward Abbey, and Gang." *Social Anarchism* no. 15 (1990): 19–29.

———. *Paul Goodman.* Boston: Twayne, 1980.

———. "The Pertinence of Modern Pastoral: The Three Versions of *Lady Chatterley's Lover.*" *Studies in the Novel* 5 (Fall 1973): 298–313.

———. "The Post-Modernist Art of Protest: Kesey and Mailer." *Centennial Review* 19 (Summer 1975): 121–35.

———. "Profiling an Erotic Prophet: Biographies of D. H. Lawrence." *Studies in the Novel* 7 (Summer 1976): 234–45.

———. "The Sociology of Literature?" *Studies in the Novel* 11 (1979): 99–105.

Works Cited

———. "The Wages of Intellectuality . . . and the Fictional Wagers of Iris Murdoch." In *Twentieth Century Women Novelists*, edited by Thomas F. Staley, 16–38. London: Macmillan, 1982.

———. *The Ways of Nihilism: Melville's Short Novels*. Los Angeles: Ward-Ritchie, 1970.

Widmer, Kingsley, Arthur Efron, and Mark Spilka. "Controversy." *Paunch* no. 27 (Oct. 1966): 83–96.

Widmer, Kingsley, and Eleanor Widmer, eds. *Literary Censorship*. Belmont, Calif.: Wadsworth, 1961.

Wilson, Edmund. *The Shock of Recognition*. Garden City, N. Y.: Doubleday, 1943.

Wiltshire, David. *The Social and Political Thought of Herbert Spencer*. Oxford: Oxford University Press, 1978.

Index

239

Index

Butler, Gerald (crit. rage), 167, 180 nn.24, 25
Butterfield, R. W. (lit. history), 211n.45

Caesar, Julius, 35, 57, 62
Callow, Phillip (L. biography), 185n.4
Calonne, David Stephen (L. annotation), 209n.23
Campbell, Joseph (mythomania), 166, 215n.37
Camus, Albert, 122
Carlyle, Thomas (L. source), 40
Carpenter, Edward (sexology), 40
Carroll, John (ideology history), 193n.44
Censorship, 132–45
Chambers, Jessie (L. memoir), 42, 78
Chapelle, Delores La (eco-ritual), 167
Christenson, Paul (Olson biography), 211n.51
Christianity (mostly as pathology), 7, 9, 10–11, 13, 14, 21, 28, 36–38, 44, 91, 97, 108, 123–24, 171
Clark, L. D. (lit. history), 193n.44, 211n.44
Clarke, Colin (lit. history), 198n.5
Clitoris ("beak," "button," "rosebud"). See Female sexuality; Lesbianism
Comfort, Alex (sexology), 81
Conversion sexuality, 9–10, 13–15, 17–18, 19, 25, 26–27, 29, 30–31, 51–52, 72, 76, 78–79, 81–83, 84–85, 103, 106, 114, 116–17, 120, 133, 147, 165–66, 166, 201n.12
Cooper, James F. (L. source), 29
Corke, Helen (semi-lesbianism), 12, 42, 78, 199n.9
Cowley, Malcolm (obscenity defense), 139

Cox, James T. (editor), 199n.9
Crane, Hart (L. influence), 125, 129, 211
Cushman, Keith (L. annotation), 202n.14

Dahlberg, Edward (anti-gay L. influence), 127–29, 212
Dalleski, H. M. (L. criticism), 116, 149
Danto, Arthur C. (Nietzsche criticism), 52, 54, 192n.41, 195n.50
Dark prophecy, 4, 33–39, 41–69, 70, 150–56
Davie, Donald (L. influence), 165
Dax, Alice (L. friend), 183n.32
Death insistence, 7, 22, 151. See also Christianity; Nihilism
Declassing (de-proletarianizing), 92–95, 205n.24. See also Lawrence, D. H.: *Lady Chatterley's Lover, Sons and Lovers*
Delaney, Paul (Marxism), 168–69, 219n.54
Delavenay, Emile (L. sources), 40, 49, 135–36, 183n.35, 185n.3
Democracy, 30–39, 45
Derrida, Jacques (lit. scientism), 192n.41
Desire/negation ideology, 2, 6–39, 46–47, 60–69, 70–71, 109, 158–59
Dialectical stance, 1–5, 6–10, 40–69. *See also* Desire/negation ideology
Diogenes (the great), 18, 132, 173
Dionysianism, 47, 50–61, 97, 98, 109. *See also* Desire/negation ideology; Nietzsche
Dix, Carol (feminism), 152
Dos Passos, John, 111
Dostoyevsky, Fyodor, 27, 35, 36, 37, 41, 99, 107, 128, 191n.33, 192n.42

240

Index

Douglas, William O. (obscenity law), 139

Durkheim, Emile (social organicism), 160

Ebbatson, Roger (social Darwinism), 183–84n.35

Efron, Arthur (neoReicheanism), 133, 159, 167, 217n.45

Ehrenfeld, David (eco-theory), 220n.64

Eliot, George (L. source), 41, 42

Eliot, T. S. (polemic), 8, 108

Ellis, David, and Howard Mills (L. survey), 180n.23

Empson, William (criticism), 204n.23

Euripides, 132

Evernden, Neil (eco-theory), 180–81n.25, 221n.64

Female sexuality, 29, 77–93, 106, 116–17, 145–157, 163. *See also* Conversion sexuality

Feminism, 9, 19, 75, 132, 134, 138, 145–57. *See also* Misogyny

Fiedler, Leslie (L. method), 129–30, 212n.58

Flaubert, Gustave (contrast), 85, 135, 144

Ford, Ford Madox, 41–42, 96, 122, 186n.8

Foster, John Burt, Jr. (loose survey), 49, 122

Foucault, Michel (deconstructionism), 161–63, 218n.47

Francis, Saint (silly anthropomorphism), 33

Freudianism, 13, 18, 41, 61, 77, 80, 120, 133, 148, 150, 159–61, 165–66, 197n.5, 215–16n.37

Frye, Northrop (lit. scientism), 206n.28

Garnett, Edward (L. censoring), 213n.7

Gertzman, Jay A. (L. censorship), 213n.12

Gill, Stephen (Marxism), 202n.16

Gillan, Patricia (sex therapy), 166

Goodheart, Eugene (fashion history), 49, 218n.46

Goodman, Paul (L. libertarianism), 113, 159, 217n.44

Gray, Ronald (L. annotation), 49

Green, Eleanor (lit. history), 49

Green, Martin (eccentric history), 185–86n.6

Greer, Germaine (feminist dogmas), 114, 132–33, 144

Gutierrez, Donald (L. criticism), 198n.5, 212n.1, 215n.32

Hardin, Sam, 200n.10

Hawthorne, Jeremy (L. origins), 180n.20

Hayman, Ronald (Nietzsche biography), 193n.44

Heidegger, Martin (on Nietzsche), 192n.41

Heilbrun, Carolyn G. (feminist canon), 152, 215n.37

Hemingway, Ernest (parallels), 73, 84, 118, 155

Herbert, Michael (L. annotation), 188–89n.22

Herodotus, 216n.40

Hinz, Evelyn J. (mythomania errors), 204–5n.23, 206–7n.1

Holderness, Graham (Marxism), 203n.16

Holmes, Colin (L. origins), 179n.20

Homoeroticism, 11, 23, 26–27, 31, 52, 55–56, 58, 63, 65, 79, 95, 114–16, 128–29, 136–37, 208n.23. *See also* Lawrence, D. H.: sexual peculiarity

Humma, John B. (lit. history), 49, 191n.30, 203n.18

Index

Incest, 18, 19
Inhumanism (biocentrism), 3, 6, 22, 30–38, 40–69, 149, 163–73

Jackson, Dennis (compilation), 2–3, 205n.23
Jacobson, Dan (social criticism), 169
James, Henry (contrast), 17, 88
James, William (source?), 84, 88, 183n.32
Johnson, Diane (cultural fashion), 167, 219n.53
Johnson, Spud (editor), 167
Jong, Erica (L. influence), 151, 197n.4, 215n.31
Joyce, James, 77, 85, 108, 109, 165

Kaufmann, Walter (on Nietzsche), 192n.41
Kazin, Alfred (lit. publicist), 139
Keller, Karl (gay critic). *See* Homoeroticism
Kermode, Frank (lit. history), 195n.56
Kesey, Ken, 68
Kessler, Jascha (mythomania), 193n.44
Kibard, Declan (anti-feminism), 154, 181n.27
King, Richard (sex politics), 113
Knight, G. Wilson (symbolmania), 77

Laclos, C., 53, 120
Larkin, Philip, 171
Larrett, William (L. annotation), 191n.30
Lawrence, D. H.: Dionysianism, 50–61; films of, 220n.61; literary aesthetic, 83–86; paintings, 137; profile, 61–67; sexual peculiarity, 25, 31, 77–83
—works: *Aaron's Rod*, 49, 52–55, 62, 107, 114, 137, 145, 150, 190n.30, 208–9n.23; "A Propos

Lady Chatterley's Lover," 6–7, 162; "Aristocracy," 35–36, 57; "Blessed Are the Powerful," 36; "The Blind Man," 190n.28; "The Border Line," 51, 52; *The Captain's Doll*, 32, 51, 98, 146; "The Christening," 158; "Cocksure Women and Hensure Men," 147; "The Crown," 2, 7, 52, 106, 177n.3; "Daughters of the Vicar," 9, 98; "Democracy," 37, 184n.40; "Education of the People," 178n.12, 195n.57, 206n.26; "England, My England," 44, 187–88n.15; *Etruscan Places*, 187n.10; *Fantasia of the Unconscious*, 160–61; *The First Lady Chatterly*, 83, 86–90, 203n.17; "Fish," 35, 149; *The Fox*, 32; "A Fragment of Stained Glass," 10; "Give Her a Pattern," 146; "Him with His Tail in His Mouth," 36–37; "The Horse-Dealer's Daugher," 10; "On Human Destiny," 26, 195n.60; "Insouciance," 177n.5; "Is England Still a Man's Country?" 147; "Jimmy and the Desperate Woman," 148; *John Thomas and Lady Jane*, 83, 86–90, 203n.17, 205n.24, 206n.27; *Kangaroo*, 55–58, 150; *The Ladybird*, 24, 52; *Lady Chatterley's Lover*, 4, 9, 17, 20, 26, 27, 32, 51, 52, 55, 61, 70–99, 102, 103, 110, 111, 112, 114, 132–44, 154, 166, 171, 195–206, 199–200n.10; *The Lost Girl*, 9, 28–30, 32, 47, 98, 122, 145, 182n.31, 188n.20; "Love," 178n.14; "The Lovely Lady," 156; ". . . Love Was Once a Little Boy," 33–34; *The Man Who Died*, 7, 10, 60, 98, 136, 137, 147, 161; "The Man Who Loved Islands," 7, 32, 158; "Master in

Index

Index

Johnson, and Robert C. Kolody
(female orgasm), 167
May, Keith M. (semi-history), 50
Melville, Herman, 119–29
Meyers, Jeffrey (L. biographies), 81,
111, 136, 179n.20, 183n.32,
198n.7
Michaels-Tonks, Jennifer (lit.
history), 49
Miller, Henry, 4, 68, 100, 101–10,
114, 116, 117, 118, 119, 140,
149, 155, 206–9
Millet, Kate (feminist polemic), 114,
150–51, 154
Milliaras, Barbara A. (feminism),
216n.37
Milton, Colin (lit. history), 49–50
Misogyny, 8–9, 11–12, 18, 23, 25,
31, 34–38, 59, 61, 64–65, 70–89,
90–119, 145–57, 192–94. *See
also* Feminism
Montherlant, Henri de (misogynist),
154
Moore, Harry T. (L. biography),
152, 183n.35, 185n.4
Moramarco, Fred (lit. history),
212n.55
Morris, William (L. source), 91, 97,
167
Moynahan, Julian (fashion history),
204n.20
Murdoch, Iris (novelist), 120,
210n.37
Murfin, Ross C. (compiler), 215n.34
Murphy, Robert F. (anthropology),
138
Murry, John Middleton, 51, 105,
148, 167, 214n.24

Nehamas, Alexander (phil. history),
187n.13
New, Peter (lit. history), 182n.27
Nietzsche, Friedrich, 4, 8, 20, 36,
37, 40–69, 72, 101, 107, 109,
120, 154, 185–95

Nihilism, 2, 3, 5, 13, 14, 15–16, 22,
24, 30, 33, 40–67, 124–25, 161,
See also Desire/negation ideology
Nin, Anaïs (memoirs), 101, 118,
148–49, 207n.2
Nixon, Cornelia (L. criticism),
181n.27, 188n.16
Nott, Kathleen (essay), 149, 214n.29

Oates, Joyce Carol (L. criticism),
181n.27
Obscenity, 74–77, 102–3, 131–49,
196–97n.4, 213–14. *See also*
Censorship
Olson, Charles (criticism), 125–27,
128, 129, 211
Otto, Rudolf (theology), 180n.25

Paganism, 90–99. *See also*
Dionysianism
Paglia, Camille (anti-feminism), 118,
216n.40
Pally, Marcia (anti-censor), 212–
13n.5
Pan. *See* Dionysianism
Pastoral, 90–99, 204 nn. 20–23. *See
also* Utopianism
Peek, Andrew (L. annotation),
211n.44
Peters, Joan D. (L. annotation), 198–
99n.8
Peters, John (L. annotation), 197n.5
Plato (as ideological enemy), 36, 37,
71–72, 88, 105, 191n.33
Political correctness. *See* Censorship;
Feminism; Racism
Porter, Katherine Anne (polemic),
142
Pound, Ezra (climate), 55, 108, 122
Pre-Raphaelite (L. source), 96
Proust, Marcel (contrast), 85, 108
Pseudo-scientific criticism, 2–21
Pullin, Faith (feminism), 152

Index

Racism (mostly Lawrencean), 36, 53, 56, 59, 62, 79, 199–200n.10

Radford, Jean (Mailer criticism), 113

Ragnissis, Michael (semi-semiotics), 182n.27

Rahv, Philip (Miller criticism), 102

Read, Allen Walker (linguistics), 196n.4

Reich, Wilhelm (left-Freudianism), 32, 162, 167

Religion. *See* Christianity; Desire/ negation ideology; Dionysianism

Rembar, Charles (obscentiy law), 139, 140–41, 213n.11

Rexroth, Kenneth (on L.), 194n.45

Renyer, J. R. L. (L. annotation), 199n.9

Rieff, Philip (Freudian theory), 149, 160–61, 214n.29, 217–18n.46

Robinson, H. M. (theology), 50

Rolph, C. H. (gentleman-editing), 144–45

Rossman, Charles (meliorist criticism), 151, 152, 193n.44

Rylance, Rick (L. politics), 185n.41

Sabin, Margery (L. annotation), 182n.27

Sade, Marquis de, 134

Sagar, Keith (L. biography), 170–71, 220n.59

Sanders, Scott (Marxist pattern), 203n.16

Scholes, Robert (semiotics of clitoris), 82, 200–201n.12

Schopenhauer, Arthur (on will), 43, 48, 193n.44

Schorer, Mark (editing), 139, 171, 172, 220n.63

Sentimentality, 3, 12, 24, 32, 33–34. *See also* Spilka, Mark

Shakespeare, William (negative view of), 125, 210n.44

Simpson, Hilary (lit. history), 153

Sissman, L. E. (arch-moralism), 202–3n.16

Smith, Anne (feminism), 151–52

Smith, Bradley (Miller journalism), 207n.4

Snow, C. P. (polemic), 168

Social Darwinism, 34–38, 42, 46, 57, 59, 60, 66, 60, 66, 178n.14, 183–84n.35, 192n.42

Socialism, 36, 53, 93

Social marginality, 13, 21–22, 27, 32–33, 41–55, 90–99, 163–73

Solomon, Robert C. (on Nietzsche), 54, 67

Sontag, Susan (culture fashion), 100, 217n.46

Spencer, Herbert (social Darwinism), 34, 184n.35

Spengler, Oswald (doom), 101, 106

Spilka, Mark (sentimental criticism), 4, 81, 82, 152, 172, 183n.33, 194.47, 201n.12, 215n.35, 219n.57

Springer, Mary Doyle (Catholic apology), 213n.10

Squires, Michael (L. annotation), 197n.4, 203n.17, 204n.20

Steele, Bruce (L. annotation), 186n.9

Steinhauer, H. (lit. history), 49

Stern, J. P. (on Nietzsche), 193n.44

Stevens, C. J. (L. biography), 198n.8

Stirner, Max (individualism), 193n.44

Stoehr, Taylor (biography), 217n.44

Strindberg, August (misogyny), 68, 155

Swigg, Richard (lit. history), 185n.2

Talese, Gay (sex history), 166

Tallman, Warren, 180n.24

Teunissen, John J. *See* Hinz, Evelyn J.

Thatcher, David S. (lit. history), 49

Tolstoy, Leo (L. source), 95, 144

Index

Trilling, Diana (high journalism), 148, 169–70
Turner, John (L. criticism), 178n.16

Unterecker, John (on Hart Crane), 211n.46
Updike, John (anal sex), 77, 198n.6
Utopianism (social radicalism), 27, 32, 36, 46, 60, 65, 67, 94, 70, 90–99, 108, 160–73. *See also* Pastoral

Vidal, Gore (polemic), 173, 221n.66
Vivas, Eliseo (censor), 197n.5, 213–14n.18

Walker, Alice (female sexuality), 201n.12

Weaver, Raymond M. (lit. history), 121, 123
Weber, Max (social theory), 21, 22
Welch, Colin (L. censure), 197n.5
Wells, H. G. (counter-utopia), 37
Wenke, Joseph (on Mailer), 112
Whitman, Walt (L. source), 37, 41, 107
Will, 8–9, 23–25. *See also* Misogyny; Nietzsche, Friedrich
Williams, Penny (feminism reversed), 166
Williams, Raymond (Marxism), 219n.54
Williams, Tennessee (L. influence), 118
Wilson, Edmund (criticism), 121
Wiltshire, David (on Spencer), 184n.35
Wordsworth, William (as silly poet), 33

246